THE
WONDER BOOK
OF
VOLCANOES AND
EARTHQUAKES

BY
PROFESSOR EDWIN J. HOUSTON

THE WONDER BOOK OF VOLCANOES AND EARTHQUAKES
CHAPTER I

THE VOLCANIC ERUPTION OF KRAKATOA IN 1883

Krakatoa is a little island in the Straits of Sunda, about thirty miles west of the island of Java, and nearly the same distance east of the island of Sumatra. It is uninhabited and very small, measuring about five miles in length and less than three miles in width. Its total area is only thirteen square miles. This little piece of land made itself famous by what took place on it during the month of August, 1883.

Krakatoa is one of the many islands that form the large island chain known as the Sunda Islands. The most important islands of this chain are Sumatra, Java, Sumbawa, Flores, and Ceram. Between Sumatra and Java, the largest two of these islands, there is a channel called the Straits of Sunda that connects the waters of the Indian Ocean with those of the Pacific Ocean. The Straits of Sunda is an important piece of water that forms one of the great highways to the East. Shipping is, therefore, always to be found in its waters.

As can be seen by the map, Krakatoa is not far from the Equator, being situated in lat. 6° 7' S. and long. 105° 26' E. from Greenwich. Since there are about sixty-nine[Pg 2] miles in every degree of latitude, Krakatoa is about 420 miles south of the Equator, and is about twenty-five miles from Java. Java is part of the Dutch East Indies, which includes Java, Celebes, the Spice Islands, and parts of Borneo and Sumatra. Batavia, the principal seaport of Java, near the northwest coast, is a great shipping centre, visited by vessels from nearly all parts of the world. It has, however, no harbor, but is approached from the ocean by means of a canal two miles in length, the sides of which are provided with massive brick walls. Besides Batavia, which is situated about one hundred English miles east of Krakatoa, there are many smaller towns or villages, the most important of which is Anjer, a thriving seaport town, where sailing vessels obtain their supplies of food and fresh water. Before the eruption of Krakatoa, Anjer was provided with a strong, stone lighthouse.

Java is especially noted for its production of coffee, in which it is second only to Brazil. Its area is about the same as that of the State of New York. Java is one of the most densely populated parts of the world, containing nearly four times as many people as the whole State of New York.

These facts about the situation and surroundings of Krakatoa are necessary to an understanding of the wonderful thing that happened on it during the month of August, 1883. In that month Krakatoa suffered a most tremendous explosive volcanic eruption, for it is a volcano.

[Pg 3]

FIG. 1. THE SUNDA ISLANDS

A volcano is a mountain or hill, generally conical in shape, having at the top a nearly central opening, called a *crater*, from which at times melted rock and lava, vapor and gases escape. The lava either flows down the side of the mountain in a liquid condition, or is thrown upwards into the air. If the distance the lava is thrown upwards is sufficiently great the melted matter solidifies[Pg 4] before it falls to the earth. In such cases the largest fragments form what are called *volcanic cinders*, the smaller pieces,*volcanic ashes*, and the extremely small particles, *volcanic dust*. If, however, the lava is thrown to a comparatively small height, it is still melted when it falls, and is then known as *volcanic drops* or *driblets*.

FIG. 2. KRAKATOA BEFORE THE ERUPTION

It is not surprising that Krakatoa is a volcanic island, since it lies in one of the most active belts of volcanic islands in the world, and near the coasts of the most active of these islands; i. e., Java. This belt, as shown in the map, includes, besides the Sunda Island chain, parts of Gilolo, Celebes, Mindanao and the Philippine Islands. These islands lie between Asia on the northwest and Australia on the southeast.

FIG. 3. KRAKATOA AFTER THE ERUPTION

There is no other part of the world with, perhaps, the[Pg 5] single exception of Japan, where so many active volcanoes are crowded in so small a space. The island of Java, small as it is, has nearly fifty volcanoes, of which at least twenty-eight are active. They are situated in a lofty range running from east to west, some of the peaks of which are more than 10,000 feet above the level of the sea. Volcanic eruptions are so frequent that the island is seldom free from them.

As will be seen from the map shown in Fig. 2, Krakatoa consists of three groups of volcanic mountains, the southern group giving the name of Krakatoa to the island. Strictly speaking, this mountain was called *Rakata*, but as it is now generally known as Krakatoa, it would be unwise to attempt to call it by any other name. The central mountain or group of mountains is known as Danan, and consists largely of part of an old crater. The group of mountains which lies near the northern end of the island was known as Perboawatan. From the centre of this latter group of mountains are several old lava streams consisting of a variety of lava resembling a dark-colored glass, known to mineralogists as *obsidian*, or *volcanic glass.*

Although Krakatoa was always a volcano, yet between the years 1680 and 1883, it was in the condition of a sleeping or extinct volcano. There had been a severe explosive eruption in the year 1680, that caused great loss of life and property, but ever since that time all activity had ceased and it seemed that the volcano would never again burst out. In other words, it was generally regarded as a trustworthy, sedate, quiet, inoffensive and perfectly safe volcano, that had become extinct.

The long continued quiet of Krakatoa was broken on the 20th of May, 1883, when the inhabitants of Batavia on the island of Java were terrified by noises like the firing[Pg 6] of great guns, that were first heard between ten and eleven o'clock in the morning. These noises were accompanied by the shaking of the ground and buildings. The sleeping volcano of Krakatoa was evidently growing restless, but no great damage was done and soon all was again quiet. The disturbances were merely the forerunner of the terrible eruption soon to follow, and confidence was soon restored. But suddenly, on Sunday, August 26th, 1883, almost without any further warnings, Krakatoa burst into terrible activity and began an explosive eruption that has never been equalled in the memory of man.

That memorable Sunday of August 26th, 1883, came during a season of the year known as the *dry monsoon*, a name given the season of the periodical winds from the Indian Ocean. Batavia, and the surrounding country, greatly needed rain, for in this part of the world it seldom rains from April to October, although the air is very moist and damp. For this reason the beginning of the wet season is always welcomed. When, therefore, the rumbling sounds of the approaching catastrophe of Krakatoa were heard in Batavia, the people, believing that the noises were due to peals of thunder, rejoiced, for all thought they heralded an earlier setting in of the wet monsoon. But when the rumbling sounds increased and reports were heard like heavy artillery, it was clear that the sounds were the beginning of a volcanic eruption, a phenomenon with which they were only too well acquainted, but, as volcanic eruptions were far from being uncommon in Java, no one was very greatly frightened.

But this time the noises increased to such an extent that the people became alarmed. Throughout the night the appalling sounds continued and were accompanied by shakings of the earth sufficiently strong to shake the[Pg 7] houses violently. Sleep was out of the question. Many of the people left their houses and remained all night in the open air, fearing the shocks would bring the houses down over their heads.

The morning instead of heralding the dawn of a beautiful tropical day, with its bright, cheerful sunlight, brought with it skies covered with gray clouds that completely hid the sun. The rumbling sounds, however, had decreased, and the people were beginning to congratulate themselves that the dangers were over, when suddenly, the sky grew darker, and there began a shower of ashes that soon covered the streets and houses of the city. About seven o'clock on the morning of August 27th, a most tremendous crash was heard. The sky rapidly became so dark that it was soon necessary to light the lamps in the houses of Batavia, and some of the neighboring towns in the western part of Java. In addition to this the air was filled with vapor, while every now and then earthquake shocks were again felt. These

2

shocks were accompanied by terrific noises like those produced by the explosion of heavy artillery. The noises rapidly increased in number and intensity until they produced a nearly continuous roar, the nature of which it is almost impossible to describe since it is probable that such sounds had never been heard before by man. It is a curious fact, which, I believe, has never been satisfactorily explained, that in most cases the people in the immediate neighborhood of the volcano, as, for example, those on board vessels in the Straits of Sunda, did not hear the terrific noises at all. Possibly they were too loud and simply gave a single inward impetus to the drum of the ear and then held it in position.

Probably some of my readers may remember that witty description given by Dr. Oliver Wendell Holmes of an[Pg 8] alleged effort made by all the people of the world to find out whether or not there is a man in the moon. This wonderful plan was as follows:

Careful calculations were made to ascertain when it would be the same time over all the earth so that all the people of the earth could simultaneously shout at the top of their voices. In this way it was hoped that the man in the moon, if there were such a person, would notice the noise.

The story goes on to tell how when the time approached for the great experiment, and all were ready to shout as loud as they could, that each person reasoning to himself or herself, that amid so great a noise no one could notice whether his or her voice was omitted, determined to remain silent, so as to be able to hear the noise and the better to observe what the man in the moon would do when the sound reached him. The result was that every person on the earth remained silent and simply listened, so that the earth was never so quiet before.

Had Oliver Wendell Holmes, or any other person conceiving the witty idea, lived during the time of the great explosive eruption of Krakatoa, on that memorable August 27th, 1883, he might have taken the opportunity of observing the man in the moon, had he not been frightened by what was occurring, for certainly never before were such tremendous or terrifying sounds produced, for these sounds, as we shall see shortly, were actually heard for distances of more than 3,000 miles from the volcano.

There were two different kinds of waves produced in the air by the tremendous forces at work in the eruption of Krakatoa; namely, atmospheric waves and sound waves.

The atmospheric waves showed their presence in the air by means of changes produced in the atmospheric[Pg 9] pressure. Now, while these changes cannot readily be felt by man, yet their presence can be easily shown by the use of instruments called *barometers*.

There are in different parts of the world, buildings called *meteorological observatories*, that are provided, among other instruments, with recording barometers. These instruments caught the great atmospheric waves that were produced by the eruption of Krakatoa. In this manner, the astounding fact was learned that the waves starting from the volcano travelled no less than seven times around the world. When we say astounding, it must not be understood that the formation of such waves was at all contrary to the known laws of physics. On the contrary, provided the force of the eruption was sufficiently great, such waves must have been produced in the great ærial ocean. The astonishing, or wonderful thing, was that the force setting up these waves was so great that it caused them to move seven times around the globe.

The atmospheric waves were so powerful that it will be worth our while to describe them in detail. Starting from the volcano of Krakatoa, as a centre, these waves moved outwards in all directions, becoming gradually larger and larger until they reached a point halfway round the globe, or 180° from Krakatoa. The waves did not, however, stop here, but continued moving onward, now growing smaller and smaller until they reached a point in North America, immediately opposite Krakatoa. Such a point on a globe is called an *antipodal point*.[1] The waves did not stop at this point, but again advanced moving toward Krakatoa, growing larger and larger until they again reached a point halfway around the globe, or 180° from Krakatoa, when they again continued[Pg 10]moving but now continually growing smaller and smaller, until they reached Krakatoa. Here they again began moving completely around the globe, and this was continued for as many as seven times. It must not be supposed that the waves ceased on the seventh time around. On the contrary, they, probably, kept on moving for many additional times, but they were then so feeble that even the sensitive recording barometers were unable to detect their presence.

There was another kind of waves in the atmosphere that did not require barometers for their detection. These were the sound waves, and can readily be detected by the human ear.

Now, in the case of the great eruption of Krakatoa, the intensity of the sounds was so great that the sounds could be heard distinctly at distances of several thousand miles from Krakatoa.

The sound waves so closely resembled the explosion of artillery that at Acheen, a port on the northern coast of Sumatra, 1,073 miles from Krakatoa, the authorities, believing that an attack was being made on the port, placed all their troops under arms to repel the invaders. The sounds were also distinctly heard at Bangkok, in Siam, a distance of 1,413 miles from the volcano. They were also heard at the Chagos Islands, a group of islands situated in the Indian Ocean about 2,267 miles from Krakatoa.

Two steamers at Singapore, 522 miles distant, were despatched to find the vessel that was believed to be firing guns as distress signals.

The sounds were distinctly heard in parts of South Australia, 2,100 miles distant, and in Western Australia, at 1,700 miles distance.

But it will be unnecessary to give any further details[Pg 11] of the great distances at which these sounds were actually heard. It will suffice to say that they were heard as far off as about 3,000 miles.

It is difficult to picture to one's self such great distances. Assuming the greatest distances to be in the neighborhood of 3,000 miles, it would be as if a sound produced, say, in Boston, New York, or Philadelphia, was so loud that it could be heard in Amsterdam, London, or Paris.

Some idea of the intensity of these sounds can be had from the fact that in Batavia, when, in accordance with usage, a gun was fired from one of the forts at eight o'clock in the morning, two hours before the greatest intensity of the sounds had been reached, the sound of the gun could scarcely be heard above the continuous roar.

While, of course, the principal reason the sound waves were carried so far was the great force causing the eruption, yet these distances were increased by the fact that the explosion occurred in a region almost entirely surrounded by great bodies of water. The waves could, therefore, be readily carried along the surface of the sea. Had there been a high mountain wall, like the Andes of South America, on one side of the volcano they would probably have been shut off in this direction a short distance from where they were produced.

[Pg 12]

CHAPTER II

SOME EFFECTS OF THE ERUPTION OF KRAKATOA

Besides the sound waves in the air, there were waves in the waters of the ocean. Suddenly, without any warning, the people of Batavia were surprised by a huge wave that, crossing the Straits of Sunda, entered the ship canal before referred to as connecting the city with the ocean, and, rising above the brick wall, poured over the surrounding country.

Although Batavia was 100 English miles from Krakatoa, yet after travelling this distance the wave was sufficiently strong to enter the city and flood its streets with water to a depth of several feet. Fortunately, the loss of life was small in the city of Batavia, but very great in the surrounding towns and villages.

The ocean waves varied in height at different times of the eruption. The greatest were from fifty to eighty feet high. Just imagine the effect of a wave twice the height of an ordinary house. The waves caused great damage to the shipping in the neighborhood. In one instance, a vessel was carried one and a half miles inland and left on dry land thirty feet above the level of the sea.

The total loss of life by the waves has been estimated at 35,000 people; besides this, of course, there was a great amount of property destroyed. The greatest loss was in the

4

immediate neighborhood of Krakatoa. Gigantic waves swept over the lowlands lying near the shores of Sumatra and Java, where over areas several miles in width[Pg 13]nearly everything was destroyed, the houses, trees, and people being swept away and the surface of the land greatly changed. The towns of Karang and Anjer, as well as numerous smaller villages, were almost completely destroyed.

The seaport town of Anjer, by far the most important of the above towns, was almost completely swept away. The heavy stone lighthouse was so completely obliterated that no traces of its heavy stone foundations could afterwards be found. The Rev. Phillip Neale, formerly a British chaplain at Batavia, from whose account of the eruption of Krakatoa some of the above facts have been taken, tells of the brave action of the keeper of the lighthouse at Anjer. Besides his work as lighthouse keeper, to see that the light was constantly burning during the night, he was charged with telegraphing to Batavia the names of all passing vessels. On the fateful morning of the great catastrophe, observing that the sun did not rise, he kept the light of the lighthouse burning, and, notwithstanding the danger to which he was exposed, continued at his post in order to send word to Batavia of the passing of an English steamer. While doing this the lighthouse was swept away and the brave man perished.

The following verbal account of the destruction of the port of Anjer was given by a Dutch pilot stationed at Anjer. This description is quoted by the Rev. Mr. Neale from an article prepared by him for publication in "The Leisure Hour."

"I have lived in Anjer all my life, and little thought the old town would have been destroyed in the way it has. I am getting on in years, and quite expected to have laid my bones in the little cemetery near the shore, but not even that has escaped and some of the bodies have actually been washed out of their graves and carried out to[Pg 14] sea. The whole town has been swept away, and I have lost everything except my life. The wonder is that I escaped at all. I can never be too thankful for such a miraculous escape as I had.

"The eruption began on the Sunday afternoon. We did not take much notice at first, until the reports grew very loud. Then we noticed that Krakatoa was completely enveloped in smoke. Afterwards came on the thick darkness, so black and intense that I could not see my hand before my eyes. It was about this time that a message came from Batavia inquiring as to explosive shocks, and the last telegram sent off from us was telling you about the darkness and smoke. Towards night everything became worse. The reports became deafening, the natives cowered down panic-stricken, and a red, fiery glare was visible in the sky above the burning mountain. Although Krakatoa was twenty-five miles away, the concussion and vibration from the constantly repeated shocks were most terrifying. Many of the houses shook so much that we feared every minute would bring them down. There was little sleep for any of us that dreadful night. Before daybreak on Monday, on going out of doors, I found the shower of ashes had commenced, and this gradually increased in force until at length large pieces of pumice stone kept falling around. About six A. M. I was walking along the beach. There was no sign of the sun, as usual, and the sky had a dull, depressing look. Some of the darkness of the previous day had cleared off, but it was not very light even then. Looking out to sea I noticed a dark, black object through the gloom, travelling towards the shore.

"At first sight it seemed like a low range of hills rising out of the water, but I knew there was nothing of the kind in that part of the Sunda Strait. A second glance—and[Pg 15] a very hurried one it was—convinced me that it was a lofty ridge of water many feet high, and worse still, that it would soon break upon the coast near the town. There was no time to give any warning, and so I turned and ran for my life. My running days have long gone by, but you may be sure that I did my best. In a few minutes I heard the water with a loud roar break upon the shore. Everything was engulfed. Another glance around showed the houses being swept away and the trees thrown down on every side. Breathless and exhausted I still pressed on. As I heard the rushing waters behind me, I knew that it was a race for life. Struggling on, a few yards more brought me to some rising ground, and here the torrent of water overtook me. I gave up all for lost, as I saw with dismay how high the wave still was. I was soon taken off my feet and borne inland by the force of the resistless mass. I remember nothing more until a violent blow aroused me. Some hard, firm substance seemed within my reach, and clutching it, I found I had gained a place of safety. The waters swept past, and I found myself clinging to a cocoanut palm-tree. Most of the trees near the town were uprooted and thrown down for miles, but this one fortunately had escaped and myself with it.

"The huge wave rolled on, gradually decreasing in height and strength until the mountain slopes at the back of Anjer were reached, and then, its fury spent, the water gradually receded and flowed back into the sea. The sight of those receding waters haunts me still. As I clung to the palm-tree, wet and exhausted, there floated past the dead bodies of many a friend and neighbor. Only a mere handful of the population escaped. Houses and streets were completely destroyed, and scarcely a trace remains of where the once busy, thriving town originally stood. Unless you go yourself to see the ruin you will[Pg 16] never believe how completely the place has been swept away. Dead bodies, fallen trees, wrecked houses, an immense muddy morass and great pools of water, are all that is left of the town where my life has been spent. My home and all my belongings of course perished—even the clothes I am wearing are borrowed—but I am thankful enough to have escaped with my life and to be none the worse for all that I have passed through."

As is common in cases of earthquake waves a great depression in the level of the sea occurred at places great distances from Krakatoa. For example, at the harbor of Ceylon, the water receded so far that for about three minutes the boats were left high and dry, and then a huge wave carried them with it as it rushed over the land.

Perhaps one of the best evidences of the immense power of ocean waves is to be seen in the massive blocks of white coral rock that were washed up by the waves, on parts of the coast of Java for distances of from two to three miles from the ocean. Many of these blocks weighed from twenty to thirty tons. Indeed, some of them reached the weight of from forty to fifty tons.

It is probable that the island of Krakatoa and its neighboring smaller islands formed portions of a huge cone about eight miles in diameter, that has been broken up at some very remote but unknown time by, perhaps, a greater catastrophe than that of August, 1883.

In the Straits of Sunda the water was raised fifty feet to eighty feet above the ordinary level, and produced tremendous destruction especially on the coasts of Java and Sumatra, sweeping away many villages and drowning many thousands of people. The wave had a velocity of progression of nearly 400 miles per hour, or eight times faster than an ordinary express train.

When it is said that the *velocity of progression of the[Pg 17] wave* was nearly 400 miles per hour, it is not meant that a body floating on the ocean, such, for example, as a ship, would have been carried forward at this high velocity, but would merely rise and fall in a to-and-fro swing to about the height of the wave; that is, fifty to eighty feet according to what may have been the height. As in the case of the sound waves these motions of water covered or passed over nearly all the waters of the earth. The waves progressing toward the west, crossed the Indian Ocean reaching to the coast of Hindostan, and Madagascar, and sweeping around the southern part of Africa, finally reached the coasts of France and England, as well as the eastern part of North and South America. Sweeping towards the east, they reached the coasts of Australia, New Zealand, and crossing the vast Pacific Ocean were felt at Alaska and the western coasts of North and South America.

But besides the enormous waves caused by the eruption, there were marked changes in the level of the land. Large portions of the coast of Sumatra and Java were almost annihilated, much of the original surface near the coast being submerged, and places that were formerly dry land are now covered with water to a depth of from 600 to 900 feet.

The enormous amount of material thrown into the air by the forces of the eruption is especially characteristic of this phenomenon. Such quantities of pumice stone and ashes fell from the clouds that, sinking in the water and collecting on the bed of the channel, they changed the depth of the water, so as to render navigation dangerous. Indeed, the Sebesi Channel, lying on the north of the island of Krakatoa was completely blocked by a huge bank of volcanic material, portions of which projected above the water, forming two smaller islands.[Pg 18] These, however, have since been washed away by the waves.

We will not attempt to give at present any explanations as to the causes of this great volcanic eruption, since the different theories as to the cause of volcanoes will be better understood when other volcanic eruptions have been described. It is sufficient here to say that if a large quantity of water should have suddenly reached a great mass of molten rock, frightful explosive eruptions would have occurred, and if the island was resting on a submerged crater its sudden disappearance may be explained.

Another great wonder connected with the explosive eruption of Krakatoa was the enormous heights to which the fine dust was thrown up into the air. It has been asserted that during the most intense of these eruptions the particles reached elevations of perhaps more than twenty-five miles above the level of the sea. Carried by the winds, the fine particles remained suspended in the air for many months, and gave rise to magnificent sunlight effects, such as early dawn, lengthened twilights, lurid skies, and gorgeous sunsets of a reddish tint. There were also caused curious haloes, as well as green and blue moons.

The fine dust particles consisted of minute crystals of feldspar and other minerals, and when examined under the microscope presented the appearance shown in Fig. 4.

These mineral substances permitted a portion of the light to pass through them, thus producing wonderful optical effects in the atmosphere either because they acted like minute prisms and so produced rainbow colors, or because they turned the rays of light out of their course as to produce what is called interference by color effects of a nature similar to the colors seen in mother-of-pearl, rainbow coal, or in the wing cases of many beetles. The[Pg 19] explanations of these phenomena are too difficult for a book of this character.

An explosive volcanic eruption is a very terrifying and wonderful phenomenon. Frightful roaring sounds are suddenly heard, the earth shakes for many miles around, when suddenly a vast quantity of molten rock, and sometimes huge stones, are thrown out of the crater high up into the air. So great is the force that throws these materials out of the opening that heavy masses of rocks often are ejected very much faster than the projectiles from the largest guns that are used in any of the navies of the world.

Fig. 4. Volcanic Dust as it Appears Under the Microscope

As the molten lava cools and falls in the form of prodigious clouds of ashes, cinders and dust, for many miles around the volcano, even the light of the sun is obscured, and one cannot see the hand before the face. Some of the materials in these clouds are so light that they remain suspended in the air for many hours, often indeed for many days, and sometimes even for years. The heavier particles, however, soon begin to fall, and before long the earth's surface both around the volcano, and often at considerable distances from it, is covered with a thick layer of ashes.

The sounds accompanying a volcanic eruption are often terrifying. Amid shakings and tremblings of the earth's crust, known as earthquakes, there are occasionally heard noises like the explosion of huge guns. Sometimes these sounds follow one another so rapidly that they produce an[Pg 20] almost continuous roar. Through the roar of the explosion a curious crackling noise can be heard, due to the fragments of stone hurled out of the crater striking against one another, especially as the stones which are thrown out of the crater and have commenced to fall back again to the earth, are struck by others that are still rising.

Immense quantities of ashes, stones, vapor and gases are thrown upwards for great distances into the air, while, at the same time, a lava stream pours over the lowest side of the crater. As the column of ashes and cinders reaches its greatest height in the air, it begins to spread outward on all sides, rapidly growing like a huge dark mushroom. This soon shuts out the light of the sun, and from it showers of red hot ashes and cinders fall to the earth.

It would be extremely dangerous to be on the side of the volcanic mountain during an explosive eruption; for, even should you escape falling into an opening in the side of the mountain, you might be killed by the huge stones that are constantly falling on all sides around the opening, or might be buried under the vast showers of red hot ashes that are poured down from the dense clouds overhanging the mountain, or suffocated by clouds of sulphur vapor that rush down its sides.

When at a safe distance the sight is certainly magnificent. There is no light from the sun. All would be in pitch darkness but for the reddish glare thrown upwards by the red hot lava, by the glowing showers of ashes that are being rained down on the sides of the mountain, or by terrific lightning flashes, due to the discharge of the immense quantities of electricity produced by the forces of the eruption.

Naturally a great volcanic eruption can cause a considerable loss of life and property. When a large lava[Pg 21] stream begins to flow down the sides of the mountain, it cannot be stopped, and should it flow toward a village or town it is likely to destroy the town completely. Besides this, the vegetation of the country for many miles around is destroyed by the showers of red hot ashes that fall from the sky. The houses of neighboring cities are similarly ruined by the great conflagrations thus set up. Further destruction is also caused by large streams of mud that rush down the slopes of the mountain, or by huge waves set up in the ocean. If the volcano is situated, as most volcanoes are, near the coast, the showers of ashes and falling stones may set fire to vessels in the neighborhood, or the progress of such vessels may be seriously retarded by layers of ashes or pumice stone that float on the surface. Sometimes these layers are so thick as actually to bring ships to a complete standstill.

It must not be supposed that volcanoes are in a constant state of eruption. On the contrary, nearly all volcanoes, after an eruption, become *quiet* or *inactive*. The air soon clears by the ashes settling, and the sunlight again appears. A crust forms over the surface of the lava, which rapidly becomes hard enough to permit one to walk over it safely. The vegetation, which has been destroyed by the hot ashes, again springs up, and, if the volcano happens to be situated within the tropics, where there is an abundance of moisture, the land soon again becomes covered by a luxuriant vegetation. Most of the people, who have escaped sudden death during the eruption, return to the ruins of their houses; for it is a curious fact that no matter how great has been a volcanic eruption, or how far-reaching the ruin, the survivors, as a rule, do not appear to hesitate to return to their old neighborhood. In a few years the fields are re-cultivated, the villages are rebuilt, and the people apparently forget they are living over a[Pg 22] slumbering volcano, which may at any time again burst forth in a dangerous eruption.

A volcano that throws out molten rock, vapor and gases is known as an *active volcano*. An active volcano, however, is only correctly said to be in a state of eruption when the quantity of the molten rock, lava or vapor it throws out is greatly in excess of the ordinary amount.

Sometimes the volcanic activity so greatly decreases that the molten rock or lava no longer rises in the crater, but, on the contrary, begins to sink, so that the top of the lava in the crater is often at a considerable distance below its edges. The lava then begins to harden on the surface, and, if the time is sufficient, the hardened part extends for a considerable distance downward. In this way the opening connecting the crater with the molten lava below becomes gradually closed, the volcano being thus shut up, or corked, just as a bottle is tightly closed by means of a cork driven into the opening at its top so as to prevent the escape of the liquid it contains.

It may sound queer to say that a volcano has its crater so corked up as to prevent the escape of the lava, but the idea is nevertheless correct and helpful. To realize the size of these huge volcanic corks one must remember that the craters of some volcanoes are several miles across. A volcano thus choked or corked up is said to be *extinct*.

When we speak of an extinct volcano we do not mean that the volcano will never again become active. A volcano does not cease to erupt because there are no more molten materials in the earth to escape, but simply because its cork or crust of hardened lava has been driven in so tightly that the chances of its ever being loosened again seem to be very small. But small as the chances may seem we must not forget that the volcano may at[Pg 23] any time become active, or go into its old business of throwing out materials through its crater. A volcano in an extinct condition is not unlike a steam boiler, the safety valve of which has been firmly fixed in place. If the steam continues to be generated in the boiler, it is only a matter of time when the boiler will blow up, and the explosion will be all the greater because the safety valve did not allow the steam to escape earlier.

Sometimes an intermediate class of volcanoes called *dormant* is introduced between active volcanoes on the one hand and extinct volcanoes on the other. The name dormant volcano, or, as the word means, *sleeping volcano*, is objectionable, since it might lead one to think that an extinct volcano is not sleeping but dead, and this is wrong.

Since the plug of hardened lava in the volcanic crater is generally at a much lower level than the top of the crater, the crater will soon become filled to a greater or less depth with water, produced either by the rain, or by the melting of the snow that falls on the top of the mountain. Crater lakes, often of very great depths, are common in extinct volcanoes.

Of course, when an extinct volcano again becomes active, two things must happen if the eruption is explosive. In the first place, the force of the explosion must be sufficiently great to loosen the stopper or plug of hardened lava which stops it. In doing this the mass is broken into a number of fragments that are thrown forcibly upwards into the air. After rising often for great heights they soon fall again on the sides of the mountain.

But besides the breaking up of the stopper, the lake in the crater of the volcano is thrown out along with the cinders or ashes, producing very destructive flows of what are called aqueous lava or mud streams. These streams flow down the sides of the mountain, carrying with them[Pg 24] immense quantities of both the ashes thrown out during the eruption, or those that have collected around the sides of the crater during previous eruptions. Very frequently, these streams of aqueous lava produce greater destruction than the molten lava.

If you have ever watched common ants at work clearing out or enlarging their underground homes, in a piece of smooth gravel walk in your garden, you can form some idea why the mountain immediately around a volcanic crater is conical in shape. If the colony of ants happens to be fairly large, you can see an almost unbroken stream of these industrious little animals, each bearing in its mandibles a small grain of sand or gravel brought up from some place below the surface.

Carrying it a short distance from the opening, it throws it on the ground, rapidly returning for another load. In this way there is heaped up around all sides of the opening a pile of sand or gravel, the outward slopes of which gives the pile a conical form. You have, probably, noticed that the steepness of the slopes depends on the size of the grains; for the larger these grains the sharper or steeper the slopes, the very fine grains producing flat mounds or cones.

It is the same with a volcanic cone. The materials that are thrown upwards into the air, falling again on the mountain, collect around the crater on all sides, thus giving it the characteristic cone-like shape of the volcanic mountain. Where nothing occurs to disturb the formation of the cone its height above the level of the sea will gradually increase. Very frequently, however, during explosive eruptions, a large part of this cone will be blown away by the force of the eruption only to be again built up during some later eruption. Indeed, in the case of volcanic islands, the force of a great volcanic eruption is sometimes so great that not only is a large volcanic mountain blown[Pg 25] entirely away, but a hole is left, where it had been standing, that extends further downwards below the level of the sea than the top of the mountain extended previously above it. The above are some, but by no means all, the wonders attending volcanic eruptions. We shall refer to others in subsequent chapters in describing particular eruptions.

[Pg 26]

CHAPTER III

THE VOLCANIC ISLAND OF HAWAII

The volcanic island of Hawaii, the largest of the Sandwich Island chain, is situated in the mid Pacific, south of the Tropic of Cancer. As shown in Fig. 5, this island chain consists of Hawaii, Maui, Molokai, Oahu, Kauai, Nihau, and about eight large islands, together with numerous small islands, extending in a general northwest direction from Hawaii to Nihau, a distance of about 400 miles. Like most volcanic islands they lie in more or less straight lines, probably along fissures, in this case in two nearly parallel lines. The island of Nihau, however, is an exception, the direction of the greatest length being almost straight across the two parallel lines.

The Sandwich Islands lie 2,000 miles from San Francisco in deep water, between 2,000 and 3,000 fathoms, or between 12,000 and 18,000 feet in depth. This island chain consists of great volcanic mountains, that had, at one time, fifteen active volcanoes of the first class. These are now all extinct but three, and all of these are on the island of Hawaii.

In his report to the United States Geological Survey for 1882-83, Dutton states that the summit of Mt. Haleakala on East Maui is 10,350 feet above the sea level. Oahu has peaks on its eastern side 2,900 feet high, and peaks on the western side 3,850 feet high. The summit of Kauai is probably 6,200 feet above the sea.

[Pg 27]

FIG. 5. THE HAWAIIAN ISLANDS
From U. S. Geological Survey

It can be shown by deep-sea soundings that all these[Pg 28] volcanic piles are the summits of a gigantic mountain mass that rises abruptly from the bed of the Pacific. There are reasons for believing that this submarine chain continues for many hundreds of miles in the same direction beyond Kauai.

The extinct volcano, Haleakala, on East Maui appears to have been in eruption at a much later day than Mt. Kea, which is also an extinct volcano. But the natives have no traditions of any eruptions.

The volcanoes on the other islands have been extinct for a very long time judging from the extent of their erosion. Dutton is of the opinion that the western islands of the chain have been extinct for much longer times than the remaining islands.

The Sandwich Islands, also known as the Hawaiian Islands, are one of the colonial possessions of the United States. The island of Hawaii is about 2,000 miles from San Francisco. Honolulu, on the island of Oahu, the principal seaport of the chain, has a pleasant climate, and is an important coaling station for warships, commercial vessels, whalers, and trading ships generally.

The principal product of the island is sugar cane.

The island of Hawaii, as shown in map, Fig. 6, consists of five volcanic mountains and some small coral reefs. These mountains are: Mt. Kea, on the north, 13,805 feet in height; Mt. Haulalai, in the west central part of the island, 8,273 feet in height; Mt. Loa, in the south central part of the island, 13,675 feet in height; Mt. Kilauea, twenty miles east of the crater of Loa, 4,040 feet high at the Volcano House, and 4,158 feet on the highest point on the west, and Kohala, 5,505 feet in height, running through the northwestern part of the island, and the Kohala mountains in the northwestern part.

[Pg 29]

FIG. 6. HAWAII
From Dana's Manual of Geology

[Pg 30]

Of these mountains, Mt. Loa and Kilauea are the only active volcanoes, and are in frequent eruption. Mt. Haulalai was in eruption during 1804. Mt. Kea has not been active during historical times, while Mt. Kohala has been inactive for so long a time that its slopes are deeply gullied wherever the rivers flow down them.

As you can see from the map, Hawaii is very large. It has a length of ninety-three miles from north to south, and a breadth of eighty miles from east to west, its area is about 6,500 square miles. With the exception of small patches of coral reefs, Hawaii is formed entirely of lava, and is the largest pile of lava in the world with the single exception of Iceland.

Where the islands of the Hawaiian chain have coral reefs extending off their coasts, excellent harbors are found in the deep waters between the islands and the reefs. Hawaii, however, has no extended reefs of this character, and, consequently, no first-class harbors. Hilo, on the eastern coast, is the best harbor, and is, therefore, the principal settlement.

10

A very brief examination of the map of Hawaii will show you that there are no rivers on the island, except on the sides exposed to the wind, that is, on the northern and northeastern slopes. Since the yearly rainfall on Hawaii is large, being in the neighborhood of a hundred inches, you will understand that considerable rain water falls on the island. In those parts of the island where it does not run off the surface it must drain downward through the loose piles of broken rocks or cinders. A rainfall of one hundred inches a year means that if all the rain which falls on each square foot of surface was collected in a flat vessel one foot square with vertical sides it would fill the vessel to the depth of one hundred inches, or over eight feet. The drainage of the rainwater[Pg 31] downwards through these parts of the island, must, therefore, be large.

Another curious fact you can notice on the map, is that the lava streams of the past fifty years from Mt. Loa indicated by heavy dotted lines, in no cases begin at the crater, but start at fairly considerable distances from it. Later on in this chapter we shall explain the reason for this curious fact.

Since practically the whole of Hawaii has been formed from the streams of lava that have flowed at one time or another, you can understand how great these flows must have been. But to do this fully you must not only take into consideration the portions of the island that lie above the ocean and reach into the air at its greatest height to 13,805 feet above its surface, you must also remember that this mountain rises from a deep ocean, so that if all the water were removed, you would see Hawaii towering up above the former level of the sea to the height of about 31,000 feet, or higher than Mt. Everest, the highest point on the earth above the present sea level. This would be, approximately, five and eight-tenths miles. You can understand, therefore, how great the flow of lava must have been.

We shall begin the description of Hawaii with the active volcano of Mt. Loa, or, as it is sometimes called in Hawaii, "The White Mountain."

You will remember that the eruption of Krakatoa was of the explosive type. Practically no melted rock or lava escaped from the crater. Indeed, if it had escaped it would not have been seen; for, not only the cone near the crater, but also much of the mountain itself was blown completely out of sight and covered by the waters of the ocean.

The eruptions of Mt. Loa are of an entirely different[Pg 32] type. In Loa there are no explosions, the eruptions being what are called the non-explosive or quiet volcanic eruption type. It will be necessary to explain some of the peculiarities of this kind of eruptions.

There is a great difference in the liquidity or the ease with which different kinds of lava flow. Some lava is very thick or viscid, or is sticky like thick molasses or tar, and therefore flows very sluggishly. Other lava is thin or mobile, more closely resembling water in the ease with which it flows. Now, in the case of a volcanic mountain of fairly considerable height, where the lava possesses marked liquidity, the lava as it rises from great depths in the tube of the volcano seldom flows over the top or rim of the crater. This is not because the force that brings the lava up is unable to carry it a few thousand feet higher, so that it can run over the brim of the crater, but because the walls of the volcanic mountains are unable to stand the great pressure which the mass of liquid lava exerts against their sides.

It can be shown that a column of liquid lava 500 feet high, will exert a pressure on the walls of the crater of about 625 pounds to the square inch. Therefore, in very high volcanic mountains, long before the lava can reach the edge of the crater and overflow, the pressure becomes so great, that cracks or fissures are made in the sides of the mountain, through which the lava is quietly discharged; when, of course, the level of the lava in the crater falls considerably. In volcanoes of the explosive type, no matter what may be the condition of lava, should a large quantity of water suddenly find an entrance to a large body of molten lava at some distance below the surface, the lava would be suddenly thrown explosively into the air, where being chilled, it would afterwards descend in showers of ashes, cinders, or volcanic dust.

[Pg 33]

In some volcanic mountains such as Mt. Loa, the crater, instead of being situated at the top of a conical pass of ashes or other material, consists of a pit-like depression, generally occupying a level tract or plain at the top of the mountain. This pit is known as a *caldera*, or *caldron*, or what you might, perhaps, call a huge kettle or boiler. The pit has more or less vertical sides that extend downwards for unknown depths to the place from which the lava comes. The vertical walls of the caldera are not, however, smooth, but exhibit numerous horizontal ledges, that mark places where portions of the floor of the caldera were situated at different times.

At the bottom of the large pit or caldera on the summit of Mt. Loa can be seen the level floor formed of hardened lava. This floor is surrounded by vertical walls on which can be seen the broken edges of the old lake bed.

Captain Dutton, in a paper on Hawaiian volcanoes, prepared for the United States Geological Survey, and published in its Fourth Annual Report for 1882-83, thus describes the appearance at the great crater as it was in 1882.

"The summit of Mauna Loa (Mt. Loa), is a broad and large platform about five miles in length and four miles in width, within which is sunken the great caldera called Mokuaweoweo. The distance from the point where we first reach the summit to the brink of the pit is about a mile and a half. The surface of the platform is much more rugged than the slopes just ascended. It is riven with cracks, and small faults,[2] and piles of shattered rock are seen on every hand. Nowhere is there to be seen the[Pg 34] semblance of a cinder cone. Doubtless many eruptions have broken forth from the various fissures on this summit, but only here and there can insignificant traces of such catastrophes be definitely distinguished. The absence of fragmental ejecta (broken rock that are thrown out) is extraordinary. The shattered blocks, slabs, and spalls (chips) which everywhere cumber the surface appear to have resulted from the spontaneous shivering and shattering of the lava sheets by their own internal tensions as they cooled.

Fig. 7, taken from Dutton's report, gives the general shape of this great caldera. Dutton's description of the same is as follows:

"The length of the main caldera is a little less than three miles and its width about a mile and three-quarters. Its floor, viewed from above, appears to be composed of a series of flat surfaces occupying two distinct levels, the higher upon the surface of the black ledge, the lower lying within the ledge. Upon the western side is a small cinder cone standing close upon the border of the black ledge. It is the only one visible, either within the caldera or upon the surrounding summit. Its height is about 125 or 130 feet. It was seen in operation, throwing up steam, clots of lava, and lapilli (some of the larger pieces of fragmentary lava) in the year 1878. The only other diversifications of the floor are many cracks which traverse it, the larger of which are distinctly visible from above. Some of them are considerably faulted. There is no difficulty in recognizing the fact that the whole floor has been produced by the sinkage of the lava beds which once continued over the entire extent of the depression, their undersides having been melted off most probably by the fires beneath. The lava beds in the immediate vicinity of the brink upon the summit platform wear the aspect of some antiquity.[Pg 36]They have become brown and carious by weathering, and, although no soil is generated, little drifts of gravel are seen here and there mixed with pumice. Since the caldera was formed there is no indication that the lavas have anywhere overflowed its rim. And yet it is a very strange fact that within a half mile, and again within a mile to a mile and a half, lavas have been repeatedly erupted within the last forty years from the summit platform, and have outflowed at points situated from 700 to 900 feet above the level of the lava lake within. Traces may also be seen, at varying distances back of the rim, of very many eruptions in which the rocks betoken great recency, although no dates can be assigned to their occurrence."

FIG. 7. PANORAMA OF MOKUAWEOWEO
From U. S. Geological Survey

FIG. 8. VIEW OF THE CRATER OF KILAUEA FROM THE VOLCANO HOUSE
From U. S. Geological Survey

During his visit to this great pit, Captain Dutton succeeded in climbing down the almost vertical walls on the side of the crater, and, reaching the surface of the hardened lake, walked over it. It must have required no little courage to thus venture on the thin floor of a lake which he knew was filled to great depths with red hot boiling lava, for he was walking over the surface of a slumbering volcano, that might at almost any moment awaken, and opening, swallow him and his companions. Through enormous cracks in the floor, he could feel the heat from the molten mass, while, through the same openings came suggestive whiffs of sulphur vapor.

During the eruption of this mountain, on January 23d, 1859, the light from the glowing lava streams was bright enough to read fine print at Hilo, a distance of thirty-five miles.

During the eruption of 1852, a stream of white-hot lava was thrown up into the air from one of the fissures to a height of from 300 to 400 feet.

STONES AND LAVA THROWN UPWARDS—ERUPTION OF MOKUAWEOWEO, HAWAII, JULY 4-21, 1899
From a Stereograph, Copyright, by Underwood & Underwood

When an eruption takes place in Mt. Loa the column of lava slowly rises in the crater, threatening to overflow[Pg 37] its lowest edges, but before this can take place the pressure becomes so great that some portion of the mountain below the crater is fractured and the lava quietly escapes.

During some conditions of the mountain every fifteen or twenty minutes a column of highly glowing lava is shot upwards like a fountain to a height of 500 feet and over, falling back into the lake in fiery spray. Unusual heights of these streams are generally followed by an eruption.

These curious jets of molten rock certainly cannot be due to the pressure of higher columns of lava, since the crater itself is near the top of a high plain. They are believed to be due to steam formed by the penetration of the rain water that falls on this part of the mountain.

You can now understand why the lava streams escaping from Mt. Loa as shown on the map, in Fig. 6, do not begin at the level of the crater; for the discharge of the lava does not take place over the rim of the crater, but through the cracks or fissures formed further down the sides of the mountains. It must not be supposed, however, that the fissures are limited to the sides of the mountain where they can be seen. They probably occur in many places below the surface of the water on some part of the bed of the ocean.

The crevices that are formed in this manner in the sides of the mountain vary greatly in size, some being so narrow that the lava scarcely flows through them at all but simply fills up the crevice, hardens on cooling, and mends the cracks in the mountains, in the way that a crack is mended in a piece of china by the use of glue or in a wall of masonry by mortar. Through the largest crevices or cracks, however, large lava streams may continue to flow often for several weeks, or even longer.

Sometimes, especially towards the close of the eruptive[Pg 38] flow, the lava may escape disruptively, so that small cones are formed along the lines of the fissures. Cones of this character are called lateral cones, and in the case of a volcanic island, where the lava flows out below the level of the water, the lateral cones sometimes project above the water and form volcanic islands or dangerous shoals that impede navigation.

When the lava pours out of a crevice in the side of the mountain, a river of molten rock rushes down the slopes, at first like a torrent, but on reaching the more nearly level ground, it spreads out in great lava lakes or fields, the surface of which takes on the characteristic black appearance of basalt, a certain kind of glass, for the lavas of Mt. Loa are generally basaltic. After an eruption the hardened floor of lava in the caldera, being no longer supported by the liquid mass formerly below it, falls in, leaving a large cavity with only the edges of the old floor clinging to the sides of the pit.

It will be interesting to give a short account of some of the great lava streams that have been poured out at different times from Mt. Loa.

In the great eruption of August 11th, 1855, the lava escaped through fissures from two to thirty inches in width. Then, flowing in a continuous stream, it did not stop until it was within five miles of Hilo.

In the eruption of January 23d, 1859, the lava stream flowed towards the northwest on the east side of Haulalai, reaching the sea in eight days.

The eruption of March 27th, 1868, was characterized by severe earthquake shocks, one of which, occurring on the second of April, destroyed many houses and produced huge fissures in the earth. These shocks produced great earthquake waves that reached distant coasts.

Mt. Kilauea, lies at a lower level towards the east.[Pg 39] This crater is situated at 4,040 feet above the level of the sea, and is nearly 6,000 feet below the caldera on the top of Mt. Loa.

Fig. 8, taken from the United States Geological Survey, Fourth Annual Report, for 1882-83, shows a view of Kilauea from the Volcano House. Dutton gives the following description of the appearance of Halemaumau, the pit crater or caldera of Kilauea.

"In front of us and right beneath our feet, over the crest of a nearly vertical wall, more than 700 feet below, is outspread the broad floor of the far-famed Kilauea. It is a pit about three and a half miles in length, and two and a half miles in width, nearly elliptical in plan and surrounded with cliffs, for the most part inaccessible to human foot, and varying in altitude from a little more than 300 feet to a little more than 700 feet. The altitude of the point on which we stand is about 4,200 feet above the sea....

"The object upon which the attention is instantly fixed is a large chaotic pile of rocks, situated in the centre of the amphitheatre, rising to a height which by an eye estimate appears to be about 350 to 400 feet. From innumerable places in its mass volumes of steam are poured forth and borne away to the leeward by the trade wind. The color of the pile is intensely black....

"Around it spreads out the slightly undulated floor of the amphitheatre, as black as midnight. To the left of the steaming pile is an opening in the floor of the crater, within which we behold the ruddy gleams of boiling lava. From numerous points in the surrounding floor clouds of steam issue forth and melt away in the steady flow of the wind. The vapors issue most copiously from an area situated to the right of the central pile, and in the southern portion of the amphitheatre. Desolation and horror reign supreme. The engirdling walls everywhere hedge it in.[Pg 40] But upon their summits, and upon the receiving platform beyond, are all the wealth and luxuriance of tropical vegetation heightening the contrast of the desolation below...."

FIG. 9. CRATER OF KILAUEA
From Dana's Manual of Geology

Fig. 9 represents the pit-like crater of Kilauea as it appeared after the eruption of 1886. Here, as will be seen, there are several lakes of lava, the largest of which is known as Halemaumau. The eruption of 1886, like all the eruptions of Kilauea, consisted of the escape of the lava from an opening on the side of the mountain below the crater, and a sinking in of the hardened floor of the crater. The figure also shows the position of the New Lake that lies east of Halemaumau. The extent and appearance of each of these lakes are constantly changing, both as to height and area.

Dutton gives the following description of the appearance of the lake of lava, and some curious phenomena that occur on its surface. He is describing the general appearance of[Pg 41] the pool of molten lava covered as it is with a hardened black crust:

"The surface of the lake is covered over with a black solidified crust showing a rim of fire all around its edge. At numerous points at the edge of the crust jets of fire are seen spouting upwards, throwing up a spray of glowing lava drops, and emitting a dull, simmering sound. The heat for the time being is not intense. Now and then a fountain breaks out in the middle of the lake and boils freely for a few minutes. It then becomes quiet, but only to renew the operation at some other point. Gradually the spurting and fretting at the edges augment. A belch of lava is thrown up here and there to the height of five or six feet, and falls back upon the crust. Presently, near the edge, a cake of the crust cracks off, and one edge of it bending downwards descends beneath the lava, and the whole cake disappears, disclosing a naked surface of liquid fire. Again it coats over and turns black. This operation is repeated edgewise at some other part of the lake. Suddenly a network of cracks shoots through the entire crust. Piece after piece of it turns its edge downwards and sinks with a grand commotion, leaving the whole pool a single expanse of liquid lava. The lake surges feebly for awhile, but soon comes to rest. The heat is now insupportable, and for a time it is necessary to withdraw from the immediate brink."

It is very curious to think of cakes of hardened lava floating on the surface of molten lava, but, of course, this is just as natural as cakes of ice floating on the surface of water; for a cake of hardened lava is, as you will understand, only a cake of frozen lava, and, being lighter than the molten lava, must, of course, float on its surface.

The disappearance of these cakes of frozen lava and their remelting is still more curious, and can be explained[Pg 42] as follows: The frozen or solidified mass of black basalt is a trifle lighter than the lava on which it is floating only while its temperature is high, and therefore expanded by heat. As soon as it cools, its density increases, and when it becomes a little greater than that of the liquid lava, it begins to sink and soon disappears.

FIG. 10. SECTIONS OF KILAUEA AT DIFFERENT PERIODS
From Dana's Manual of Geology

Professor Dana, who has made a careful study of the phenomena of Kilauea, shows in Fig. 10, a cross section of Kilauea at different times. Before the eruption of 1823, the depth of the crater was from 800 to 1,000 feet. At the eruption the bottom 600 to 800 feet, making the depth of Kilauea over this deeper central part about 1,500 feet. The varying depths at different dates are clearly marked on the drawing.

The eruptions of Kilauea generally occur as follows:

First there is a slow rising of the lava in the crater. This rising continues until the pressure is so great that the mountain is ruptured at some lower place. Next a discharge of the lava and a sinking to a level in the conduit that will depend on the position of the crevice. Then a gradual falling in of the hardened floor of the lake, a portion of the horizontal walls remaining on the sides of the caldera.

The eruption of Kilauea, however, has not always been of the quiet type. There was an eruption in the year 1789 that would appear to have been of the explosive variety. The following account is given by Dana as taken from a[Pg 43] history of the Sandwich Islands by the Rev. I. Dibble, published in 1843:

"The army of Keoua, a Hawaiian chief, being pursued by Kamehamoha, were at the time near Kilauea. For two preceding nights there had been eruptions, with ejections of stones and cinders. The army of Keoua set out on their way in three different companies. The company in advance had not proceeded far before the ground began to shake and rock beneath their feet, and it became quite impossible to stand. Soon a dense cloud of darkness was seen to rise out of the crater, and, almost at the same instant, the thunder began to roar in the heavens and the lightning to flash. It continued to ascend and spread around until the whole region was enveloped, and the light of day was entirely excluded. The darkness was the more terrific, being made visible by an awful glare from streams of red and blue light, variously combined through the action of the fires of the pit and the flashes of lightning above. Soon followed an immense volume of sand and cinders, which were thrown to a great height, and came down in a destructive shower for many miles around. A few of the forward company were burned to death by the sand, and all of them experienced a suffocating sensation. The rear company, which was nearest the volcano at the time, suffered little injury, and after the earthquake and shower of sand had passed over, hastened on to greet their comrades ahead on their escape from so imminent a peril. But what was their surprise and consternation to find the centre company a collection of corpses! Some were lying down, and others were sitting upright, clasping with dying grasp their wives and children, and joining noses (the mode of expressing affection) as in the act of taking leave. So much like life they looked that at first they supposed them merely at rest, and it[Pg 44] was not until they had come up to them and handled them that they could detect their mistake." Mr. Dibble adds: "A blast of sulphurous gas, a shower of heated embers, or a volume of heated steam would sufficiently account for this sudden death. Some of the narrators who saw the corpses, affirm that though in no place deeply burnt, yet they were thoroughly scorched." As you will see in Chapter XI, this sudden and awful death due to highly heated air and dust particles, caused even a greater loss of life in the catastrophic eruption of Pelée, in Martinique on May 8, 1902.

By reason of its situation at a lower level on the slopes of Mt. Loa, Kilauea was at one time thought to be one of the craters lower down on the slopes of Loa. This was the opinion of Professor Dana when he examined the district in 1840. Since this time the region has been more carefully studied, and Mt. Loa and Kilauea, are now generally regarded as separate and independent volcanoes, neither of which acts as a safety valve for the other.

We shall not attempt in this chapter to say anything concerning the sources or places from where these great supplies of lava have been drawn. This will be left to some subsequent chapter, after we have described still other volcanoes.

The outlines of mountains like Mt. Loa or Kilauea differ greatly from mountains like Vesuvius; their slopes, like the slopes of all other Hawaii volcanoes, have an inclination which does not exceed 10°. The lava streams, therefore, as they flow down the mountains, move more slowly than they would were the slopes more precipitous, as in mountains like Vesuvius.

There have been many eruptions of Kilauea. That which occurred in the year 1840, was of great magnitude (see map, Fig. 6), and began in a fissure southwest of[Pg 45] the crater. The principal eruption, however, broke out about twelve miles from the sea coast, and about twenty-five miles east of Kilauea. Here an enormous mass of lava forming a stream nearly three miles wide reached the ocean at Nanawale.

When an eruption takes place on Mt. Loa through a fissure at the height of 10,000 to 13,000 feet the length of the lava streams is frequently as great as twenty-five to thirty miles. Often the lava though hardening at the surface will continue to flow underneath through huge tunnels, of which the top and sides are composed of solidified parts of the same lava stream. After the flow has ceased long hollow tunnels often remain. If the lower end of such a tunnel containing molten lava is momentarily closed, the pressure of the lava above may not only burst through the obstruction, but may even throw the lava upwards in jets 300 to 700 feet high. Probably most of you have seen illumined fountains where jets of water are beautifully lighted up by different colored electric lights placed below them. Such fountains, however, can but poorly compare either in beauty or grandeur with these wonderful lava fountains, common on the slopes of Mt. Loa during an eruption.

[Pg 46]

CHAPTER IV

THE VOLCANIC ISLAND OF ICELAND

The island of Iceland consists of a number of volcanic mountains some of which are still active. As can be seen from the map, shown in Fig. 11, Iceland lies in the North Atlantic Ocean, immediately below the Arctic Circle, about 250 miles east of Greenland, and 600 miles west of Norway. Its length from east to west is about 300 miles, and its breadth about 200 miles, its total area, including the adjacent islands, being more than 40,000 square miles.

Were all the water removed from the North Atlantic Ocean, it would be seen that Iceland rests on the bed of the Atlantic, on a submarine plateau or highland; for, in this part of the ocean the water is only from 1,500 to 3,000 feet deep. This submarine plateau extends as far as Norway on the east, Greenland on the north, and the island of Jan Mayen on the northeast. Immediately north of the plateau the ocean suddenly drops to a depth of 12,000 to 15,000 feet.

[Pg 47]

FIG. 11. ICELAND

Toward the south the plateau extends with but few interruptions through the middle of the ocean to a shoal known as the *Dolphin Shoal*, as far as lat. 25° N. This part of the ocean, which can only relatively be called a shoal, is not generally deeper than 9,600 feet, although in some places the water is more than 12,000 feet deep. On each side of the Dolphin Shoal the water is much deeper, being in places 15,000 feet on the east, while on[Pg 48] the west there are depths as great as from 17,000 to 21,000 feet.

This sunken plateau, possibly including the shallower plateau on the north, is believed by some to be the remains of the fabled continent of *Atlantis*, to which we shall refer in another part of this book.

The coast line of Iceland is unbroken on the southeast, but the remainder of the coast is deeply indented with bays or fiords in which are many excellent harbors.

Iceland is liable to frequent earthquake shocks and volcanic eruptions. From careful records that have been preserved in the history of the island, we learn that since the beginning of the twelfth century there have practically never been intervals longer than forty years, and more generally not longer than twenty years, in which there has not been a great earthquake or a great volcanic eruption. These volcanic eruptions are often very protracted. For example, one eruption of the volcano Hecla continued for six years without ceasing. Sir Charles Lyell, the great English geologist, writes as follows about Iceland:

"Earthquakes have often shaken the whole island at once, causing great changes in the interior, such as the sinking down of hills, the rending of mountains, the desertion of rivers by their channels, and the appearance of new lakes. New islands have often been thrown up near the coast, some of which still exist, while others have disappeared, either by subsidences or the action of the waves.

"In the interval between eruptions innumerable hot springs afford vent to the subterranean heat, and solfataras discharge copious streams of inflammable matter. The volcanoes in different parts of the island are observed, like those of the Phlegræan Fields, Italy, to be in activity by turns, one vent often serving for a time as a safety[Pg 49] valve for the rest. Many cones are often thrown up in one eruption and in this case they take a linear direction, running generally from southeast to northwest."

The volcanic eruptions of Iceland belong for the greater part to the fissure type. During a volcanic eruption in Iceland the ground is split in fissures or cracks, generally parallel to each other, and varying in width from a few inches to several yards. These fissures extend for great distances across the country. The lava quietly wells out along the fissures not unlike the way quiet spring waters flow from their reservoirs.

According to Dr. Th. Thoroddsen, the Icelandic geologist, there are two systems of fissures extending through Iceland, from southwest to northeast in the southern part of the island, and from north to south in the northern part. Where two lines of fissures cross each other the points of intersection may be especially active.

Dr. Th. Thoroddsen arranges the volcanoes of Iceland under three heads, i. e., *cone-shaped volcanoes, lava cones*, and *chains of craters*, the last being the commonest. Out of 107 volcanoes examined by him in Iceland, eight were of the Vesuvian type, or were built up of layers of lava and volcanic ashes; sixteen were of the lava-cone type, similar to Mt. Loa, of the Hawaiian Islands, and the remaining eighty-three were of the type of crater chains.

The volcano of Snaefell Jökul, 4,710 feet above the level of the ocean, is built up of alternate layers of lava and hardened volcanic mud. It is not, however, a true cone-shaped mountain.

The largest volcano in Iceland, the Dyngjufköll, with its immense crater of Askja, has an area of some twenty-five square miles. In its form it resembles Snaefell.

Volcanoes of the lava-cone type have been built up entirely of lava and have a slight angle of inclination.[Pg 50] These volcanoes range in size from small hillocks to the largest mountains on the island. Their cones generally stand on a base of wide circumference and frequently rise to great heights, the top being occupied by a caldera, or pit crater like that on Mt. Loa or Kilauea.

Volcanoes of the type of chain-craters follow the natural fissures in the crust. These craters are generally low, seldom being more than 350 feet high.

There are also seen in Iceland caldron-shaped depressions that have been formed by explosive eruptions. One of the best instances of such craters is Viti, on the side of Mt. Krafla. This crater was formed by the sudden eruption of May 17th, 1724.

The lava sometimes quietly runs out of the entire length of the fissure without forming any cone. This was the case of a great fissure known as the Eldgja Chasm. Here three lava streams covered an area of 270 square miles.

As the lava comes out of the fissures, it generally produces long ramparts of slags, and blocks of lava that are piled up on either side of the fissure. Sometimes a line of low cones is built up. These cones consist of heaps of slag, cinders, and blocks of lava. Their craters are not rounded as in the case of volcanoes of the Vesuvian type, but are oblong, or have their greatest diameter extending in a direction of the fissure.

Icelandic lava as it escapes from the fissures is peculiar in that it is very viscid or plastic and can be readily drawn out into long threads that can be spun into ropes. When such lava runs down the sides of a steep slope, it often splits on cooling into separate blocks. Where it runs over flat, level ground, however, it spreads uniformly on all sides, producing vast level lava deserts that are as flat as the surface of a well built floor.

There are many rivers in the north and the west of[Pg 51] Iceland. Now, as the lava streams flow out of the fissures they enter the channels of the rivers so that the streams of water must find new paths to the sea, and this operation may be repeated again and again. Often the time between eruptions is long enough to give the rivers opportunity to cut deep channels or gorges in their new channels; but on the next escape of the lava these gorges and valleys are again filled with the molten rock, and the rivers must begin their channel cutting all over.

You will note the frequent use of the word Jökul, as Snaefell Jökul, Skaptar Jökul, Orefa Jökul, etc. The name Jökul means a large mass of ice, or a mountain that is continually covered with snow, for example, Snaefell Jökul, is a beautifully shaped, snow-covered mountain situated on a point of land on the western coast of the island, extending out nearly fifty miles into the sea, between the Faxa Fiord and the Briela Fiord. It is a very conspicuous object, being visible to passing ships at considerable distances from the island. Orefa Jökul is the highest mountain in Iceland. Skaptar Jökul is one of the active volcanoes of Iceland.

There can be no doubt that Iceland has been formed entirely by lava thrown up from the bottom of a submarine plateau, until it extended above the surface of the waters. To make an island entirely of lava with an area of 40,000 square miles, must, of course, have required many cones or craters that continued to pour forth lava for periods of time much longer than those during which man has lived on the earth.

The surface of Iceland is far from attractive. The interior is practically a vast lava desert, covered with snow-clad mountains or Jökuls. There is no plant life except in marshy lands near the coasts, and even here scarcely enough grass is raised to feed the few cattle and[Pg 52] horses owned by the inhabitants. There is no agriculture, owing to the very short summers, so that all grain is brought from Europe. Every now and then the grass crop is destroyed by accumulation of Polar ice on the northern and western coasts. Such failures are always attended by great famines, when many of the people die.

Should you ever visit Iceland you would probably be surprised to hear the people speaking about their forests. You might go over all the coasts of the island without seeing anything larger than a birch bush, not much higher than six feet. These are what the Icelanders like to speak of as their forest trees, and I suppose there is no harm done, if one only understands just what they mean by "trees."

While, however, Iceland has practically no trees, yet it has no difficulty in obtaining a plentiful supply of timber, since in the deep fiords or bays on the western and southern coasts there can always be found much drift timber brought there by the ocean currents from the forests of America.

The principal town or settlement in Iceland is Reykjavik, the capital of the island, on the southwestern coast; this is the chief trading place on the island. Thingvalla is also an important town.

The lavas that form the entire mass of Iceland were thrown out both before and since the glacial age. It is the opinion of Geikie that these outflows have continued uninterruptedly since that age to the present time. It is known that the lavas of Iceland were thrown out both before and after the glacial age, because during the glacial age, deep cuttings or groovings were made on the surface of the earth by the glaciers as they slowly moved over it. Now lava beds containing the glacial scratches have been found and resting on them are other lava streams. The[Pg 53] scratched lavas must, therefore, have been thrown out before the glacial age, and the second lavas after that age.

Let us now examine some of the more active volcanoes of Iceland and their eruptions. We will begin with the well-known volcano of Skaptar Jökul.

The following description of this volcano has been taken from a book on Iceland by E. Henderson, published in Boston, 1831. Skaptar Jökul lies in the south central part of Iceland about forty odd miles from the coast. It takes its name from the Skaptar River, down whose channel the lava flowed its entire distance of forty miles from the ocean. Skaptar Jökul consists of about twenty conical hills lying along one of the fissures that extends from northeast to southwest.

It appears from Henderson's account that people living in the neighborhood of Skaptar Jökul were greatly alarmed by repeated earthquakes that were felt at different times from the first to the eighth of June, 1783. These earthquake shocks increased in number and violence, so that the people left their homes and awaited in terror the coming catastrophe. On the morning of the eighth a prodigious cloud of dense smoke darkened the air, and the surrounding land soon became covered with ashes, pumice, and brimstone. As is common with eruptions in Iceland, that have been preceded by long periods of rest, the heat produced by the escaping lava and the sulphurous gases, melted such quantities of ice that great floods were produced in the rivers.

On the 10th of June vast torrents of lava that had been escaping from the craters entered the valley of the Skaptar River, and commenced flowing through its channel. Immense quantities of steam were produced, and, in less than twenty-four hours, the river was completely dried up, for the lava had collected in the channel, which in[Pg 54]many places flows between high rocks from 400 to 600 feet in height and nearly 200 feet in breadth, and had not only filled the river to its brink, but had overflowed the adjacent fields to a considerable extent, and flowing along the cultivated banks of the river destroyed all the farms in its path.

On gaining the outlet, where the channel of the Skaptar emerged into the plain, it might have been supposed that the burning flood would have at once spread over the low fields, which lay immediately before it, but, contrary to all expectations, this flow was for a time stopped by an immense unfathomed abyss in the river's bed, into which it emptied itself with great noise. When this chasm was at last filled, the lava increased by fresh flows, rose to a prodigious height, and breaking over the cooled mass, proceeded south towards the plain.

In the meantime the thunder and lightning, together with subterranean roars, continued with little or no intermission.

On the 18th of June, 1783, another dreadful eruption of red hot lava came from the volcano. This flowed with great velocity and force over the surface of the cooling stream that had been thrown out principally on the tenth of the month. Floating islands consisting of masses of flaming rock were seen on the surface of the lava stream, and the water that had been banked up on both sides of the stream was thrown into violent boiling.

In the meantime people living along the Hverfisfloit, the next largest river to the east of the Skaptar, had not yet been visited by the lava streams. It is true that their vegetation had been destroyed by showers of red hot stone and ashes, and that both atmosphere and water were filled with poisonous substances. The land had also been plunged in utter darkness, so that it was scarcely possible[Pg 55] at noonday to distinguish a sheet of white paper held up at the window from the blackness of the wall on either side. But the molten lava streams had not yet reached the people of this valley and they hoped that the eruption would soon be over, and that the lava flow would continue to follow the Skaptar. On the 3d of August, however, they were alarmed by seeing steam escaping from the River Hverfisfloit, and soon all its water was dried up, and a fresh lava flow poured down upon them. As in the case of the Skaptar, the melted rock completely filled the empty channel to the brink, and then overflowing, covered the low grounds on both sides, so that by the ninth of August it had reached the open and level country near its mouth and in the course of a few hours spread itself for a distance of nearly six miles across the plain. This flow continued after the end of August, and, indeed, even as late as the month of February, 1784, when a new eruption took place in this part of the country.

Hecla, another well-known volcano in Iceland, situated about thirty miles from the southern coast, consists of three peaks, the central of which is the highest. Its craters form

19

vast hollows on the sides of these peaks, and at the time of the eruption in 1766 were covered with snow. Hecla is believed to have been an active volcano long before Iceland was inhabited. No less than twenty-three eruptions have been recorded between A. D. 1004 and the great eruption of 1766-68.

Volcanic history frequently repeats itself. There had been no great eruption of Hecla for a period of about twelve years, and the people living in the neighborhood were congratulating themselves on the belief that the mountain was becoming actually extinct, and that therefore they need not trouble themselves about eruptions. Others, however, more farseeing, pointed out the fact that[Pg 56] the lakes and rivers in the vicinity did not freeze, and that the amount of water they contained was greatly decreased.

The following description of the great eruption of Hecla that was remarkable both for its violence, as well as for the time during which it continued, is taken from Symington's "Sketches of Faroe Islands and Iceland":

"On the 4th of April, 1766, there were some slight shocks of an earthquake, and early next morning a pillar of sand, mingled with fire and red hot stones, burst with a loud thundering noise from its summit. Masses of pumice, six feet in circumference, were thrown to the distance of ten or fifteen miles, together with heavy magnetic stones, one of which, eight pounds weight, fell fourteen miles off, and sank into ground still hardened by the frost. The sand was carried towards the northwest, covering the land, 150 miles round, four inches deep, impeding the fishing boats along the coast, and darkening the air, so that at Thingore, 140 miles distant, it was impossible to know whether a sheet of paper was white or black. At Holum, 155 miles to the north, some persons thought they saw the stars shining through the sand-cloud. About mid-day, the wind veering round to the southeast, conveyed the dust into the central desert, and prevented it from totally destroying the pastures. On the 9th of April, the lava first appeared, spreading about five miles towards the southwest, and on the 23d of May, a column of water was seen shooting up in the midst of the sand. The last violent eruption was on the 5th of July, the mountains, in the interval, often ceasing to eject any matter; and the large stones thrown into the air were compared to a swarm of bees clustering around the mountain-top; the noise was heard like loud thunder forty miles distant, and the accompanying earthquakes were more severe at Krisuvik, eighty miles westward, than at half the distance[Pg 57] on the opposite side. The eruptions are said to be in general more violent during a north or west wind than when it blows from the south or east, and on this occasion more matter was thrown out in mild than in stormy weather. Where the ashes were not too thick, it was observed that they increased the fertility of the grass fields, and some of them were carried even to the Orkney Islands, the inhabitants of which were at first terrified by what they considered showers of black snow."

The largest volcano in Iceland is Dyngjufjoll. This has on its summit the gigantic crater of Askja, some twenty-five square miles in area. This crater is of the intermediate form; the most general form of volcanoes on the island consisting of a number of craters that closely follow fissures.

Professor Johnstrup, in a report to the Danish Government, on this volcano, states that the valley of Askja has been gradually filled by repeated flows of lava from enormous craters on the edge of the mountain. In many places the surface of the earth is covered with bright red pumice stone that was thrown out during an eruption March 29th, 1875. Some of these craters are filled with steam that escapes with an almost deafening roar. The surprising feature of this eruption was the immense quantity of pumice stone that escaped.

The volcanoes in the Nyvatus Oraefi are entirely different. This barren plain is thirty-five miles in length and thirteen miles in breadth. Suddenly on the 18th of February, 1875, a volcano appeared in the centre, and four other craters were formed at subsequent dates. The mass of lava that was thrown out of these openings has been estimated at 10,000,000,000,000 cubic feet, or eighteen times the estimated mass of lava that has been emitted from Vesuvius between 1794 and 1855. This lava is basalt.

[Pg 58]

CHAPTER V

VESUVIUS

The old Greeks and Romans had but little knowledge of volcanoes. They only knew the volcanic mountains in the Mediterranean Sea. Here there are three volcanic regions:— one in the neighborhood of Naples; one including Sicily and the neighboring islands, and the other that of the Grecian Archipelago.

Some idea can be had of these three regions from a map of the Mediterranean shown in Fig. 12. The principal volcanoes are Vesuvius, Etna, Stromboli, and Vulcano, a mountain, by the way, that gave its name to all volcanic mountains. In this chapter we will describe the volcano of Vesuvius, the most active, though by no means the largest of the volcanoes of the Mediterranean.

But, before doing this, it will be well first to describe briefly the volcanic districts surrounding Vesuvius.

As shown in Fig. 13, this district includes Vesuvius, Procida, and Ischia.

[Pg 59]

FIG. 12. THE MEDITERRANEAN

Ischia is a small island measuring about five miles from east to west, and three miles from north to south. There were such terrific volcanic eruptions on this island long before the Christian Era, that several Greek colonies were forced to abandon it. A colony established long afterwards, about 380 B. C., by the king of Syracuse also had to depart. Strabo, the Grecian geographer (born about 63 B. C.), states that, according to tradition, terrific earthquakes occurred on the island a little before his time,[Pg 60] and its principal mountain threw out large quantities of molten rock, which flowed into the sea. At the time of this eruption there were earthquake waves in the sea, the waters of which slowly receded, leaving large portions of the bottom uncovered, and rushing, afterwards, violently over the land, caused great destruction. It was during this disturbance, so Strabo asserts, that the island of Procida was formed by being violently torn from Ischia.

FIG. 13. THE VOLCANIC DISTRICT AROUND VESUVIUS

The Phlegræan Fields was a name given by the ancients to some of the lowlands in the neighborhood of Naples; they were believed to be under the special protection of the Roman gods. When the frequent earthquake shocks shook these fields, the Roman people believed that conflicts were taking place between their gods and slumbering giants confined in the regions below the surface.

[Pg 61]

It is more than probable that Mt. Vesuvius has always been the centre of these volcanic disturbances. Long before the Christian Era, however, Vesuvius, or Somma, the name given to the old crater that then occupied the summit of the mountain, had been an extinct crater. Indeed, it had been so quiet that the people who lived on its slopes did not appear to know they were living on the slopes of a slumbering volcano. Their knowledge of volcanic mountains must have been very limited, for this mountain with the huge pit at its summit had all the appearance of a volcanic crater. When they climbed to the top of the mountain, which, of course, they frequently did to look after the vineyards they were cultivating on the slopes, and looked down into the deep pit from the rocks on its edge, they could see at the bottom of a great central pit three miles in diameter, a lake, with room here and there to enable one to walk along its borders. The walls of the precipice were covered with luxuriant vines.

When we say that none of the people even suspected that Vesuvius had ever been in a state of eruption, we must except some of their learned men. For both Diodorus Siculus, a native of Sicily, who lived about 10 B. C., and wrote an Universal History, containing some forty volumes, of which only about one-third remain, and Strabo, the Geographer, pointed out in a general manner, that Vesuvius, and much of the surrounding country, looked as if it had been eaten by fire. Then, too, a Roman philosopher who lived between A. D. 1 and A. D. 64, spoke of Vesuvius being "a channel for the eternal fire!"

21

Let us now endeavor to obtain some idea of the appearance of this region a short time before A. D. 79, when Vesuvius burst forth in a terrific eruption. The slopes of the mountain were covered with the rich vegetation that[Pg 62] characterizes this part of Italy. When most volcanic ashes and lava have been exposed for some time to the atmosphere they make a very fertile soil. Now, this soil on the slopes of Vesuvius made the vineyards that covered the mountain slopes and the fields for miles around its base, bear very plentifully, so that the people lived very comfortably. Here and there on the slopes of the mountain large towns like Herculaneum and Pompeii had long been established, while, in the distance, was the large city of Naples. Besides these there were numerous populous towns and villages scattered here and there over the plain or on the lower mountain slope.

You have all probably read of the Roman gladiator, Spartacus. Spartacus was a Thracian by birth, and while a shepherd had been taken prisoner by the Romans and sold to a trainer of gladiators at Capua. Chaffing under the tyranny of the Romans, who forced him to fight in the arena with men and beasts, he revolted against his masters, and with a band of some seventy followers, fled to a mountain fastness in the crater of Vesuvius. Proud Rome sent a few men to recapture him, with scourges for his punishment, but they were beaten by Spartacus. Every day dissatisfied men like himself escaped from the Romans and joined his ranks. Rome sent a larger body of men against Spartacus, but they also were beaten. At last, recognizing the gravity of the position, the Roman Prætor, Clodius, was sent against Spartacus with an army of some three thousand men. Clodius caught Spartacus in the crater and guarded the only space by which it seemed possible for Spartacus to escape. Using the vines that covered the precipitous walls of the crater, Spartacus did escape, and falling unexpectedly on the armies of Clodius, routed them. After this victory, Spartacus with an army of over 100,000 men overran southern Italy,[Pg 63] and sacked many of the cities of the Roman Campania. During this time Spartacus defeated one Roman army after another, until finally, in the year 71 B. C., Crassus was sent against him and vainly endeavored to conquer him. Being unsuccessful, Crassus urged the Roman Senate to recall Lucullis from Asia and Pompey from Spain, and finally poor Spartacus was cut down in a fight he made against Crassus and Lucullis.

But let us come to the great eruption of Vesuvius in A. D. 79. The people living on the slopes of Vesuvius were not without plenty of warnings of the dreadful catastrophe that was coming. As early as A. D. 63 there was a great earthquake that shook the country far beyond Naples. In Pompeii, then a flourishing city, the Temple of Isis was so much damaged that it had to be rebuilt.

Even if the earthquake shocks had not foretold the coming eruption, there were other signs. The height of water in the wells decreased. Springs that had never before been known to fail, dried up completely. These changes, as we well know, were due to the red hot lava being slowly forced up from great depths into the tube connected with the crater.

The earthquake shocks continued at irregular intervals for sixteen years, until, on the 25th of August, A. D. 79, about one o'clock in the afternoon, Vesuvius burst forth in the terrible eruption that destroyed the towns of Pompeii and Herculaneum. Pompeii was a seaport town situated near the mouth of the River Sarno, about fifteen miles southeast of Naples. It was a beautiful place, containing many splendid temples. Its people for the greater part lived luxuriously, for Pompeii was the summer resort of the richer people of Naples, some of whom lived there during the hottest months of the year.

Herculaneum, the other town, was nearer Naples, only[Pg 64] five miles from the city. It was also, like Pompeii, a beautiful town, and contained many splendid buildings. In each town there were magnificent baths and a large theatre. The inhabitants spent so much of their time in the open air, or in the baths, that it was not necessary for them to build very large houses. The houses, however, were well built, and though generally consisting of practically a single story, were provided with all the luxuries that great wealth could command.

On August 25th, A. D. 79, severe earthquake shocks again visited this part of the world and Vesuvius suddenly threw up from its crater an immense column of black smoke, which, rising high in the air, spread out in the form of a huge mushroom, or, perhaps, more like the umbrella pine tree of the neighborhood. Rapidly spreading on all sides, the smoke soon completely shut out the light of the sun, and wrapped the earth in an inky darkness, except for a red glare from columns of molten rock that rushed out of the crater.

From the dark cloud immense quantities of red hot stones, pumice, and volcanic ashes descended on the earth. At the same time there fell a deluge of rain, caused by the sudden condensation of the enormous amount of water vapor that was thrown out from the crater during the eruption. Fortunately, very few of the people were killed in either of the cities of Pompeii and Herculaneum, although some bodies were found in the ruins. Most of the people escaped through the darkness and gloom, continuing to flee from the city for at least three days.

Both cities were covered so deep with ashes or mud that the tops of the tallest buildings were no longer visible. Pompeii was buried by showers of ashes or volcanic cinders, and Herculaneum mainly by vast floods of aqueous lava.

[Pg 65]

So completely were these cities covered that their very existence was at last forgotten. It is true that Titus, who was then Emperor of Rome, endeavored to clear away the ashes and rebuild Pompeii, but the task was so great that he finally abandoned it.

During the year 1592, the architect Fontana, while superintending the building of an aqueduct, came across some ancient buildings. At a much later date, in 1713, some workmen, while digging a well in the village of Portici, uncovered three marvellously beautiful marble statues. In the year 1738, the same well was dug deeper, when traces of the old theatre of Herculaneum were discovered. Some effort was then made to excavate the city and many of the public buildings and private houses were uncovered, and statues, mosaics, wall paintings, and charred manuscripts of papyrus were found. A few of these have been unrolled and deciphered, but owing to the difficulty of doing this, without destroying them, the greatest number still remain unread.

In 1860, the Italian Government began a systematic excavation of the buried cities, and now both Pompeii and Herculaneum are thrown open to the sunlight so that one can walk through the old streets, and look into the houses, in which, before A. D. 79, the people lived so happily.

Many interesting stories are told about the discoveries that were made during the government excavations. The skeleton of one of the inhabitants was found grasping a money bag. He might have escaped, but had gone back to get his money. He got it, but remained with it. In another place, the skeletons of a number of people were found in an underground room or cellar of a house, where were also found some mouldy bread and empty water flasks. Instead of leaving the city, which they might[Pg 66]have done, they had retreated to the underground room for safety, but the fine volcanic dust drifted in and suffocated them.

The younger Pliny, the historian, has given an excellent account of some features of this great eruption. It appears that his uncle was stationed with the Roman fleet, in the Bay of Naples, at the time of the eruption. He describes the dark cloud of ashes that was formed over Vesuvius. He refers to the rapidity with which it spread, and to the showers of ashes, cinders, and stones that it rained down on the earth. His uncle, the elder Pliny, landed on the coast, and was afterwards killed by a cloud of sulphurous vapor that swept down the side of the mountain.

The following letter from the younger Pliny, describing his flight with his mother from Misenum, is quoted from Dana's "Characteristics of Volcanoes."

"It was now seven o'clock [on the morning of August 25th], but the light was still faint and doubtful. The surrounding buildings had been badly shaken, and although we were in an open spot [a little yard between his uncle's house and the sea], the space was so small that the danger of a catastrophe from falling walls was great and certain. Not till then did we make up our minds to go from the town.... When we were free from the buildings we stopped. There we saw many wonders and endured many terrors. The vehicles we had ordered to be brought out kept running backward and forward, though on level ground; and even when blocked with stones they would not keep still. Besides this, we saw the sea sucked down and, as it were, driven back by the earthquake. There can be no doubt that the shore had advanced on the sea, and many marine animals were left high and dry. On the other side was a dark and dreadful[Pg 67]cloud, which was broken by zigzag and rapidly vibrating flashes of fire, and yawning showed long shapes of flame. These were like lightning, only of greater extent....

"Pretty soon the cloud began to descend over the earth and cover the sea. It enfolded Capreæ and hid also the promontory of Misenum." ... The flight was continued. "Ashes now fell, yet still in small amount. I looked back. A thick mist was close at our heels, which followed us, spreading out over the country, like an inundation." ... Turning from the roar in order to avoid the fleeing, terror-stricken throng, they rested. "Hardly had we sat down when night was over us—not such a night as when there is no moon and clouds cover the sky, but such darkness as one finds in close-shut rooms. One heard the screams of women, the fretting cries of babes, and shouts of men....

"Little by little it grew light again. We did not think it the light of day, but a proof that the fire was coming nearer. It was indeed fire, but it stopped afar off; and then there was darkness again, and again a rain of ashes, abundant and heavy, and again we rose and shook them off, else we had been covered and even crushed by the weight.... At last the murky vapor rolled away, in disappearing smoke or fog. Soon the real daylight appeared; the sun shone out, of a lurid hue, to be sure, as in an eclipse. The whole world which met our frightened eyes was transformed. It was covered with ashes white as snow."

Young Pliny and his mother returned to Misenum, and survived the perils to which they were exposed.

It was during this eruption that a large part of the old crater was blown off the mountain by the tremendous force at work.

There have been many eruptions of Vesuvius since the[Pg 68] great eruption of A. D. 79. One of these occurred during the reign of Severus, A. D. 203. It was during this eruption that an additional part of the old crater of Somma was blown away.

Another great eruption occurred A. D. 472. Then great quantities of volcanic dust were thrown up into the air, and falling, covered practically all parts of Europe, producing darkening of the sun and great fear as far as the city of Constantinople.

But what was perhaps a still greater eruption occurred during December of 1631. This eruption spread great quantities of ashes over the country for hundreds of miles around, and great streams of mud rushed down the slopes of the mountain. Buccini gives the following account of this eruption:

"The crater was five miles in circumference, and about 1,000 paces deep. Its sides were covered with brushwood, and at the bottom there was a plain on which cattle grazed. In the woody parts wild boars frequently harbored. In one part of the plain, covered with ashes, were three small pools, one filled with hot but bitter water; another with water saltier than the sea, and a third with water that was hot but tasteless. But at length these forests and grassy plains were consumed, being suddenly blown into the air and their ashes scattered to the winds. In December, 1631, seven streams of lava poured at once from the crater and overflowed several villages, on its flanks, and at the foot of the mountain. Reisna, partly built over the ancient city of Herculaneum, was consumed by the fiery torrent. Great floods of mud were as destructive as lava. This is no unusual occurrence during these catastrophes for such is the violence of the rains produced by the evolution of aqueous vapors that torrents of water descend the cone and become charged with impalpable[Pg 69] volcanic dust, and rolling among ashes, acquire sufficient consistency to deserve the ordinary appellation of aqueous lava."

Of course, you will understand that we have given only a few of the most notable of the eruptions of Mt. Vesuvius. Since the yea A. D. 1500 there have been no less than fifty-six recorded eruptions, that of the year 1857 being especially violent.

Omitting these eruptions we at last come to the great recent eruption of 1872.

Fortunately, the eruption of 1872, as well as still more recent eruptions that have occurred, have been more accurately described than have most volcanic eruptions, for the Italian Government, recognizing the value to the natives of Italy of a knowledge of what was going on at the crater of Vesuvius, has maintained for the past thirty years an observatory on the western part of the mountain. This observatory has been placed in charge of Prof. Luigi Palmieri, a well-known student of volcanoes and earthquakes. At this place records are kept of the behavior of the volcano, of all earthquake disturbances, as well as other phenomena. At the same time, by the use of photography, excellent pictures have been obtained showing the appearance of the sky during an eruption.

Vesuvius had been in a quiet state from November, 1848, to the year 1871, when small quantities of lava flowed continuously for several months. Again, early in 1872, other quiet eruptions of lava continued for weeks at a time. Finally, on April 26th, of that year, a violent explosive eruption occurred. The following account has been taken from Palmieri's report, entitled, "The Eruption of Vesuvius in 1872."

On April 23d the recording earthquake instruments, the seismographs, were greatly affected. On the evening[Pg 70] of the 24th lava streams flowed down the cone in various directions. These streams were continued on the 25th and the 26th, so that on the night of the 26th the observatory lay between two streams of molten lava that threw out so much heat that the glass windows in the observatory were cracked, and a scorching smell was quite perceptible in the rooms. The cone of the mountain was deeply fissured, lava escaping freely from all the fissures, so that the molten rock appeared to ooze from over its entire surface, or as Palmieri expressed it, "Vesuvius sweated fire."

This great cracking or fissuring of the cone was accompanied by the opening of two large craters at the summit, that discharged, with a great noise, immense clouds of steam, dust, lapilli, and volcanic bombs. These latter are very curious and consist of masses of soft lava that are thrown high into the air by the outrushing columns of steam. Being rotated or spun, as they rise in the air, they assume a spherical shape. Some of these volcanic bombs were thrown to a height estimated by Palmieri to have been nearly 4,000 feet above the top of the mountain. When the height of a projectile is known, the velocity with which it left the opening from which it was projected or thrown can be estimated, so that the volcanic bombs must have left the crater at a velocity of about 600 feet per second.

On the 27th, in the evening, the lava streams ceased flowing, but the dust and lapilli continued to fall during the 28th and the 29th. On the 30th the detonations decreased and by the 1st of May the eruption was entirely over.

Palmieri calculated that the quantity of molten rock thrown out during this eruption was sufficient to cover an area of about 1.8 square miles to an average depth of about thirteen feet.

[Pg 71]

As we can see from the above descriptions, the volcanic activity of Vesuvius is characterized by long periods of rest followed by periods of activity. The periods of rest are measured by years, and often by centuries; the periods of activity by days or hours.

But Vesuvius was not to have a long period of rest after its eruption of 1872. On the contrary, shortly after the great disaster of Martinique in 1906, it again became active, and on the 5th of April, 1906, began throwing large blocks of lava out of its central cone, and on the next day began to throw out large streams of lava, which, on April 7th, destroyed a village in the neighborhood. At the same time rumbling sounds were heard, and violent earthquake shocks shattered the windows of the houses.

Professor Matteucci, the present director of the Vesuvius Observatory, made the following report on April 8th.

"The eruption of Vesuvius has assumed extraordinary proportions. Yesterday and last night the activity of the crater was terrific, and is increasing. The neighborhood of the observatory is completely covered with lava. Incandescent rocks are being thrown up by the thousands, to a height of 2,400 feet or even 3,000 feet, and falling back form a large cone. Another stream of lava has appeared.... The noise of the explosion and of the rocks striking together is deafening. The ground is shaken by strong and continuous seismic movements, and the seismic instruments [instruments employed to record the time, direction, and intensity of earthquake movements] threaten to break. It will probably be necessary to abandon the observatory, which is very much exposed to the shocks. The telegraph is interrupted, and it is believed the Funicular railroad has been destroyed."

On April 9th Matteucci made the following report:

[Pg 72]

"The explosive activity of Vesuvius, which was so great yesterday, and was accompanied by very powerful electric discharges, diminished yesterday afternoon. During the night the expulsion of rocks ceased, but the emission of sand increased, completely enveloping me and forming a red mass from six to ten centimeters deep, which carried desolation into these elevated regions. Masses of sand gliding along the earth, created complete darkness until seven o'clock. Several blocks of stone broke windows in the observatory. Last night the earthquake shocks were stronger and more frequent than yesterday, and displaced the seismic apparatus. Yesterday afternoon and this morning, torrents of sand fell."

On April 10th Matteucci sent the following report:

"Last night was calm, except for a few explosions of considerable force from time to time. At four o'clock this morning the explosions became more violent. The seismic instruments recorded strong disturbances."

The eruption of Vesuvius of 1906 was especially noted for the great quantities of sand and ashes thrown out of the crater. The amount of sand that fell on the roof of the market house at Monti Olivetto was so great that the roof fell in. In this eruption there were some six lava streams that poured down the mountain. The most formidable of these was that which descended towards Torre Annunziata. Here it stopped just short of the wall of the cemetery outside of the town.

During this eruption of Vesuvius, as in previous eruptions, clouds of volcanic dust collected in the air, shutting off the light of the sun. Naples was in a state of semi-darkness. The roofs of the houses were covered to a depth of several inches with an exceedingly fine reddish dust. In some places this dust had drifted into heaps fully a yard in depth.

[Pg 73]

CHAPTER VI

OTHER VOLCANOES OF THE MEDITERRANEAN

The relative positions of the other volcanic mountains of the Mediterranean Sea; i. e., Etna, Stromboli, and the volcanoes of the Santorin group of the Grecian Archipelago, are shown in the map, Fig. 12.

We will begin with the volcanic mountain of Etna, under which, according to mythology, the angry gods had buried the rebellious Typhoon.

Etna is situated on the island of Sicily, immediately southwest of Italy. It is a much larger mountain than Vesuvius, rising, as it does, from a circular base about eighty-seven miles around, to a height of 10,840 feet above the level of the Mediterranean. It forms a conspicuous object when seen either from the Mediterranean, or from distant parts of Italy.

The height of Etna is so great that its slopes can be divided into three distinct climatic zones or belts. The lowest of these lies between the sea and a height of 2,500 feet. In this zone the mountain slopes are covered with cultivated fields, olive groves, orchards, and vineyards. The middle zone lies between 2,500 feet and 6,270 feet. This zone is covered with forests of chestnuts, oaks, beeches, and cork trees. The third and highest zone includes the rest of the mountain, and may be called the desert zone, since it is a sterile region, covered with huge blocks of lava and scoriæ, and terminating, in the higher portions, in a snow-covered plain, from which the central cone rises.

[Pg 74]

Etna is continually sending up columns of steam and sulphur vapor. Every now and then it starts in eruption, throwing out large quantities of lava either from the crater on its summit, or from some of the 200 smaller cones or craters that occupy portions of its slopes. On account, probably, of its height the eruptions are most frequently on the sides. Etna affords a magnificent example of a huge volcanic pile of the Vesuvian type, which has been slowly built up by the gradual accumulation of materials that have escaped from its craters.

One of the most interesting features of the higher regions of Etna is an immense chasm rent in a side of the cone near the summit, and known as the Val del Bove. This chasm forms a vast amphitheater.

The great force that removed such an immense mass of matter from the cone could not have been the eroding power of water, since the materials of the cone are too porous to permit streams of any size to rush down the slopes. The force is most probably to be found in some explosive eruption of the mountain, when a portion of the crater was suddenly blown off, just as was done in Vesuvius when a large part of the old crater of Somma was blown away. What is especially interesting about the Val del Bove is the opportunity it affords for studying the interior structure of the mountain, for it practically enables one to enter to almost the heart of this great volcano.

The Val del Bove has the shape of a great pit five miles in diameter. It has almost vertical walls, the height of which varies with their position. Those which reach highest up the mountain vary from 3,000 to 4,000 feet in height.

Like Vesuvius, Etna has been split or fissured into great crevices that have been filled with lava during the many[Pg 75] eruptions of its central crater. On hardening, these lava streams form what are known as dikes. As the sides of the mountain are worn away by erosion, the dikes, being harder than the rest of the cone, project from its sides like huge walls. An excellent opportunity for seeing them is afforded in the walls of the Val del Bove.

Sir Charles Lyell, the English geologist, who has carefully studied Mt. Etna, asserts that this mountain began to be formed during a geological period known as the Tertiary Age, through a crater that opened on the floor of the Mediterranean Sea. The material thus thrown out, collected around the crater and produced a mountainous pile that gradually emerged above the level of the sea, and on fresh materials continuing to be thrown out, at length reached its present height. It would appear that at some former time in its history, there were two vents near the top of the mountain, the second crater being formed immediately under the Val del Bove. Soon, however, the second and lower crater was closed, the upper one alone remaining active. The mountain, therefore, continued to be slowly raised in the air by the materials brought out through this opening. Then came the great explosive eruption during which the side of the mountain was blown off to form the great chasm of the Val del Bove.

Because of its almost constant activity, Mt. Etna must have been well known to the ancients, who described some of its most violent eruptions. The following brief notes concerning these eruptions have been taken from Lyell.

According to Diodorus Siculus, an eruption that occurred before the Trojan war, caused the people living in districts near the mountain to seek new homes. Thucididies, the Greek historian, states that in the sixth year of the Peloponnesian war, which would be about the spring[Pg 76] of 425 B. C., a lava stream caused great destruction in the neighborhood of Campania, this being the third eruption that had occurred in Sicily since it had been settled by the Greeks.

Seneca, during the first century of the Christian Era, calls the attention of Lucullus to the fact that during his time Mt. Etna had lost so much of its height that it could no longer be seen by boatmen from points at which it had before been readily visible.

But passing by these very early eruptions of Etna we come to the great eruption of 1669. This eruption was preceded by an earthquake that destroyed many houses in a town situated in the lower part of the forest zone, about twenty-five miles below the summit of the mountain, and ten miles from the sea at Catania. During this eruption two deep fissures were opened near Catania. From these such quantities of sand and scoriæ were thrown out, that, in the course of three or four months, a double cone was formed 450 feet high, which is now known as Monte Rosso. But what was most curious was the sudden opening, with a loud crash, of a fissure six feet broad reaching down to unknown depths that extended in a somewhat crooked course to within a mile of the summit of Etna. This great fissure was twelve miles in length and emitted a most vivid light. Five other parallel fissures of considerable length opened, one after another, throwing out vapor, and emitting bellowing sounds which were heard at a distance of forty miles. These fissures were afterwards filled with molten rock, and in this manner were formed the long dikes of porphyry and other rocks that are seen to be passing through some of the older lavas of Mt. Etna.

[Pg 77]

FIG. 14. MT. ETNA
From Map of State and Government

The great lava streams which flowed down the side of the mountain during this eruption, destroyed fourteen[Pg 78] towns and villages, and at length reached Catania. A great wall had been raised around this city to prevent the lava from entering it. The molten rock, however, accumulated, until it rose to the top of the wall, which was sixty feet high, and then pouring over it in a fiery cascade, overwhelmed part of the city. It is said that during the first part of its journey, the lava streams moved over thirteen miles in twenty days, or at the rate of 162 feet an hour. Beyond this, after the lava had thickened by cooling, it had a velocity of only twenty-two feet per hour.

Fig. 14 represents a plan of Mt. Etna reduced from a map by the Italian Government. During the eruption of 1865, a rent was made in the mountain extending from Mount Frumento (B in the preceding map) for one and one-half miles, and six cones from 300 to 350 feet in height were formed along the fissure.

During the eruption of 1874, great fissures three miles in length were formed in the mountain.

There exists on the slopes of Mt. Etna vast subterranean grottoes formed by the sudden conversion into steam of great quantities of water that were overwhelmed by the molten mass. These immense volumes of steam produced enormous bubbles in the molten lava. When the lava hardened irregular grottoes were left. Lyell describes one of these as follows:

"Near Nicolosi, not far from Monte Rosso, one of these great openings may be seen, called the *Fossa della Palomba*, 625 feet in circumference at its mouth and seventy-eight deep. After reaching the bottom of this, we enter another dark cavity, and then others in succession, sometimes descending precipices by means of ladders. At length, the vaults terminate in a great gallery ninety feet long, and from fifteen to fifty broad, beyond which there is still a passage, never yet explored, so that the extent of[Pg 80] these caverns remains unknown. The walls and roofs of these great vaults are composed of rough bristling scoriæ of the most fantastic forms."

Besides the eruptions mentioned there have been many others, such as those of 1811, 1819, and 1852. The last of these was greater than any eruption except that of 1669. It began in August, 1852, and continued until May, 1853, and was remarkable for the immense quantity of lava thrown out.

FIG. 15. STROMBOLI, VIEWED FROM THE NORTHWEST, APRIL, 1874

We come now to the volcano of Stromboli. Stromboli, one of the Lipari islands, is situated about sixteen miles west of the Straits of Messina. Its general appearance is shown in Fig. 15. The form of the mountain is that of an irregular four-sided pyramid, which rises about 3,090 feet above the level of the Mediterranean, and stands on the bottom of the sea in water about 3,000 feet deep.

If you carefully examine the appearance of Stromboli, as shown in the preceding figure, you will notice that the flat cloud which hangs over the island is made up of a number of globular masses of vapor, formed during the peculiar action of the volcano.

When examined by night Stromboli presents a still more curious appearance. Since the mountain stands alone, its height permits it to be seen readily at sea for distances of at least a hundred miles. At night a curious glow of red light may be seen on the lower surfaces of the cloud. This light is not continuous, but increases in intensity from a faint glow to a fairly bright red light, then gradually decreases, and finally dies away completely. After awhile the light again appears, again gradually decreases, and disappears, and this continues until the rising sun prevents the red glow from being any longer visible. Stromboli, therefore, acts not unlike the flashing lighthouses so common on the sea coasts of all parts of[Pg 81] the world. Indeed, it is actually used by sailors in the Mediterranean for the purpose of showing them their direction. For this reason Stromboli is commonly called "The Lighthouse of the Mediterranean."

As Judd remarks, from whom much of the information concerning some of the volcanic districts of the Mediterranean has been obtained, the flashing light of Stromboli differs from that of the ordinary flashing light in two important respects; viz., in the intervals that elapse between the successive flashes, and in the intensity of the light emitted. As you know, it is necessary that the different lighthouses placed near one another on a coast must have their lights of such a nature that they can be readily distinguished. In order to do this, the flashing light has been devised. In flashing lighthouses, the lights only appear at intervals, one lighthouse being distinguished from another in its neighborhood by the intervals between successive flashes, or, sometimes, indeed, by the color of some of the flashes. Now, in the case of Stromboli, the intervals between the successive glowings of the red lights are very irregular, varying between one and twenty flashes per second. Moreover, the intensity of the light also varies greatly from time to time.

You naturally inquire as to the cause of these flashes of light that are emitted by Stromboli. If, as Judd suggests, you should climb to the summit of the mountain, during the daytime, and look down the inside of the crater, you could see its black slag bottom crossed by many cracks and fissures. From most of the smaller fissures the vapor of water is quietly escaping. This vapor rises in the air in which it soon disappears. There are, however, larger cracks on the bottom of the crater from which, at more or less regular intervals, masses of steam are emitted with loud snorting puffs not unlike those produced by a locomotive.[Pg 82] From some of the openings molten matter is seen slowly oozing out, collecting in parts of the crater and moving up and down in a heaving motion. Every now and then a bubble is formed on the surface of this liquid. The bubble swells to a gigantic size, and suddenly bursts. The steam it contained escapes, carrying fragments of scum which are thrown high into the air. The masses of steam, formed below the surface of the sticky, boiling, lava, in endeavoring to escape, force their way through the mass, blow huge bubbles, which, on bursting, produce the roaring sounds that are heard, and throwing great columns of vapor in the air, produce the rounded masses of clouds you can see floating high up in the air over the mountain. At the same time the scum is partially removed from the red hot surface, its light illumines the lower surface of the overhanging cloud, which flings it back again to the earth. With the bursting of each bubble, and the clearing of the scum from the surface of the red hot mass, the light begins, increases in intensity, and then as the scum again begins to collect on the surface, decreases, and finally disappears, and not until the bursting of the next bubble is it again visible.

But let us make a study of some of the peculiarities of Vulcano, another of the Lipari islands, which lies north of Sicily.

Vulcano affords a curious example of a volcano that has been harnessed by man, or made to do work for him. All volcanoes bring from inside of the earth different kinds of chemical substances, in the form of vapors, gases, or molten materials. Now, these materials acting on one another, produce chemical substances some of which, such as sal ammoniac, sulphur, and boracic acid, possess commercial value. This is especially true in the case of Vulcano, and since the eruptions are not generally[Pg 83] violent, a chemical works has actually been erected by a Scotch firm on the side of the mountain, where the materials are collected from the crevices.

This effort to harness a volcano was for a time so successful that the same people contemplated the building of great leaden chambers over the principal fissure at the bottom of the crater, so that the large volumes of ejected vapors might be condensed and collected. But Vulcano, like all other volcanoes, could not be relied on continually to keep the peace. One day it suddenly burst forth more fiercely than usual, so that the workmen were compelled to abandon the factory and fly down the mountain for their lives, but not, however, before some of them were severely injured by the explosions.

Vulcano is an instance of a volcano in an almost exhausted or dormant condition. It has had, however, many eruptions during the past few centuries, some of which have been very violent, for example, that of 1783, and that of 1786.

There still remains to be considered the volcanic region of the Santorin group of the Grecian Archipelago. The island of Santorin or Thera, is the southernmost of the Cyclades. It is an exceedingly curious island, being a submerged volcano, with most of the top of the crater remaining above the waters, so that the entire island has the shape of an irregular circle or crescent broken at several points. Its formation is, probably, due to the gradual

29

sinking of a volcanic mountain until its crater has been almost completely submerged, only the higher parts of the edges of the crater being left above the surface of the waters. Suppose, for example, a mountain like Vesuvius at the time the crater Somma existed, was sunk below the level of the Mediterranean until only the highest parts of the crater remained above the waters. If,[Pg 84] now, one or more volcanic eruptions occurred, producing craters or volcanic islands inside the submerged rim, you would have a condition of affairs seen in the island of Santorin.

[Pg 85]

CHAPTER VII

ORIZABA, POPOCATEPETL, IXTACCIHUATL, AND OTHER VOLCANOES OF MEXICO

While some of the volcanoes of Mexico are still in an active condition, most of them are either only slightly active or are dormant or extinct. Humboldt, the celebrated traveller and geographer, states that there are only four active volcanic mountains in Mexico; namely, Popocatepetl, Tuxtula, Colima, and Jorullo. But there are many others, among which may be mentioned Orizaba, Ixtaccihuatl, Xinantecatl, Tuxtula, Cofre de Perote, and Colima.

Of course, you can understand that, since extinct volcanoes may at any time become active, in parts of the world where communication with the interior is not good, many volcanic mountains that have been regarded as extinct may have broken out temporarily, during historical times, without their eruptions having been recorded.

It was at one time thought that Popocatepetl was the highest mountain in North America. More recent measurements, however, have shown that there are at least three other mountains in this part of the world, that are much higher. One of these is the active volcano of Orizaba that we will now briefly describe.

[Pg 86]

FIG. 16. MEXICO AND CENTRAL AMERICA

Orizaba is situated in the north central part of Mexico, about seventy-five miles west of Vera Cruz. Its ancient Aztec name was Cittaltepetl, or *Star Mountain.* The[Pg 87] height of the mountain is 18,200 feet. Like all high tropical mountains whose summits are snow-clad, one would pass through the same changes in climate, in going from its base to its summit, as in going along the earth's surface from the equator to the poles. Near the base of the mountain will be found a tropical climate, above that a temperate climate, while in still higher regions, the climate of the Arctic region.

According to Russell, from whose work on the volcanoes of North America much of the information concerning the volcanoes of Mexico and Central America has been condensed, Orizaba has three craters on its summit. The last recorded eruption took place about the middle of the Eighteenth Century. The mountain is now in a dormant or extinct condition, as may be seen from the fact that its three craters are for the greater part filled with snow.

Orizaba, like Etna, and many other volcanoes, has deep fissures extending through its sides. Through these, lava streams have flowed during times when it was active. There are also found on the slopes of this mountain many cones of a type known as *parasitic cones.* These cones are not caused by materials that have been brought to the surface during an eruption, but have been formed by the steam passing through lava streams that have come out of the crater during other eruptions.

Popocatepetl, or, as the word means, *The Smoking Mountain,* is the second highest mountain in Mexico. According to recent measurements made by the Mexican Government, its height is 17,876 feet. Popocatepetl is situated on the edge of the great plateau of Mexico, forty miles southeast of the City of Mexico. It is a conical mountain, and is a magnificent object when seen from the City of Mexico, rising, as it does, fully 10,000 feet from the elevation of the city, while on the east it towers for nearly[Pg 88] 18,000 feet above the level of the sea. This splendid mountain is poetically described by Russell:

"Seen from the basal plains, it sweeps up in one grand curve to nearly its full height,—a collossus of three and a quarter miles in elevation, white with everlasting frost on its summit, and bathed in the green of palms, bananas, oranges, and mangoes, at its base. Evergreen oaks and pines encircle its middle height, and above them, before the ice itself is reached, occur broad areas of loose sand into which the lavas have been changed by weathering. Soft wreaths of sulphurous vapor may at times be seen curling over the crest of the summit crater,—gentle reminders that the days of volcanic activity are not yet necessarily over."

Popocatepetl takes its name, *The Smoking Mountain* from the fact that gases and vapor are continually being emitted from its summit crater. It has a conical peak with a depression or crater on its summit. The bottom of the crater is crossed by fissures from which small quantities of steam escape, not, however, sufficient to melt all the snow which covers the slopes of the mountain to a depth of from eight to ten feet. A small lake of hot water has collected in the crater from the water derived from the melting snow. This water, sinking through the porous materials in the cone, is the source of a great number of large hot springs that occur around the base of the mountain.

Reclus states that the first to climb to the top of Popocatepetl was one of Cortez' officers, 1519.

Another snow-capped volcano, which rising from the plain of Mexico is in clear view of the city, is Ixtaccihuatl (Ets-tak'-se-wat-el), or as the word means in the ancient Aztec, *The White Woman*. This mountain, as measured by Heilprin, is 16,960 feet in height. Ixtaccihuatl is now in so[Pg 89] dormant a condition that many who have climbed to the top assert that it is not a volcano at all, since they find no crater on its summit. Nor are there any signs of volcanic heat, the summit being snow clad during summer. The conical form of the mountain, however, and the fact that the entire mountain is formed of volcanic rocks, show beyond doubt that it is an extinct volcano, whose crater has most probably been completely filled in by the washing away of its sides.

Xinantecatl is another extinct volcanic mountain situated about forty miles southwest of the City of Mexico. It is about 16,500 feet high. Its name means in the ancient Aztec language, *The Naked Lord*. It is also sometimes known as the Nevado de Toluca, or *The Snow of Toluca*. On the top of the peak are two craters filled with lakes of fresh water. Russell states that the larger of these lakes is about thirty feet in depth and contain a peculiar species of fish.

Tuxtula is another volcano of Mexico, situated on the western coast of the Gulf of Mexico, about eighty miles southeast of Vera Cruz. It was an active volcano in 1664, when it threw out molten lava. It then became dormant until March, 1793, when its long rest was broken by one of the grandest explosive eruptions of modern times. This eruption rivalled in energy the great explosive eruption which blew off the summit of Coseguina, in Central America, in 1835. As is common in the case of explosive eruptions, volcanic dust and scoriæ were blown high into the air, and, being carried by the winds, fell on the roofs of houses and on the land at a distance of 150 miles.

There have been a number of less violent eruptions of Tuxtula since 1835. Tuxtula is a comparatively low mountain, being only 4,960 feet high, because much of the mountain was blown away by the eruption of 1793.

[Pg 90]

As Russell points out, it is not safe to infer that because an eroded mountain is not lofty it cannot be young or energetic, since the very energy of some of its eruptions may, as in the case of Tuxtula, blow away a large part of the mountain. A low mountain, with an unusually large crater, generally means a mountain that has been visited by a great explosive eruption.

Another extinct volcano known as the Cofre de Perote is situated on the eastern coast of Mexico, east of Ixtaccihuatl, about thirty miles north of Orizaba. It takes its name Cofre de Perote which means the Coffin of Perote, from its peculiar box-like shape. It was called in the Aztec language "Nauhcampatepetl," or the *Four-Ridged Mountain*. Cofre de Perote is in a dormant or extinct condition.

We will conclude this brief description of the volcanoes of Mexico with the volcano of Colima, a mountain about 5,500 feet high situated on the western coast of Mexico.

Colima has been active of recent years, eruptions having occurred in 1869, 1872, 1873, and 1885. During these eruptions lava escaped from lateral openings in the sides of the mountain, these openings being termed by the natives the *Sons of Colima.*

[Pg 91]

CHAPTER VIII

COSEGUINA AND OTHER VOLCANOES OF CENTRAL AMERICA

Central America has a great number of volcanoes extending along nearly all its western coast, or on the Pacific side of the country.

Central America consists of a high plain or table-land sloping gently towards the northeast, but terminating abruptly on the southwest. In the opinion of geologists this table-land consists of the surface of a huge tilted block of the earth's crust, or, perhaps, more probably, of a series of such blocks, that are limited on the southwest by a narrow belt of intersecting fractures. It is in these fractures that scores of volcanoes are situated, together with active craters, solfataras, and hot springs. The volcanoes are mainly of the Vesuvian type. There are so many volcanoes in this part of the world that it will be possible to describe but a few of them.

We will begin with the volcano of Coseguina, situated on the Pacific coast of Nicaragua. Its appearance is that of a conical mountain with the top cut off, and suggests that it is most probably an explosive volcano which has had the top blown away during some of its great eruptions.

Coseguina is celebrated by reason of its tremendous eruption of 1835. Before the still more tremendous explosive eruption of Krakatoa in 1883, described in the first two chapters of this book, Coseguina shared with[Pg 92] Sombawa, on the island of Sumatra, as being the foremost of explosive volcanoes.

It had been estimated that before its eruption of 1835, Coseguina had a height of perhaps 10,000 feet, but so much of it was blown away by this eruption that it now is a little less than 4,000 feet.

The following description of the great eruption of Coseguina in 1835 has been condensed from an account prepared by Squier, published in 1850.

You will note in reading this brief account how closely many of the phenomena resemble those that occurred during the eruption of Krakatoa in 1833.

The eruption of Coseguina was heralded on the morning of January 20th, 1835, by several loud explosions that were heard for a distance of some 300 miles around the crater of the volcano. Then followed an ink black cloud formed directly over the mountain, which gradually spread on all sides shutting off the light of the sun, except for a sickly yellowish light. Fine sand was thrown from this cloud, which made it both difficult and painful to breathe. For two whole days the cloud continued to grow denser, the explosions louder and more frequent, and the rain of sand thicker. On the third day the explosions were strongest and the darkness greatest.

The amount of sand that fell from the cloud was so great that people left their houses, fearing the roofs would be crushed in by the great weight. This sand fell in large quantities over an area more than 1,500 miles in diameter, or, quoting the language of Squier:

"The noise of the explosions was heard nearly as far" (1,500 miles). "And the Superintendent of Belize, eight hundred miles distant, mustered his troops, under the impression that there was a naval action off the harbor. All nature seemed overawed; the birds deserted the air,[Pg 93] and the wild beasts their fastnesses, crouching, terror-stricken and harmless, in the dwellings of men. The people for a hundred leagues grouped, dumb with terror, amidst the thick darkness, bearing crosses on their shoulders and stones on their heads in penitential abasement and dismay. Many believed that the day of doom had come, and crowded in the tottering churches, where, in the pauses of the explosions, the voices of the priests were heard in solemn invocation to Heaven. The brightest lights were invisible at the distance of a few feet; and to heighten the terror of the scene, occasional lightnings traversed the darkness, shedding a lurid glare over the earth. This continued for forty-three hours, and then gradually passed away."

It appears that the eruption of Coseguina was followed by violent earthquake shocks and other evidences of volcanic energy over extended regions. For example, there were fearful earthquakes along the Andes, the worst of which occurred on February 20th, and continued at the rate of three or four a day up to March 6th, and, less frequently, to March 17th. It was during one of these earthquakes that the city of Concepcion, Chile, was so completely destroyed, that but a single house remained.

The same brilliant sunsets and sunrises occurred in different parts of the world after the eruption of Coseguina, due to the presence of large quantities of volcanic dust that followed the great eruption of Krakatoa.

The cause of this great explosive eruption of Coseguina was most probably the same as that which is believed to have caused the eruption of Krakatoa, namely, a large volume of water suddenly gaining access to a mass of liquid lava.

Volcán del Fuego is another of the many volcanoes of Central America. It is situated as one of a group of volcanoes[Pg 94] on the highest summit of the Isthmus. This volcanic mountain has a regular cone with regular slopes on all sides, except on the north, where a table-like projection, about 1,000 feet below the summit, is all that remains of a vast cone, the summit of which was blown away, according to Russell, in prehistoric times, just as was the crater of Somma on Vesuvius.

There have been in Central America, since the time of the Spanish conquest, some fifty volcanic eruptions sufficiently great to have been recorded. Some idea of the activity of Fuego during this time may be had from the fact that of all these eruptions some twenty were those of Fuego. At the present time, however, the volcano is dormant and apparently almost extinct.

The recorded eruptions of Fuego are nearly all of the explosive type. Among the most violent were those that occurred during 1526, 1541, and 1581. During 1582, 1585, and 1586, there were eruptions nearly every month, the most terrible being near Christmas day in 1586. Other memorable eruptions occurred in 1614, 1623, 1686, and 1705, and at other dates down to August 17th, 1860, from which date to the present time the volcano has been quiet.

We will conclude this brief description of the volcanoes of Central America with that of Volcán de Agua, or, as the word means, *The Water Volcano*. It is situated in Guatemala near the coast, and is one of the mountains that occupies the plateau on which Fuego is situated.

The Volcán de Agua is one of the most remarkable volcanoes in Central America, standing, as it does, nearly alone, and rising to an elevation of 3,350 metres (10,988 ft.), above the level of the sea. It has been extinct for a long time.

It has been supposed by some, from its name, that this is a volcano that throws out water. Others believe that[Pg 95] the name comes from the water produced by the melting of the snow that is collected on the sides of the mountain. Now there almost always escapes from the craters of volcanoes during violent eruptions immense quantities of water vapor, which, condensing, fall as vast showers of rain that often deluge the surrounding country. In snow-clad mountains, the escape of lava is often attended by floods caused by the rapid melting of the snow. The water volcano did not, however, take its name from either of these facts, but rather because at the time of the Spanish invasion, the crater of the mountain was occupied by a large lake, and that during an earthquake in 1541 the wall of the crater was broken, when the lake was poured as an immense stream of water down the side of the mountain, overwhelming a village which was situated on this slope. That this was the correct origin of the same may be seen from the fact that the crater at the present time still shows the remains of its former lake basin, and that on the sides of the broken rim an immense ravine can be seen through which the water poured down on the village below.

Daubeny describes this volcano as follows:

"The Volcán de Agua (Water-Volcano) is of enormous height, being covered with eternal snow, in the latitude of 14°. Captain Basil Hall estimates it at more than 14,000 feet, but a recent traveller states it at 12,600. It has the form of a blunted cone clothed with perpetual verdure to its summit. The crater is from forty to sixty yards in depth, and about

150 in diameter,—the sides and bottom strewed with masses of rock, apparently showing the effects of boiling water or of fire.

"By a deluge of water from this volcano in 1527, the original city of Guatemala was overwhelmed; and the next built, called the Old City, *La Antiqua*, was ruined by an[Pg 96] earthquake in 1773. The present capital is situated at a distance of eight leagues from the mountain."

Another volcano in this part of the country is described by Daubeny as follows:

"Massaya, near the lake of that name, was one of the most active vents at the time of the first discovery of the country. Its flames were visible twenty-five miles off. Its crater was only twenty or thirty paces in diameter; but the melted lava 'seethed and rolled in waves as high as towers.' A story is told of a Dominican who imagined the fluid lava was melted gold, and descended into the crater with an iron ladle to carry some away; but the ladle, it is said, melted, and the monk escaped with difficulty."

[Pg 97]

CHAPTER IX

THE VOLCANIC MOUNTAINS OF SOUTH AMERICA

The volcanoes of South America are limited to the Andes Mountain System that stretches like a huge wall along the entire western side of the continent. The names of the more important of these volcanoes are marked on the map of South America, shown in Fig. 17. As will be seen, this huge mountain wall reaches from Patagonia on the south to the Isthmus of Panama on the north. The arrangement of the volcanoes in South America is of the linear type. The craters follow one another in more or less straight lines, or are situated along the lines of great fissures that lie near the ocean. You must not, however, suppose that there is a continuous chain of active volcanic mountains from the Isthmus of Panama to the southern part of the continent. According to Lyell, from lat. 2° N., or from the north of Quito, to lat. 43° S. or south of Chile, a total distance including 45° of latitude, there is a succession of districts with active and extinct volcanoes, or at least with volcanoes that have been quiet during the last three centuries.

[Pg 98]

FIG. 17. SOUTH AMERICA

Lyell traces the volcanoes of South America as follows:

"The principal line of active vents which have been seen in eruption in the Andes extends from lat. 43° 28' S., ... to lat. 30° S.; to these thirteen degrees of latitude succeed more than eight degrees, in which no recent volcanic eruptions have been observed. We then come to the volcanoes of Bolivia and Peru, extending six degrees[Pg 99] from S. to N., or from lat. 21° S. to lat. 15° S. Between the Peruvian volcanoes and those of Quito another space intervenes of no less than fourteen degrees of latitude, in which there is said to be but few active volcanoes as far as is yet known. The volcanoes of Quito then succeed, beginning about 100 geographical miles south of the equator, and continuing for about 150 miles north of it, when there occurs another undisturbed region of more than six degrees of latitude, after which we arrive at the volcanoes of Guatemala, or Central America, north of the Isthmus of Panama."

Of course, you must not understand that there are no extinct volcanoes in these gaps. On the contrary, according to Daubeny, we find, beginning on the north in the United States of Colombia, the lofty volcano of Tolima. According to Daubeny's book published in 1848, Tolima was then constantly emitting steam and sulphur gases from its summit. Tolima is situated in the easternmost of the three mountain ranges that extend through this section of the country. It is, therefore, at a comparatively great distance from the ocean. Tolima was in eruption in 1595. It again burst out in 1826.

Coming now to Ecuador we find that this, the smallest of the South American Republics, contains numerous great volcanic mountains.

Some of the principal volcanic mountains are Chimborazo, 20,498 feet above the sea; Antisana, 18,880 feet; Cotopaxi, 19,660 feet; Pichincha (17,644 feet in 1848, Daubeny), El Altar, 16,383 feet.

These all lie in South America on the plateau of Quito. As Baron Alexander von Humboldt has pointed out, the volcanic mountains of Quito are arranged in two parallel chains that extend side by side for a distance of over 500 miles north into the State of Colombia, including between[Pg 100] them the high plateaus of Quito and Lacumbia. According to Whymper, however, who has recently studied this part of South America, there is a succession of basins between the mountains, but there is no such thing as a single valley in the interior of Ecuador. The extinct volcanoes of Cayamba, Antisana, and Chimborazo are the most important. On all three mountains there are old lava streams on their sides. Although no craters can be seen on their summits, yet it is almost certain they once had craters. There is plenty of room on the summit of Antisana for a cone as great as that of Cotopaxi. Whymper is of the opinion that the snow domes that form the summit of Chimborazo were at one time two of the highest points of the rim of the old crater.

Nearly due south of Quito is the great volcanic cone of El Altar. Like all the peaks of this high plateau, El Altar rises to a great height above the sea, being at the present time 16,383 feet above the sea. This mountain has an enormous crater that appears to be dormant or extinct, and is covered with snow. According to the traditions of Indians, El Altar, or, as they call it, *Capac Urcu* or *The Chief*, was the highest mountain near the equator, being much higher than Chimborazo. But during a prodigious eruption that occurred before the discovery of America, and continued uninterruptedly for eight years, the height of the mountain was considerably reduced. According to Boussingault, the fragments of the cone of this celebrated mountain are now spread for great distances around the mountain on the surrounding lowlands.

Pichincha in Ecuador, an extinct volcano, is situated almost immediately on the equator. It has a height as measured by Whymper by the barometer, of 15,918 feet above the Pacific. The summit is covered by blocks of pumice. Several species of lichens are found at this[Pg 101] elevation. According to Daubeny, Pichincha was extinct prior to 1539, when it became active. There were also eruptions in 1577, 1587, and 1668. It was also in activity during 1831.

Cayamba, another volcanic mountain of Ecuador, lies to the east of Pichincha, a short distance north of the equator. Its height is 19,186 feet. It is nearly extinct.

Cotopaxi, 19,680 feet, is another volcanic mountain of the high plateau of Quito. Cotopaxi is still active. Its slopes are covered with snow down to a height of about 14,800 feet. Between the lower edge of this snow line and the lower slopes of the mountain, there lies a zone of naked rock.

According to Whymper, the eruption of Cotopaxi, in 1877, was preceded by an unusual degree of activity in the earlier parts of the year. This, however, did not cause any alarm until June 25th, 1877, when, shortly after midday, an eruption, attended by tremendous subterranean roars, began, and an immense black column shot up into the air for about twice the height of the cone. This eruption was clearly visible at Quito, for the wind blew the ashes towards the Pacific. At this time the summit had not changed its appearance, but towards 6:30 A. M., on the next day, another enormous column of ashes rose from the crater. The ashes and cinders were first carried due north by the winds, and then, spreading out in all directions, were subsequently distributed through the air all over the country. At Quito, as early as 8 A. M., the sky assumed the appearance it generally has at twilight, and the darkness increased until midday, when it became as dark as at midnight. Indeed, it was so dark that one could not see his hand before his face.

During this eruption, as is very common in the eruptions of the snow-clad mountains of South America, a flood of[Pg 102] water, due to the rapid melting of the snow and ice on the summit, rushed down the mountain slopes at 10 o'clock A. M., on the 26th of the month, almost immediately after the appearance of a stream of lava that began to flow down the mountain. In a few moments the mountain was completely shut off from view by immense columns of steam and smoke. At first, a low, moaning sound was heard, which rapidly increased to a roar, when a deluge of mud, mingled with huge blocks of ice and stones, swept down the mountain, leaving a desert in its path. It is estimated that at some places this stream moved with a velocity of fifty miles per hour.

The general appearance of Cotopaxi is shown in the accompanying reproduction from the painting by Frederick E. Church in the Lenox Library, New York.

According to Whymper, who made an ascent of Cotopaxi in 1880, the crater on the summit has the form of an immense amphitheatre, 2,300 feet across from north to south, and 1,650 feet from east to west. Its crest is irregular and notched. The crater is surrounded by perpendicular cliffs. The western side of the volcano is irregular. Barometric measurements gave the height of this volcano at 19,498 feet. Its height as taken by La Condamine, during the early parts of the last century, was 19,605 feet, so that, according to Whymper, assuming as would seem probable, that this difference in height has not all been due to errors in measurements, the volcano has grown or increased in height during the last century and a half.

Chimborazo, 20,498 feet, is another lofty mountain on the plateau of Quito. This volcano is situated in lat. 1° 30' S., and is not at the present time in an active condition. It is, however, formed entirely of volcanic material. Its upper portions are covered with a layer of snow to a level of some 2,600 feet below the summit.

COTOPAXI

From a Painting by Frederick E. Church in the Lenox Collection of the New York Public Library.

By Permission

[Pg 103]

Chimborazo has an enormous volcanic summit, which, when seen from the Pacific, when the air is especially clear after the long rains of winter, is a most splendid sight. Whymper, who ascended the mountain, says:

"When the transparency of the air is increased and its enormous circular summit is seen projected upon the deep azure of blue of the Equatorial sky, it represents a magnificent sight. The great rarity of the air through which the top of the Andes is seen adds much to the splendor."

Whymper says, that as far as records are concerned, there have been no eruptions of Chimborazo, which has apparently been an extinct volcano for many years. Its crater has been completely buried by a thick cap of ice on its summit, while what lava streams exist on the mountain are either covered by large glaciers, or have been removed by erosion, or hidden by vegetation.

Chimborazo possesses less of the conical outline than Cotopaxi. There are steep cliffs towards the summit that have been named by Whymper "the northern and southern walls." They seem to him to have been formed by the violent upheavals of the explosive eruptions that have blown away portions of the cone.

There are other volcanoes in this district, but the above are all we have space for describing.

According to Lyell, the volcano of Rancagua, in Chile, lat. 34° 15' S., is continually throwing up ashes and vapors like Stromboli. Indeed, a year seldom passes in Chile without some earthquake shocks. Of these shocks those which came from the side nearest the sea are most violent. The town of Copiapo was laid waste by these shocks during the years 1773, 1796, and 1819, in both instances after intervals of twenty-three years.

Since the volcanic mountains of South America are snow-covered the occurrences of volcanic eruptions are[Pg 104] apt to be attended by great floods caused by the rapid melting of the snow, as well as sometimes by the breaking of huge subterranean cavities that are filled with water.

According to Lyell, the volcanoes of Peru rise from a plateau from 17,000 to 20,000 feet above the sea. One of the principal volcanoes of Peru is Arequipa, whose summit is 18,877 feet above the level of the sea. The mountain takes its name from the city of Arequipa, which is situated not far from its base. It is an active volcano. Another volcano, Viejo, is found in lat. 16° 55' S.

36

According to Lyell, there are active vents extending through Chile to the island of Chiloe to lat. 30° N.

Aconcagua, west of Valparaiso, in lat. 32° 39' S., 23,000 feet in height, the highest mountain in South America, is still in an active condition. According to Scrope, when the city of Mendoza was destroyed by an earthquake, that killed 10,000 people, in March, 1861, it is probable that Aconcagua was in eruption.

There are many other active volcanoes in Chile, extending as far south as the volcanoes of Patagonia, north of the Straits of Magellan as well as others of Tierra del Fuego.

[Pg 105]

CHAPTER X

VOLCANOES OF THE UNITED STATES

For some readers this may be a surprising chapter heading, for it is a general impression that there are no volcanoes in the United States. It is true that practically all of the volcanoes of this country are dormant or extinct. They have, however, at one time been exceedingly active, and, if reports are correct, some of them were active during comparatively recent times.

Nearly all of the volcanoes of the United States lie west of the meridian of Denver. These volcanoes belong to two distinct types, either the Vesuvian type with built up cones, or the plateau or fissure type already referred to.

The following brief description of the volcanoes of the United States has been collated, for the greater part, from Wallace's excellent book on the volcanoes of North America.

Crossing the United States on the Southern Pacific Railroad one's attention is caught, in Arizona, by a magnificent group of mountains known as the San Francisco Mountains. The highest peak of these mountains reaches 12,562 feet above the level of the sea, and 5,700 feet above the surface of the plateau on which the mountains stand.

[Pg 106]

FIG. 18. THE UNITED STATES

According to G. K. Gilbert, the San Francisco Mountain group is formed of a variety of lava known as trachyte, that is of comparatively recent ejection, possibly of a geological age called the Tertiary. The lava forming the mountains escaped through a number of crater cones,[Pg 107] some of which can still be seen in the neighborhood. Some of these craters are now in almost as perfect a condition as the day they were formed. Indeed, to one looking at them from a neighboring elevation, they appear so fresh, and so little affected by the climate, that one might almost believe that the lava had just flowed out of the craters, and has not yet hardened. Nevertheless, geologists are sure they have been formed long before man appeared on the earth. In one of these craters a lake of fresh water has collected.

Another extinct volcano of the United States is Mt. Taylor in New Mexico, nearly east of the San Francisco Mountains. This mountain rises from the surface of a high table-land, or, as it is called in this part of the world, a *mesa*. The surface of the plateau is covered with a thick lava stream from which Mt. Taylor rises to a height of 11,390 feet above the level of the ocean. This mesa, or table-land, is forty-seven miles in length from northwest to southeast, and about twenty-three miles in breadth. Its general elevation is about 8,200 feet. The plateau rises about 2,000 feet above the surface of the level land that surrounds it. All these 2,000 feet have been removed by erosion. The table-land from which Mt. Taylor rises has not been eroded by the action of the rain, rivers, and other weathering agencies like the surface of the country surrounding it, because of a covering of lava that has been spread over its surface to a depth of about 300 feet.

Mt. Taylor is formed almost entirely of lava that has escaped through a single opening and has built up a high cone around it. The volcano is now quite extinct, so that the original form of the mountain has been greatly changed by erosion.

You will remember, when we were discussing the general subject of volcanoes, in the beginning of this book, that[Pg 108] we spoke of volcanic mountains being bottled up after an eruption, by the hardening of the lava which remained in the crater and the tube that connects the crater with the place from which the lava had been derived. We then spoke of this hardened mass being known as a *volcanic plug*, or stopper, explaining how the volcano could never again erupt through its old crater unless it could develop sufficient force to blow out or remove this stopper.

Now besides the crater at the top of Mt. Taylor there were several others in the eroded region surrounding the mesa, or high table-land, from which Mt. Taylor rises. When, therefore, the erosion which removed the 2,000 feet of rocks on all portions of the old mesa that were not protected by the coating of lava, these old mountain plugs were too hard to be worn away or eroded, and were, therefore, left projecting into the air like vast pyramids.

If you should ever visit Mt. Taylor and should go to the eastern border of this mesa, and look over the eroded plain, you would see in the lowlands a part of the places from which the 2,000 feet of matter have been slowly eroded. Dutton describes the beautiful panorama that is to be seen as follows:

"The edge of the mesa suddenly descends by a succession of ledges and slopes, nearly 2,000 feet into the rugged and highly diversified valley-plain below. The country beneath is a medley of low cliffs and bluffs, showing the browns and pale yellows of the Cretaceous sandstones and shales. Out of this confused patchwork of bright colors rise several objects of remarkable aspect. They are apparently inaccessible eyries of black rock, and at a rough guess, by comparison with the known altitudes of surrounding objects, their heights above the mean level of the adjoining plain may range from 800 to 1,500 feet. The blackness of their shade may be exaggerated by contrast[Pg 109] with the brilliant colors of the rocks and soil out of which they rise, but their forms are even more striking."

These black piles are the *necks* or lava plugs of extinct volcanoes. They rise above the level of the plain because, being harder than the surrounding rocks, they have resisted erosion. In some cases these necks or plugs have been converted by shrinkage, on cooling, into beautiful columns, somewhat of the type of the basaltic columns of the Giant's Causeway. It would be difficult to count the number of volcanic necks that can be seen near the edge of the mesa. One's attention is at once attracted to some dozen of these piles, which are especially striking on account of their great size, and ominous black color, but the number is by no means limited to this dozen. There are hundreds of them.

Fig. 19 gives some idea of a part of the view from the edge of the mesa, and Fig. 20the appearance of two of these volcanic necks.

But besides high volcanic mountains such as the San Francisco Mountains and Mt. Taylor, there are, in different parts of the United States, to be found fragments of huge craters from which, in the geological past, immense quantities of lava have escaped. In some instances these craters are but fragments of huge craters, that, like the crater of Mt. Somma, in Vesuvius, have been nearly completely blown away by some unrecorded explosion during the far past.

[Pg 110]

FIG. 19. PANORAMA FROM THE MESA AT THE EDGE OF MT. TAYLOR
From U. S. Geological Survey

A crater of this type, known as Ice Springs Crater, is situated in the desert valley west of the Wahsatch Mountains, some 125 miles south of Salt Lake City, Utah. This crater is especially interesting from the fact that it occupies a position on a plain that was formed by the deposition of sediment in an immense lake that covered this part of the United States very long before man lived on[Pg 111] the earth. We are alluding to Lake Bonneville, a lake that existed in a geological time known as the Glacial Epoch. This lake occupied the territory now filled by the Great Salt Lake of Utah, but towards the close of the Glacial Epoch it was immensely larger than it is now. This can be shown not only by the presence of shore lines, that are clearly marked on the sides of the surrounding mountains, but also by the ancient lake beaches, and deltas, that are common in the district, so that instead of there being the comparatively limited area of Great Salt Lake as marked on the maps of to-day there was a lake that had an area of 19,750 square miles, that covered an area on which at least 200,000 people dwell.

FIG. 20. VOLCANIC NECKS, EDGE OF MESA AT MT. TAYLOR

FIG. 20. VOLCANIC NECKS, EDGE OF MESA AT MT. TAYLOR
From U. S. Geological Survey

A similar lake, known as Lake Lehontan, existed at the[Pg 112] same time, covering large areas in the western parts of Nevada.

Coming now to Ice Springs Craters in Utah, we find here three small craters formed of scoriæ and lapilli (volcanic ashes consisting of small angular stony fragments). Near them lies a fragment of a much larger crater known as the Crescent. In some respects this crater was not unlike the crater of Somma that surrounded Mt. Vesuvius. It was not, however, as large, having a diameter of only 2,200 feet. From these craters streams of basalt flowed until they covered considerable areas.

A still more recent crater known as Tabernacle Crater is situated four miles south of the Ice Springs Crater. Tabernacle Crater takes its name from the building known in Salt Lake City as the Tabernacle. According to Gilbert, this crater was formed at a time when Lake Bonneville stood at a comparatively low level, or when the water was only from fifty to seventy-five feet above the bottom of the valley on which the crater now stands. At that time an explosive volcanic eruption occurred on the bottom of the lake, and the rim of the crater, built up by this explosion, was gradually pushed above the surface of the lake, so as to shut out its waters.

Extinct volcanic craters, not unlike those of Utah, occur also near Ragtown, in Nevada, in a district known as the Carson Valley Desert, in one of the broadest areas of what was once Lake Lahontan. Ragtown is twenty-two miles southwest of Wadsworth on the Central Pacific Railroad. At the present time there are two circular depressions or volcanic craters filled with pools of strongly alkaline water known as the Ragtown Pond, or Soda Lake. The large lake covers an area of 268-1/2 acres. Its greatest diameter is over 4,000 feet. Without going into a detailed description it will suffice to say that the larger[Pg 113] crater probably was destroyed by an explosive volcanic eruption.

Another intensely alkaline lake that fills an extinct volcanic crater is the Mono Lake, situated in Mono Valley in California at the eastern base of the Sierra Nevadas. It has an area of about 200 square miles. The centre of the lake has two small islands named Pacha and Negit. Immediately south of Mono Lake are a number of craters that occupy portions of what was once apparently a fissure extending in a general north and south direction. The highest of these craters are in the neighborhood of 2,500 feet.

But leaving these inconspicuous craters, let us briefly examine some of the higher mountain peaks of the United States that are of volcanic origin. One of the most conspicuous of these is Mt. Shasta. This mountain is situated in California, at the northern end of the Sierra Nevadas. It has a height of 14,350 feet. It is a snow-clad mountain of a conical form, and is a conspicuous object in the landscape, because it stands alone.

Mt. Shasta is a double-coned mountain. Besides the cone on its summit there is a well-developed cone known as Shastina on the western side of the mountain, 2,000 feet lower than the main summit.

There are well-defined lava streams on the slopes of Mt. Shasta. One of these, which issued from the southern side of the mountain at an elevation of 5,500 feet, divided into two streams. One of these streams is twelve miles in length. The other entered the canyon of the Sacramento River, thus displacing the water.

Coming now to the Cascade Mountains, in Oregon and Washington, we will find in them a number of giant peaks of volcanic origin. The most important of these are in regular order from south to north, as follows: Mt. Pitt, 9,760[Pg 114] feet; Mt. Mazana, 8,223; Mt. Union, 7,881; Mt. Scott, 7,123; Three Sisters, Mt. Jefferson, 10,200, and Mt. Hood, 11,225, in Oregon; Mt. Adams, 9,570; Mt. St. Helen's, 9,750; Mt. Rainier, 14,525, and Mt. Baker in Washington, 10,877.

Nearly all these mountains have craters either on their summits or on their sides. They are extinct volcanic mountains, that were, for the most part, thrown up during the Tertiary Geological Period, so that they have all been greatly affected by erosion.

One of the most remarkable of the above volcanic mountains is Mt. Mazana, in Oregon. This mountain has on its summit an approximately circular cavity from five to six miles in diameter, that is occupied by a lake of water known as Crater Lake. This lake is 6,239 feet above the level of the sea, and has a depth of 1,975 feet. It is surrounded by nearly vertical walls ranging from 900 to 2,200 feet deep, so that the vast caldera of which this great depression consists has a depth of at least 4,000 feet.

Mt. Pitt, situated about sixty miles north of Mt. Shasta, in southern Oregon, has a regularly shaped volcanic cone, and the remnant of a crater at its summit. The Three Sisters and Mt. Jefferson lie to the north of Mt. Pitt. Like the others they are ancient volcanic mountains. But little is accurately known concerning them.

Mt. Hood, 11,225 feet high, rises from the crest of the Cascade range in Northwest Oregon, about twenty-five miles south of the Columbia River. Mt. Hood is an exceedingly majestic mountain. At its summit there are only portions of the walls of the original crater. When ascended in 1888, streams of sulphur vapor were escaping from fumaroles on its northeastern slopes, at an elevation of 8,500 feet above the sea.

Mt. Adams and Mt. St. Helen's lie to the north of Mt. Hood. Mt. Adams about sixty miles to the north, and[Pg 115] beyond this, Mt. St. Helen's. Accurate information concerning the summit of Mt. Adams is still lacking. Mt. St. Helen's in Washington has more of a conical summit. Russell states that according to frontiersmen, St. Helen's has been in a state of activity within the past fifty years. A French-Canadian asserts that the mountain was in actual eruption during the winter of 1841-43, that at this date the light from the volcano was sufficiently bright to enable one to see and pick up a pin in the grass at midnight near his cabin some twenty miles distant. Mt. St. Helen's was ascended in 1889, when fumaroles were found on the northeast side.

Mt. Rainier in Washington is plainly visible from Puget Sound. It is a most magnificent mountain. The summit has a bowl-shaped crater, of an almost perfectly circular form. The inside of the crater, when last ascended, was filled to within thirty or thirty-five feet of its rim with ice and snow. There was, however, evidences of heat, since numerous jets of steam were seen issuing from its interior rim.

Mt. Baker, Washington, is the northernmost of the volcanoes of the Cascade Mountains, south of the boundary line between the United States and Canada. But little is known of this mountain. The summit appears as a conical peak from Puget Sound, so that its form would seem to show that it is of volcanic origin. According to Gibbs, officers of the Hudson Bay Company, as well as the Indians, declared that Mt. Baker was in eruption in 1843, when it broke out at the same time as Mt. St. Helen's, covering the country with ashes.

There are but few volcanoes in the Rocky Mountains which extend from north to south through the United States at a considerable distance to the east of the Sierra Nevadas and Cascade Ranges. The Spanish Peaks,[Pg 116] situated in the southeastern part of Colorado about sixty miles south of Pueblo, are the remains of ancient volcanoes. Two of the most prominent of these peaks rise from 12,720 to 13,620 feet above the sea.

We shall make no effort to attempt to describe the volcanic mountains that may exist in those portions of the Rocky Mountain Ranges or the Cascade Range lying in Canada. Comparatively little is known of them, but inasmuch as volcanic activity has been manifested in Alaska, it would seem highly improbable, as Russell remarks, that volcanoes should suddenly cease at the northern boundaries of the United States and then begin again at the most southern part of Alaska. It will be sufficient to say that Mt. Edgecome, situated on an island in the neighborhood of Sitka, is of volcanic origin, and that the Aleutian Islands, beginning at Alaska on the east at the head of Cook's Inlet, extend westward through the Peninsula of Alaska to the Peninsula of Kamtschatka for a distance of nearly 1,600 miles. This belt, which is called by Russell "the Aleutian Volcanic Belt," contains numerous volcanoes that are known to have been active in historical times.

Mt. Wrangell, on the Copper River, 200 miles northeast of the head of Cook's Inlet, is a lofty volcanic mountain that is said to have been in eruption in 1819, and at the time of last report was still throwing out columns of steam. While much remains to be ascertained about the volcanoes of the Aleutian Islands, it would appear that there are active volcanoes on twenty-five of these islands, on which some forty-eight craters have been found. Eruptions are common in the district.

[Pg 117]

CHAPTER XI

THE CATASTROPHE OF MARTINIQUE AND THE VOLCANIC ISLANDS OF THE LESSER ANTILLES

The West Indies Island chain consists of two groups of islands; i. e., the Greater Antilles, including Cuba, Jamaica, Hayti, and Porto Rico, on the west, and the chain of the Lesser Antilles on the east.

The Lesser Antilles consists of two parallel chains, the westernmost of which is for the greater part mountainous with peaks several thousand feet in height. All these islands are volcanic. The chain on the east consists of low, calcareous rocks, or rocks consisting largely of lime.

In the western chain the islands beginning on the south are, Grenada, St. Vincent, St. Lucia, Martinique, Dominica, Guadeloupe, Montserrat, Nevis, and St. Eustace, while in the calcareous chain are found the Tobago, Barbadoes, and others.

Prior to 1902, the greatest volcanic eruption in this part of the world occurred on the island of St. Vincent, with the volcano of Soufrière. Although the forces displayed were exceedingly great, yet they become insignificant when compared with the appalling eruption that took place in Martinique only a short time ago; namely, May the 8th, 1902, when the volcano of Mt. Pelée, situated on the northwestern part of the island, burst into an eruption so terrible that in destruction of life it far exceeded the eruption of Krakatoa, although the amount of energy causing the eruption was much smaller.

[Pg 118]

FIG. 21. THE LESSER ANTILLES

[Pg 119]

Heilprin, in a book called "Mt. Pelée and the Tragedy of Martinique," from whom most of the information of this chapter has been obtained, calls attention to the fact that before the eruption of Pelée there were plenty of warnings for those intelligent enough to note them. For two or three weeks prior to May 8th, 1902, the volcanic activity of Pelée had been rapidly increasing, the mountain throwing out clouds of ashes and sulphurous vapors from its crater. By April 25th the sulphurous vapors had so increased in quantity as to make breathing difficult in St. Pierre. The ashes fell on the surrounding country and by the 2d of May had so covered the streets of St. Pierre as to stop traffic.

Three days later, May 6th, shortly before noon, an avalanche of mud poured down the slopes of the mountain with the rapidity of an express train. These torrents of mud and water deluged the towns and villages in the neighborhood. The activity of Mt. Pelée increased until the morning of May 8th, 1902, when, almost at exactly 8 A. M., an eruption occurred, so terrible in its effects that in two minutes the city of St. Pierre was almost completely destroyed.

St. Pierre, the principal town of Martinique, is situated on the island of Martinique, on the northwestern coast, about ten miles southwest of Mt. Pelée. St. Pierre was settled as far back as 1635. It is situated on an open roadstead without any harbor.

That there were many points of resemblance between the position of St. Pierre and the destroyed city of Pompeii will be recognized as the description of the catastrophe is given.

St. Pierre was a beautiful city, and formed the natural outlet to one of the richest districts in Martinique for the production of sugar cane and cocoa. It contained many[Pg 120]fine houses, the homes of planters, wealthy bankers, merchants, and shippers, who, besides their regular houses in the city, had constructed handsome villas on heights on the outskirts of the city. The houses were to a great extent one or two stories in height, and were in many cases surrounded by fine gardens. The city extended along the coast for about two miles. The streets were well lighted.

The eruption of Mt. Pelée on May 8th, 1902, was of a very unusual character, containing a feature that—with the exception of a volcanic eruption of Soufrière, a volcanic mountain on the neighboring island of St. Vincent, and an eruption of Kilauea in Hawaii—so far as I am aware, never before occurred. This was a blast of highly heated air, mingled with white hot or incandescent dust, that swept down the side of the mountain with a velocity of one or two miles per minute, or possibly more.

Nearly all of the people in St. Pierre were killed. From the appearance of the bodies it seemed that death was practically instantaneous, and was due either to scorching or burning, or asphyxiation by the breathing of highly heated air. The number of people so killed, including almost the entire population of St. Pierre, as well as a number of adjoining settlements, was not less than 30,000.

The zone of absolute destruction was limited to an area the extent of which did not greatly exceed eight or nine square miles. On the outskirts of this zone the destruction, though considerable, was less complete.

There was almost an entire absence of great earthquake shocks during the eruption.

Following the terrible eruption of May 8th were a number of less violent eruptions on May 20th, 26th, June 6th, July 9th, and August 31st. According to Heilprin these eruptions were of the same character as that of May 8th.

[Pg 121]

There has been considerable discussion as to the exact causes of the tornadic incandescent blast that caused the awful destruction of life. Without entering this discussion it is sufficient to say that it is now generally considered that the blast consisted of highly heated air, and super-heated steam loaded with great quantities of finely divided red hot or even white hot dust particles.

While, perhaps, the force producing the awful eruption of Mt. Pelée was greatly excelled in the case of many other volcanic eruptions; such as Papandayang, in 1772; Asamayama, in 1783; Skaptar Jökul, in 1783; Tomboro, in 1815; Coseguina, in 1835; and Krakatoa, in 1883; yet, in the words of Heilprin, "in intensity and swiftness of its death-dealing blast ... the eruption of May 8th, and of later dates, stands unique in records of volcanic manifestations."

While the amount of ashes that accompanied the blast of white hot steam and air was comparatively small, yet during the time between this and the subsequent eruptions, the amount of ashes that were thrown from the surface of Mt. Pelée was exceedingly great.

According to Russell, in a paper on the volcanic eruptions of Martinique and St. Vincent, in 1902, the amount of ashes and solid matter generally thrown out from the crater of Mt. Pelée would be equal to 40,000,000 cubic feet every minute, or one and a half times the sediments discharged by the Mississippi in the course of a whole year.

According to Heilprin, however, the actual amount of dust thrown from the crater of Mt. Pelée was, probably, 500 times greater than the amount discharged by the Mississippi River in the course of a year, and, consequently, considerably greater than that of all the rivers of the world combined, or, as he says:

[Pg 122]

"Mont Pelée has now been in a condition of forceful activity for upwards of two hundred days; can we assume that during this time it may have thrown out a mass of material whose cubical contents are hardly less than a quarter of the area of Martinique as it now appears above the waters? One is, indeed, almost appalled by the magnitude of this work, and yet the work may even be very much greater than is here stated. We ask ourselves the questions, what becomes of the void that is being formed in the interior? What form of new catastrophe does it invite? There can be no answer to a question of this kind—except in the future happening that may be associated with this special condition. But geologists must take count of the force as being one of greatest potential energy, whose relation to the modelling and the shaping of the destinies of the globe is of far greater significance than has generally been conceived."

A curious circumstance connected with the eruption of Mt. Pelée was the most pronounced electric and magnetic disturbances. Moreover, as in the case of the eruption of Krakatoa, there were the same after glows or red sunsets and sunrises due to the presence of fine volcanic dust in the higher regions of the air. These phenomena were observed over widely separated areas.

It appears that this great eruption in Martinique was preceded by severe earthquakes in the northern part of South America, especially in Colombia and Venezuela. The most marked was the great earthquake which on April 18th destroyed the city of Guatamaula; this was, perhaps, the most destructive earthquake that has occurred in the Western Hemisphere since the great earthquake of 1812, that destroyed the city of Caracas. Indeed, Professor Milne suggests that it was this earthquake that brought about the eruption of Mt. Pelée.

[Pg 123]

Soufrière, on the island of St. Vincent, had a great eruption on May 7th, 1902, one day before the awful eruption of Mt. Pelée. No lava flowed during this eruption. There were, however, great discharges of mud, due to a lake that before the eruption filled the top of a depression known as the old crater which lay southwest of a new crater, or the crater that was formed during the eruption of 1812. The old crater was nine-tenths of a mile across from east to west, and eight-tenths of a mile from north to south. The depth to the crater floor was from 1,000 to 2,400 feet. The surface of the new and shallow boiling lake which occupied the deepest part of the floor during the latter part of May, and from June to August, was estimated to be only 1,200 feet above the level of the sea. The sheet of water that occupied it before the eruption being several hundred feet higher.

Soufrière did not fail to give warnings of its coming eruption. Rumblings were heard two days before the explosion. On May 5th, 1902, fishermen who crossed the lake noticed that the water was disturbed and agitated. On the Tuesday following, May 6th, great clouds were thrown out during the afternoon, and the volcano was illumined by a reddish glare of fire. The first explosion was heard shortly before two o'clock on the following day and the volcano burst into activity. The explosions, together with great discharges of pumice, ashes, and boulders, followed one another rapidly. A column of steam was shot up into the air for a height of 30,000 feet. The severest paroxysm came shortly after ten A. M., and was succeeded by others nearly as violent during the next few hours. By this time a reddish curtain of clouds nearly shut out the island from view, and rapidly advanced over the land and descended on the sea. This eruption caused a loss of life of about 1,350.

[Pg 124]

This eruption of Mt. Soufrière was accompanied by the same tornadic blast of glowing air. There was not, however, any single blast quite as severe as that which attended the eruption of Pelée on May 8th, 1902.

[Pg 125]

CHAPTER XII

SOME OTHER NOTED VOLCANIC MOUNTAINS

Since the limits of our book will prevent any further description of volcanic districts or regions, we must content ourselves with descriptions of some of the noted of the remaining volcanoes, although many we will thus omit contain great wonders.

As we have already seen from the description of Krakatoa, the island of Java near which Krakatoa is situated is especially noted not only for the great number of its volcanic mountains, but also for the frequency and severity of their eruptions.

Perhaps the most destructive eruption of any of the volcanic mountains of Java was of a volcanic mountain called Papandayang. This volcano, situated on the southern coast of the island, is 7,034 feet in height, and was in eruption in 1772. According to Scrope, from whom the details of this eruption have been obtained, two others of the many volcanoes on Java, situated at 184 and 352 geographical miles respectively from Papandayang, broke out at the same time into active eruption, although several intervening cones were undisturbed.

The eruption of Papandayang was of the explosive type, a large part of the mountain being broken off by the great force of the eruption, and its materials scattered far and wide over the surrounding country. During this eruption forty villages with their inhabitants were buried by great showers of ashes. An area of fifteen by six miles was left[Pg 126] in the shape of a huge pit by the great eruption. It was at first believed by some that this pit was due to the actual sinking in of the ground, but a more careful study has shown that it was in reality caused by the great force of the eruption, being, in point of fact, a vast explosive crater that was formed by the expulsion of the materials that formerly filled it. Some idea of the great extent of this eruption of Papandayang may be had by the size of this huge crater that was six by fifteen miles in diameter.

Another great volcanic mountain in Java that had a terrific eruption was Galungoon, or Galung Gung. According to Lyell, from whom the facts of this eruption have been obtained, prior to this eruption the slopes of the mountain were highly cultivated and densely populated. There was a circular pit or crater on the summit of the mountain, but there had been no traditions of any eruptions prior to 1822.

In July, 1822, the waters of the Kunir River, one of the small rivers that flow down the slopes of the mountain, were observed to become hot and turbid. On the 8th of October, 1822, a terrific explosion was suddenly heard, accompanied by great earthquake shocks, when immense columns of hot water and boiling mud, mixed with burning brimstone, ashes, and lapilli, were thrown violently like a great waterspout from the opening in the mountain, with such enormous violence that great quantities fell across the River Tandoi, forty miles distant, while the valleys in the neighborhood were filled with a burning torrent. The rivers overflowed their banks and produced great destruction by floods of burning and boiling materials that washed away all the villages and cultivated fields in their path. During this eruption an extended area was covered with boiling mud in which were completely buried the bodies of many of those who perished.

[Pg 127]
So great was the violence with which the boiling mud, cinders, etc., were thrown out of the mountain that they entirely failed to fall on many of the villages in the immediate neighborhood, while the more remote villages were completely destroyed and buried out of sight under the mud.

The first eruption continued for nearly five hours. During several days following the eruption, torrents of rain fell, which produced floods in the rivers that covered the country far and wide with thick layers of mud.

Four days after the great eruption, that is, on the 12th of October, 1822, a second and still more violent eruption occurred, when immense quantities of hot mud were again thrown out of the crater. Great blocks of hardened lava called basalt were thrown a distance of seven miles from the volcano. This eruption was accompanied by a violent earthquake. It was during this eruption that a huge piece of the side of the cone was blown out, not unlike the case of the Val del Bove on Mt. Etna. The surrounding country was covered with mud. The immense quantity of materials thus thrown out of the side of the mountain produced changes in the courses of several rivers, thus causing great floods which in the single night of October 12th drowned 2,000 people. During these eruptions there were 114 villages destroyed, with a total loss of life of about 4,000.

There is a volcanic mountain on the island of Sumbawa that is noted for the very destructive eruption that occurred on it in April, 1815. If you examine the map of the Sunda Islands chain, you will see that the island of Sumbawa lies immediately east of a little island called Lombock, about 200 miles east of Java.

This eruption of Sumbawa was of the most frightful violence, and, indeed, with the exception of Krakatoa[Pg 128] and Pelée, was one of the greatest eruptions in historic times.

Like all great eruptions, that of Sumbawa gave plenty of signs of its coming. During April, 1814, the volcano manifested considerable increase in its activity, and ashes fell on the decks of vessels sailing past the island.

The eruption began on April 5th, 1815, but reached its greatest violence on the 11th and 12th of April. According to Lyell, the sound of the explosion was heard at the island of Sumatra at a distance of 970 geographical miles towards the west, and in the opposite direction it was heard for a distance of 720 miles. The destruction of life was terrible. Out of a population of 12,000 in the province of Tomboro, only twenty-six people escaped with their lives.

Like many other great eruptions the shooting upwards of the great column of matter from the crater produced a violent whirlwind that carried people, horses, cattle, and almost every movable object high into the air, and tore up huge trees by their roots.

Immense quantities of ashes fell over the surrounding country, or were carried towards Java to the west a distance of 300 miles, while on the north they were carried towards Celebes for a distance of 217 miles. Cinders covered the ocean towards the west two feet thick and several miles in length, so that ships could hardly make their way through them.

The darkness in Java produced by the dense ash cloud was greater than had ever before been experienced with the single exception of the great eruption of Krakatoa. A considerable quantity of this volcanic dust was carried to the islands of Amboyna and Banda, the last named island being at a distance of 800 miles east of the volcano.

This eruption of Sumbawa was attended by great lava[Pg 129] streams that covered vast areas of the land and afterwards poured into the sea.

As in the case of the explosive eruption of Krakatoa great waves were produced in the ocean all along the coasts of Sumbawa, and surrounding islands. The sea suddenly rose from two to twelve feet. A great wave rushed up the mouths of the rivers, and at the town of Tomboro, on the west side of Sumbawa, an area of land was sunk in the waters and remained permanently covered by eighteen feet of water.

The most important of the still active volcanoes of Japan is Assamayna. This mountain was in terrible eruption during the autumn of 1783, when dense showers of ashes thrown out of the crater darkened the sky, turning the day into night, and, falling on the cultivated fields around the mountain, changed them into deserts. During the eruption some forty-eight villages were destroyed by showers of ashes and red hot stones and thousands of the inhabitants were either killed directly by the stones and ashes, or died from starvation, since their fields were covered with ashes for miles around to a depth of from two and a half to five feet.

Another terrible eruption in Japan was in the volcanic mountain of Wunzen, or Onzen-Gatake. This occurred during 1791-93. During the last eruption of this volcano, 53,000 people lost their lives, either by reason of the eruption of the volcano, or by huge waves set up in the ocean by an earthquake.

[Pg 130]

CHAPTER XIII

JORULLO, A YOUNG VOLCANIC MOUNTAIN

You must not suppose that when we speak of Jorullo as a young volcanic mountain that we mean young in the sense that you or I might be called young, but young as regards mountains; for Jorullo, now a great mountain range, had no existence before the year 1759, and that would make the mountain a little less than 150 years old, which so far as mountains are concerned may properly be regarded as quite young.

The story of Jorullo is very interesting, and affords an excellent example of the great scale on which modern volcanic eruptions take place during historical times.

If you examine the map of Mexico on page 86 you will see that Jorullo lies 170 miles southwest of the city of Mexico, and 108 miles from the Pacific Ocean, which is the nearest large body of water. This mountain is of especial interest because, if old traditions are to be believed, it was thrown up during practically a single night. This wonderful event took place on an elevated plain or plateau, called the Plain of Malpais, that lies between 2,000 and 3,000 feet above the level of the ocean. The plain was situated in a part of Mexico that was celebrated for the growth of the finest cotton and indigo in the world. It formed the large estate of a wealthy planter, Señor Pedro de Jorullo, who lived at his ease as a wealthy planter is apt to do in tropical countries like Mexico.

Jorullo's plantation was covered by an especially fertile[Pg 131] soil, since it was formed by the deposits of volcanic ashes, dust, tufa, etc., produced, most probably, by neighboring volcanoes long before man appeared on the earth, for the plain of Malpais was bounded by hills that were composed of volcanic materials. There had, however, been no

45

signs of volcanic activity in the neighborhood. It had indeed been quiet, so far as volcanic eruptions were concerned, since the time of the discovery of America by Columbus, until the middle of the last century. The fertile fields of the Jorullo plantation were watered by two rivers, or as we would probably call them, brooks, the Cuitamba and the San Pedro.

Signs were not wanting of the coming calamity. During June, 1759, subterranean sounds were heard of a low rumbling character, which every now and then increased until they resembled in intensity the sounds produced by the firing of large guns. These sounds were accompanied by earthquake shocks that greatly terrified the people and caused them to flee from their homes. Nothing, however, occurred, so, becoming accustomed to the noises, the people returned to their houses. The noises and tremblings ceased for over two months, until, on the 29th of September, 1759, they were again heard, and a terrible eruption began. A long fissure opened in the earth, extending generally from northeast to southwest. From this fissure flames burst out, fragments of burning rock and stone, together with large quantities of ashes were thrown to great heights in the air, and were followed by streams of molten rock. Six volcanic cones were formed along the fissure. The highest of these cones is what now constitutes the volcanic mountain of Jorullo, which then reached a height of at least 1,600 feet above the level of the plain. From its cone were thrown out great quantities of lava of the same type as that which escaped from the[Pg 132] craters of many volcanic islands such as Hawaii and Iceland, namely, basaltic lavas. This eruption, which began on the 29th of September, 1759, continued until the month of February, 1760.

The account as above given was obtained by Humboldt, who visited the country some fifty-six years after the eruption. This story was told him by the Indians, but was also recorded in verse by a Jesuit priest, Raphael Landiva, a native of Guatemala. According to the account given Humboldt by the Indians, it appears that when a long time after the eruptions had quieted down, they had returned to their old homes with the hope of cultivating part of the grounds, they found the plains still too hot to permit their living on them.

According to Lyell, there was around the base of the cone, spreading from them as a centre over an area of some four square miles, a convex mass, about 550 feet in height, most of the surface of which was covered with thousands of small flattish conical mounds from six to nine feet in height. These, together with numerous large fissures that crossed the plain in different directions, served as points for the escape of sulphur vapors, as well as for the vapors of hot water.

During the escape of lava from the craters in 1759, the molten rock, spreading over the plain, ran into the channels of the river or brooks before named, driving out the water. This water reappeared at the base of the mountain in numerous hot springs.

Humboldt thought that the conical mountains had been lifted or raised by the formation of huge bubbles formed under the lava, thus causing it to assume a shape not unlike that of a huge bladder. This opinion, however, has not been accepted by geologists at the present time. Scrope points out that this was probably the origin of the[Pg 133] little conical mounds that covered the surface of the principal conical mounds but was not, in all probability, the cause of the mound itself. He says:

"With regard to the disputed question as to the origin of the raised plain of the Malpais, M. de Saussure, the last and most trustworthy visitor, entirely confirms the opinion which I ventured to proclaim in 1825, that Humboldt was mistaken in supposing it to have been 'blown up from beneath like a bladder,' and that it is merely an ordinary current of lava, which, owing to its very imperfect liquidity at the time of its issue from the volcanic vent, as well as to the overflow of one sheet or stream upon another, had acquired great thickness about its source, gradually thinning off towards the outer limit of the elliptical area it covered."

If you have been able to follow the above you will see that Mr. Scrope means that in his opinion the cone of Jorullo is a lava cone like that we have already studied on Mt. Loa or Mt. Kilauea, or, in other words, that the lava as it came out from the opening on the top of Jorullo, flowed in all directions around the opening, thus building up a mountain in the form of a flat lava cone.

Perhaps one of the reasons Humboldt had for believing the entire elevation of Jorullo to be due to the formation of a huge bladder was the fact that the plain on which the cone is situated, when struck, gave out a sound as though there was a vast hollow space below it. This was especially the case when the hoofs of the horses driven over its surface produced sounds as though they were moving over the summit of a hollow dome-like space below. But, as Lyell points out, this was probably only due to the fact that the materials forming the cone were very light and porous.

According to Burkhardt, a German mining engineer[Pg 134] who visited Jorullo in 1827, there appears to have been no other eruptions of the volcano since the time of Humboldt's visit. Mr. Burkhardt descended to the bottom of the crater and observed that small quantities of sulphurous vapors were still escaping. The small cones or *hornitos*, however, on the slopes had entirely ceased emitting steam. It appeared, too, that the twenty-four years that had passed since the time of Humboldt's visit, the rich soil of the surrounding country had permitted the successful cultivation of some crops of sugar cane and indigo.

Russell appears to doubt the reliability of the information obtained by Humboldt concerning Jorullo. He suggests that a poetical account by the Jesuit missionary from whom Humboldt obtained much of his information was not apt to possess marked scientific accuracy. While, however, this may be true, yet to a certain extent it seems entirely probable that the principal facts were as above given. The following account as given by Humboldt, is taken from a translation made in the early part of 1800:

"The affrighted inhabitants fled to the mountains of Aguasarco. A tract of ground from three to four square miles in extent, which goes by the name of Malpays, rose up in the shape of a bladder. The bounds of this convulsion are still distinguishable in the fractural strata. The Malpays, near its edge, is only twelve metres above the old level of the plain called the Playas de Jorullo; but the convexity of the ground thus thrown up increases progressively towards the centre, to an elevation of 160 metres (524.8 ft.).

"Those who witnessed this catastrophe from the top of Aguasarco assert that flames were seen to issue forth for an extent of more than half a square league, that fragments[Pg 135] of burning rocks were thrown up to prodigious heights, and that through a thick cloud of ashes, illuminated by the volcanic fire, the softened surface of the earth was seen to swell up like an agitated sea. The rivers of Cuitamba and San Pedro precipitated themselves into the burning chasms. The decomposition of the water contributed to invigorate the flames, which were distinguishable at the city of Pascuaro, though situated on very extensive table-land 1,400 metres (4,592 ft.) elevated above the plains of Las Playas de Jorullo. Eruptions of mud, and especially of strata of clay enveloping balls of decomposed basalt in concentrical layers, appeared to indicate that subterranean water had no small share in producing this extraordinary revolution. Thousands of small cones, from two to three metres in height, called by the indigenes ovens, issued forth from the Malpays....

"In the midst of the ovens, six large masses, elevated from 400 to 500 metres each above the old level of the plain, sprung up from a chasm, of which the direction is from N. N. E. to the S. S. E. This is the phenomenon of the Montenovo of Naples, several times repeated in a range of volcanic hills. The most elevated of these enormous masses, which bears some resemblance to the puys de l'Auvergne, is the great Volcan de Jorullo. It is continually burning, and has thrown up from the north side an immense quantity of scorified and basaltic lavas containing fragments of primitive rocks. These great eruptions of the central volcano continued till the month of February, 1760. In the following years they became gradually less frequent.... The roofs of the houses of Queretaro were then covered with ashes at a distance of more than forty-eight leagues in a straight line from the scene of the explosion. Although the subterranean[Pg 136] fire now appears far from violent, and the Malpays and the great volcano begin to be covered with vegetation, we nevertheless found the ambient air heated to such a degree by the action of the small ovens, that the thermometer at a great distance from the surface and in the shade rose as high as 43° C." (109° 4' F.).

[Pg 137]

47

CHAPTER XIV

MID-OCEAN VOLCANIC ISLANDS

Besides the volcanoes we have already described, there are many others situated in mid-ocean far from any continent. A brief description will be given of a few of these.

All the three great central oceans, the Pacific, the Atlantic, and the Indian, contain numerous volcanic islands, some of which rise many thousands of feet above the general level.

We will begin with a description of some of the more important volcanic islands of the Pacific. It was first pointed out by Kotzebue, and afterwards by Darwin, that all the islands of the Pacific Ocean can be divided into two great classes, the *high islands* and the *low islands*. All the high islands are of volcanic origin, while the low islands are of coral formation. It is the opinion of Dana, who has made a careful study of coral formations, especially in the Pacific, that in all probability even the low islands of the Pacific were originally volcanic, and that the deposits of coral had been made along their shores after their volcanoes had become extinct.

The islands of the Pacific, like the shores of the continents and most of their mountain ranges, extend in two great lines of trend, or general direction, which intersect each other nearly at right angles. These lines extend from the southeast to the northwest, and from the northeast to the southwest respectively, those extending in[Pg 138] a general direction from southeast to northwest being the most common in the Pacific.

Now, perhaps, the greatest number of the earth's volcanoes are arranged along fissures, or cracks in the earth's crust. The craters are situated along the cracks, the openings being kept clear at the crater, and gradually closing elsewhere, probably by pressure. In other words, most of the volcanoes follow one another along more or less straight lines. For example, in the western part of South America they follow the Andes Mountains. A similar arrangement exists in the volcanoes of Central America, Mexico, and the United States. Now, this is especially true of mid-ocean volcanoes of the Pacific which lie along lines extending from southeast to northwest, or from northeast to southwest, though mainly along the former.

Some of the volcanic islands of the Pacific have already been described or referred to, as, for example, the Aleutian Islands, which stretch in a curved line from the southwestern extremity of the peninsula of Alaska to Kamtschatka on the coast of Asia. We have already described the island of Hawaii, the great volcanoes of the Sandwich Islands chain, and besides these there are in the North Pacific the Ladrone Islands, lying east of the Philippines.

Some of the principal remaining islands are: the Fejee Islands, which are volcanic, with numerous hot springs and craters. The Friendly Islands, with the peak of Tafua, 2,138 feet high, an active volcano with a large crater always burning, and two other volcanoes, Apia, and Upala. Tahiti, to the east, is at present extinct. One of its mountains, Orobena, said to be 10,000 feet high, has a crater on its summit. The Marquesas, still further to the east, are also volcanic. All of these islands lie generally in the lines of the northeast trend.

[Pg 139]

The Tongan or New Zealand Island chain extends in the direction of the northeast trend. This, as you will see, is the direction in which the two islands of New Zealand extend. The Tongan Island chain is continued to the south through Auckland and the Macquaire Islands to 58° S. Towards the north, in almost the same line, are the Kermadec Islands near 30° S.

There are several active volcanoes in New Zealand. An explosive eruption of Tarawera, in New Zealand, in 1883, continued for several days, and was followed, three days afterwards, by an outburst in an active volcano in the Bay of Plenty, and two months afterwards, by a violent outburst in a volcano on the island of Ninafou in the Tongan Islands.

Coming now to the Atlantic Ocean we find a number of volcanic mountains in the deep waters near mid-ocean. The principal of these, besides Iceland, are the Azores, the Canaries, Cape Verde Islands, Ascension Island, St. Helena Island, and Tristan d'Acunha. The Peak of Pico, in the Azores, rises to a height of 7,016 feet. The Peak of Teneriffe, in the

Canaries, reaches the height of 12,225 feet. Teneriffe is a snow-capped mountain. It has a cone on its summit with precipitous walls like Vesuvius. Sulphurous vapors are continually formed at its summit, but no flames can be seen.

In the Cape Verde Islands is to be found the active volcanic mountain of Fuego, rising 7,000 feet above the sea. It has a central cone that has been broken down on one side like that of Somma on Vesuvius. Fuego was in eruption in 1785, and also in 1799.

Ascension Island, south of the equator, is formed entirely of volcanic materials. This island rises from an apparently granite floor on the bed of the ocean, in water 12,000 feet deep.

[Pg 140]

St. Helena lies further to the south. It is an extinct volcano, and has the remains of a crater on its summit with lava dikes in various parts of the island.

Tristan d'Acunha is an isolated mountain that lies in the South Atlantic, south of St. Helena, 1,500 miles from Africa, the nearest land. It is an extinct volcano that rises from a depth of 12,150 feet to a height of 7,000 feet above the sea. It has a truncated cone on its summit and a lake of pure water in its old crater.

There are only a few volcanic islands in the Indian Ocean. Kerguelen Island lies in the southern waters. St. Paul and Amsterdam to the north, lying near 40° S. lat., as well as the Crozet Islands, are extinct volcanoes.

In the Arctic Ocean is the volcanic island of Jan Mayen. In the Antarctic Ocean, as far as is known, there are only two volcanoes, Mt. Erebus and Mt. Terror. Mt. Erebus, 12,400 feet high, is an active volcano. Mt. Terror, 10,990 feet high, is an extinct volcano.

[Pg 141]

CHAPTER XV

SUBMARINE VOLCANOES

A submarine volcano is a volcano that erupts on the bed of the ocean with its crater covered by the waters. Many of the great volcanic mountains of the world began as submarine volcanoes. A crater first opened on the floor of the ocean, and lava escaping, was heaped up around the opening, until it emerged above the surface as an island. As we have seen, the island of Iceland is believed to have begun in this way. Such, too, in all probability, was the origin of Hawaii, Vesuvius, Etna, and Santorin.

But besides the volcanic mountains that were thrown up during the geological past, there are others that have been called into existence while man has been living on the earth. We will now describe a few islands that have been formed in this manner by submarine volcanic eruptions.

That volcanic eruptions, or at least something that greatly resembles eruptions, occur on the bed of the ocean too far below the surface to permit them to be directly seen from above, has been shown in a number of cases where the captains of vessels have reported that in certain parts of the ocean, jets of water, or steam, and pillars of flame have been seen rising to great heights from the surface of the water, and that in certain regions sulphurous smoke has also been seen. During such occurrences, the water is agitated, as if it were being violently boiled.[Pg 142] Moreover, these parts of the ocean are shaken by severe earthquake shocks.

Another evidence of submarine volcanic eruptions is to be found in great quantities of ashes, scoriæ, or pumice stone, that are seen spread out over the surface of the ocean after the commotions referred to in the preceding paragraph. Still another proof is that parts of the ocean whose waters were previously very deep are found to have suddenly shoaled.

Of course, the best proof is the appearance of rocky reefs or small islands thrown up above the surface of the water, especially where volcanic cones appear. While in many cases the new islands thus thrown up are subsequently washed away by the waves, yet some have continued above the water.

One of the most noted instances of the formation of an island by a submarine volcano was Sabrina, which was thrown up in 1811, in the Atlantic Ocean, off the shores of St. Michael in the Azores Islands. Sabrina had a cone that was 300 feet in height. It did not

49

long remain above the waters, however, being soon washed away by the waves. It is interesting to note that in the same part of the ocean where Sabrina appeared, other islands have appeared and disappeared, at times long before 1811; that is, during the year 1691, as well as during 1720.

Another instance of a submarine island is Graham's Island, that was thrown up in 1831, in the Mediterranean Sea, between the west coast of Sicily and the nearest part of Africa, on which ancient Carthage was situated. The part of the sea where the island was thrown up had previously a depth of 600 feet.

The general appearance of Graham's Island is represented in Fig. 22.

Graham's Island was formed by accumulations of loose[Pg 143] scoria and cinders, together with blocks of lava and fragments of limestone. It reached a height of 200 feet above the water, but only remained above the surface for a few months, when it was washed away, leaving a submarine bank some twelve miles in width, that was covered by water of about 150 feet, but which, however, increased rapidly in depth towards the edge until depths of from 1,200 to 2,000 feet were reached.

FIG. 22. GRAHAM'S ISLAND—A RECENT VOLCANIC ISLAND

According to Lyell, on the 28th of June, 1831, before Graham's Island appeared, a ship passing over this portion of the sea felt severe earthquake shocks. On July[Pg 144] 10th of the same year, the captain of a vessel from Sicily reported that as he passed near this part of the Mediterranean, a column of water, 800 yards in circumference, was seen to rise from the sea to a height of sixty feet, and that afterwards a column of steam rising to a height of 1,800 feet was seen in the same place. On again passing the same region on July 18th, this captain found a small island about twelve feet in height, with a crater in its centre, that was throwing out volcanic materials, together with immense masses of vapor.

The island thus formed grew rapidly, both in size and height. When visited at the end of July, it had attained a height of from fifty to ninety feet, and was three-quarters of a mile in circumference. By August 4th, it had reached a height of 200 feet, and was then some three miles in circumference. From this time, however, the island began to decrease in size, as the waves began to wash it away. By August 25th, it was only two miles in circumference. On September 3d, it had decreased to three-fifths of a mile in circumference, and continued to decrease until it entirely disappeared, so that in the year 1832, there were, according to measurements, some 150 feet of water over its former site.

The Mediterranean Sea between Sicily and Greece is also especially liable to submarine activity. New islands appear and disappear so frequently that in this region they are almost regarded as common phenomena.

There are many other parts of the ocean where submarine volcanic eruptions are common. This is especially the case in the narrowest part of the Atlantic Ocean between Africa and South America. Here there is a region situated partly above the equator, though for the greater part south of the equator, frequently visited by submarine eruptions, that are accompanied by earthquakes, by the[Pg 145] agitation of the water, by the appearance of floating masses of ashes and scoriæ, as well as by columns of steam or smoke. Floating masses of ashes and scoriæ sometimes occur so thick as to retard the progress of vessels.

But what forms, perhaps, one of the best instances of a large island formed by submarine eruptions during historical times, is Bogosloff Island in Behring Sea, some forty miles west of Unalaska Island. This island, the position of which is seen on the accompanying map, is known to the Russians as Ioanna Bogoslova, or St. John the Theologian. It is situated in lat. 53° 58' N., long. 168° west. It is said that during the year 1795, some of the natives of Unalaska Island saw what they thought was a fog in the neighborhood of a small rock, which they had known for a long time to project above the sea in these waters. This rock was marked on some Russian chart dated 1768-69. It was seen by Captain Cooke, in 1778, and was named by him Ship Rock.

But it was not a fog that the Unalaskans had seen in the neighborhood of Ship Rock; for, to their great surprise, the fog continued in sight although everywhere else the air was quite clear. Of course, this was a great mystery to the people. During the spring of 1796, one of them, who possessed either greater curiosity than the rest, or greater courage, or both, visited the rock. He returned, telling the strange story that all the ocean around the rock was boiling, and that the mist or fog was caused by the rising steam. What was taking place was a submarine eruption. During May, 1796, sufficient matter had been brought up from below to increase greatly the area of the small rock.

[Pg 146]

FIG. 23. ALEUTIAN ISLANDS

During later years several attempts have been made to visit Bogosloff Island. For example, the island was visited during 1872 and 1873, when it was found to have[Pg 147]increased in height to 850 feet. But no appearance of any volcanic crater was to be seen.

During October, 1883, a great volcanic eruption occurred there. Considerable changes were produced in its shape, as well as in the depth of the surrounding water. During this eruption, clouds of steam completely hid the island. Great quantities of ashes obscured the light of the sun. After the eruption, a new island was thrown up near the old one, in a place where the water had previously been deep enough for the ready passage of ships. The new island was about half a mile from the old one. It was conical in form, from 500 to 800 feet in height, and about three-quarters of a mile in diameter.

The new island was visited in 1884 by the U. S. Revenue Marine Steamer *Corwin*. Lieutenant Cartwell, who visited the island at this time, described it as follows:

"The sides of New Bogosloff rise with a gentle slope to the crater. The ascent at first appears easy, but a thin layer of ashes, formed into a crust by the action of rain and moisture, is not strong enough to sustain a man's weight. At every step my feet crushed through the outer covering and I sank at first ankle-deep and later on knee-deep into a soft, almost impalpable dust which arose in clouds and nearly suffocated me. As the summit was reached, the heat of the ashes become almost unbearable, and I was forced to continue the ascent by picking my way over rocks whose surfaces being exposed to the air, were somewhat cooled and afforded a more secure foothold.

"On all sides of the cone there are openings through which steam escaped with more or less energy. I observed from some vents the steam was emitted at regular intervals, while from others it issued with no perceptible intermission. Around each vent there was a thick deposit of sulphur, which gave off suffocating vapors."

[Pg 148]

CHAPTER XVI

DISTRIBUTION OF THE EARTH'S VOLCANOES

Having now considered at some length the principal volcanoes of the earth, and endeavored to obtain some idea of the many wonders they exhibit, especially as regards the vast quantities of material they bring from the inside of the earth, as well as the great force with which they sometimes throw these materials out of their craters, it will be well to point out where such volcanoes are to be found.

It may have seemed to you, when you have carefully followed what has been said about the earth's volcanoes, that they are to be found pretty nearly everywhere, at least so far as latitude is concerned; and in this supposition you are correct; for there are volcanoes in the Arctic Ocean, as in the volcanic island of Jan Mayen between Iceland and Spitzbergen, there are Mt. Erebus and Mt. Terror in the Antarctic Ocean, besides very numerous volcanoes in the Atlantic, Pacific, and Indian Oceans, and their shores in both the temperate and the torrid zones.

There is, however, one thing that you have probably especially noticed and that is that volcanoes are seldom found at very great distances from the ocean, except on some of its arms or seas, such as the Mediterranean Sea. I do not mean by this that all the earth's volcanoes are either situated directly on the coast of the continents or on islands, since, in such a large body as the earth, a distance of a few hundred miles from the ocean is hardly[Pg 149] to be regarded as being very far from it. But it is true that all the earth's volcanoes are either situated on the coasts of the continents, or on islands, and, moreover, they are situated to a greater or less extent along lines, which, as we have already pointed out, are believed to mark weak portions of the earth's crust that have been fissured or fractured.

In order that you may have some idea of this distribution, I think it will be well to give you a number of interesting facts that have been pointed out by Dana. According to this authority, there are something in the neighborhood of 300 active volcanoes on the earth. Of these, no less than five-sixths, or 250, lie either on the borders of the Pacific Ocean, or on some of its many islands. Thirty-nine either lie within or on the borders of the Atlantic, of which thirteen are in Iceland, or near the Arctic Circle, three in the Canaries, seven in the Mediterranean Sea, six in the Lesser Antilles, and ten in the Atlantic Oceanic Islands. The Indian Ocean contains only a few active volcanoes. There are, however, a much greater number of extinct volcanoes, which may at any time again become active.

The following is the distribution of the earth's volcanoes as given by Dana. As you will see, from an inspection of Fig. 24, all of the regions of volcanoes lie either on the borders of the continents, or on islands in the oceans. The districts are as follows:

1. *Scattered Over the Pacific Ocean.*—This district includes the following active volcanoes; i. e., the Hawaiian Islands, nearly in mid-ocean, almost directly below the Tropic of Cancer; in the west central parts of the South Pacific; in the New Hebrides; in the Friendly Islands, the Tongan or New Zealand Islands, in the Santa Cruz Islands, and in the Ladrones.
[Pg 150]

FIG. 24. MAP OF THE WORLD, SHOWING LOCATION OF ACTIVE AND RECENTLY EXTINCT VOLCANOES

[Pg 151]

2. *On the Borders of the Pacific.*—This district includes the volcanoes that extend from the southern part of South America at intervals along the Andes Mountain range. Of these there are thirty-two in Chile, seven or eight in Bolivia and Southern Peru; about twenty in the neighborhood of Quito. Further north there are thirty-nine in Central America, and seven in Mexico. Proceeding northwards through the United States, there are a number of volcanic mountains, generally extinct, in portions of the Sierra Nevadas and Cascade Ranges. Probably a number of volcanic mountains exist in portions of Canada lying between the northern boundaries of the United States and Alaska, and a number in Alaska; some twenty-one volcanic mountains in the Aleutian Islands; some fifteen or twenty in Kamtschatka; thirteen in the Kuriles; some twenty-five or thirty in Japan and the neighboring islands; some fifteen or twenty in the Philippines; several along the northern coasts of New Guinea; a number in New Zealand and south of Cape Horn; the volcanoes of the Deception Island with its hot springs, and also in the South Shetlands 62° 30' S.

3. *In the Indian Ocean.*—On the western border of the Indian Ocean there are a few volcanoes in Madagascar; in the Island of Bourbon; Mauritius; the Comoro Islands; and in Kerguelen Land on the south. There are also volcanoes on the western border of the Indian Ocean where the lofty peak of Kilima Ndjro, 18,000 feet, is volcanic.

4. *Over the Seas that Separate the Northern and the Southern Continents and in their Vicinity.*— This is an especially active region of volcanoes. For the sake of convenience the continents of the world are sometimes divided into three pairs or double continents; namely, North and South America, connected by the Isthmus of[Pg 152]Panama; Europe and Africa, connected by the Isthmus of Suez; and Australia and Asia, completely separated by a sunken isthmus, the summits of which form the Sunda Island chain. In the first of these regions we have the very active group of the West Indies, where there are ten volcanic islands. In the second pair of double continents we have the volcanoes of the Mediterranean and Red Seas, and their borders, such as Sicily, Vesuvius, and other parts of Italy, Spain, Germany, the Grecian Archipelago, Asia Minor, and extending eastward through the Caspian, Mt. Ararat, Demavend, on the south shores of the Caspian, Mt. Ararat, and some few others along the borders of the Red Sea.

In the East Indies we find the most intense centre of volcanic activity in the world. Here there are some 200 volcanoes of which there are nearly fifty in Java alone, more than half of which are still active. There are nearly as many volcanoes in Sumatra, and many in the small islands near Borneo, the Philippines, etc.

5. *On the Borders of the Atlantic and Elsewhere.*—It is an interesting fact that there are no volcanoes on the eastern borders of the Atlantic north of the West Indies Island chain. In the South Atlantic the only volcano on the borders is one of the Cameroons Mountains. In the Atlantic Ocean we have Iceland, the Azores, the Canaries, Cape Verde, Ascension, St. Helena, and Tristan d'Acunha.

This curious distribution of the volcanoes of the world near the oceanic waters appears to be dependent rather on the very early shapes of the continents and the ocean beds than on their present shapes.

[Pg 153]

CHAPTER XVII

VOLCANOES OF THE GEOLOGICAL PAST

The question is often asked whether the volcanic eruptions of the geological past were not much more violent and destructive than the volcanoes of the present time. Now, while this is a matter that properly belongs to the subject of geology, and will be treated at greater length in the Wonder Book on Geology, yet a short mention should be made of it here.

It is the opinion of Dana that while there have been volcanoes during the different geological ages, yet volcanic activity has increased through the geological past until the age that immediately preceded the appearance of man on the earth. He thinks there is no reason for believing that there were any very great volcanic eruptions during the earliest geological time known as the Archæic. Dana speaks as follows concerning this:

"In this connection it is an instructive fact that in eastern North America, at epochs when there was the greatest amount of friction and crushing ... those of the making of the Green Mountains and the Appalachians ... no volcanoes were made, and little took place in the way of eruptions through fissures."

On the other hand, Prestwich seems inclined to think that the absence of well-marked cones of volcanic material in the rock of the older geological ages is not to be regarded as proof that no eruptions then took place, since the very great amount of erosion that occurred between that time[Pg 154] and the Tertiary Age before the appearance of man, would, probably, have completely obliterated any cones, and even the volcanic materials would have undergone such changes as completely to alter their general character. He agrees, however, with Dana that, probably, the most violent and explosive volcanoes of the geological ages have been those of the Tertiary Age.

Without, however, attempting anything more than a brief reference to the volcanoes of the geological past, it may be said that many of the more important of the active volcanoes of the earth's present time were begun in the Tertiary Age. Mt. Etna, Vesuvius, and Mt. Hecla are believed to have commenced at this time.

There is an interesting region of geological volcanoes in the neighborhood of Auvergne in Central France. Here they occur in three separate groups that extend over a high granite platform from north to south for a distance of about 100 miles, and from twenty to eighty miles from east to west. The eruptions began in the earlier portions of the Tertiary Age, and continued down to the latter periods of prehistoric times. Some of these volcanic craters remain to-day almost as unaffected by erosion as if they had been formed but recently.

Other regions of geological volcanoes are to be found in parts of Spain near the foot of the Pyrenees Mountains, in parts of Italy and Germany, as well as in regions in the Caucasus Mountains.

In Asia Minor there exists a group of almost thirty extinct volcanoes in the neighborhood of the Gulf of Smyrna. Both Little and Great Ararat contain volcanic cones: that in the latter mountain was active during historical times. There are also extensive volcanic districts in the Taurus Mountains. In addition to these there are groups of extinct volcanoes in portions of Central Asia.

[Pg 155]

Aden, on the Red Sea, is the centre of an extensive volcanic district. Indeed, on both shores of the Red Sea there are a few volcanoes that are still active, while in Sinai, and in the districts of the south, there are several extinct craters.

But it is in the New World, especially on the Pacific coast of North America, that volcanic activity was especially great during the geological past. There is a district containing volcanic rocks that extends through various parts of western North America, from New Mexico and North California, to Oregon and British Columbia. This district has a width of from eighty to 200 miles, and a length of not quite 800 miles. This great area of nearly 150,000 square miles is covered with great sheets of volcanic rocks except where mountain ranges rise from them, or where the rivers have cut deep valleys through them. In portions of California and New Mexico these plateaus rise to heights of from 8,000 to 10,000 feet, while in parts of Colorado, where they form huge dome-like mountains, they reach a thickness of 14,000 feet. In Oregon the sheet of lava is 2,000 feet thick, and, indeed, in some places, is estimated to have a depth of 7,000 feet.

In the opinion of nearly all American geologists these great lava flows in western North America were not of the type known as crater eruptions, but were what are called fissure eruptions. Some of them are believed to have occurred during geological times as early as the Eocene. Prestwich, however, is of the opinion that the eruptions of the past in these portions of the world were not confined to fissure eruptions, but that crater eruptions also occurred; and that it was towards the close of the Tertiary Age that crater eruptions occurred with great lava flows. Indeed, as we have seen, in portions of Utah[Pg 156] and the neighborhood the remains of true craters can be found.

Besides the above there are evidences of geological volcanoes of still older times. In portions of Deccan, in southern Hindostan, there is an immense plateau formed of trap rock, that extends from east to west for a distance of 400 miles, and from north to south through from 700 to 800 miles. This district, with an area of almost 200,000 square miles, is covered with a vast lava sheet. It was, in the opinion of Prestwich, from whom many of the facts of the geological volcanic eruptions have been obtained, probably still more extensive. The plateau of Deccan rises gradually from the east to the west, where, in some parts of the Ghauts Mountains, it reaches a height of from 4,000 to 5,000 feet.

One of the greatest of these prehistoric volcanoes of Scotland was a volcano in the Isle of Mull in the Hebrides. This volcano was probably nearly thirty miles across at its base, and was from 10,000 to 12,000 feet high. It is now only 3,172 feet in height.

According to Judd the Island of Skye in Inverness-shire is the remains of a volcano that was active in Tertiary times, probably many millions of years ago. This volcano was very large, probably about thirty miles across at its base, with a height of perhaps as great as 12,000 or 15,000 feet. Now there are only left some granite and other similar rocks that form the Red Mountains and Coolim Hills of Skye that reach about 3,000 feet above the sea level.

There are many other parts of the world containing volcanoes that were active during the geological past. The above, however, is as far as we can describe such volcanoes in this book.

[Pg 157]

CHAPTER XVIII

LAPLACE'S NEBULAR HYPOTHESIS

LaPlace's nebular hypothesis is the name given to an ingenious hypothesis proposed by LaPlace, a celebrated French astronomer, in an endeavor to explain how the solar system has been evolved.

You will notice that this is called a hypothesis and not a theory. The word hypothesis is properly applied to a more or less intelligent guess or assumption, that has been made for the purpose of trying to find out in the cause of any natural phenomenon. A theory is an expression of a physical truth based on natural laws and principles that have been independently established. A theory, therefore, is much more complete than a hypothesis. A hypothesis, as Silliman remarks, bears the same relation to a theory or law, that a scaffolding does to a completed building, since it forms a convenient means for erecting the building.

LaPlace's work is properly called a hypothesis, because it is not to be considered as any more than a means for enabling one intelligently to inquire into the probable manner in which the solar system has reached its present condition, by gradual steps or stages during the almost inconceivable length of time since its creation.

Before describing LaPlace's hypothesis it will be necessary to give you some ideas concerning what is known by astronomers as the solar system.

The solar system consists of the sun, and the eight large bodies called planets that revolve around the sun.[Pg 158] It also includes a number of moons or satellites revolving around the planets, a number of small bodies, called planetoids or asteroids, together with numerous comets and meteorites. Besides these there is probably a system of meteoric bodies that are believed to revolve around the sun, and to produce, by the reflection of the light from their surfaces, what is known as the *zodiacal light.*

The principal bodies of the solar system are the planets. These constitute eight large bodies named in their order from the sun, beginning with the nearest: Mercury, Venus, Earth, Mars, Jupiter, Saturn, Uranus, and Neptune. The last four planets, Jupiter, Saturn, Uranus, and Neptune are much larger than the others, and are therefore known as the *major planets* in order to distinguish them from Mercury, Venus, Earth, and Mars, which are called the *minor planets.* You can remember the order in which the last three planets come by their initial letter, S-aturn, U-ranus, and N-eptune, spelling the word SUN, around which they all revolve.

It may be interesting to state here that the ancients knew of seven only of these planets. Since, as they asserted, there were only seven days in the week, and seven openings into the head; i. e., two for the eyes, two for the nostrils, two for the ears, and one for the mouth, it was natural that there should be but seven planets. During later years, however, an eighth planet was discovered and named Neptune. It would be interesting to explain to you how the position of this planet was reasoned out by mathematical calculations, that is, in other words, how, as a result of such calculations, an astronomer was told that if he would point his telescope to a certain part of the heavens he would discover a new planet. He did this and located the planet Neptune. However interesting this story may be it belongs properly[Pg 159] to astronomy, and will be described in full in the Wonder Book of Astronomy.

In the opinion of some astronomers it is quite probable that a ninth planet will be found far beyond the orbit of Neptune. There may also be some additional planets discovered between Mercury and the Sun.

Besides the eight known planets there exist, somewhere between the orbits of Mars and Jupiter, many smaller planets called *asteroids,* or *minor planets.* A long time ago it was pointed out by Bode that a curious relation exists between the distances of the planets from the sun. This relation or law is generally known, after the name of the astronomer who first called attention to it, as *Bode's Law.* No reason has been discovered for this arrangement of the planets, so that Bode's Law may be regarded as empirical. It may, however, be mentioned here that the distances of all the planets from the sun agrees with the law very closely, with the single exception of Neptune, which is quite at variance with the law.

It was noticed at an early date, that a gap existed between Mars and Jupiter, so that astronomers began to believe that there was probably a missing planet in that space, and this belief was greatly strengthened when Neptune was discovered in 1781. Without going any further into this story in this book, it may be said that it is the general opinion of astronomers that the planetoids or asteroids were formed possibly from the fragments of the missing planet, or, more probably, from the breaking up of some of the outer rings on the planet Mars.

The distances of the planets from the central sun vary from the nearest planet, Mercury, which is about 36,000,000 miles from the sun, to the furthest, or Neptune, which is 2,766,000,000 miles from the sun.

All the major planets have a single moon, or more,[Pg 160] revolving around them. For example, Jupiter has four moons; Uranus, six; Saturn, eight; Neptune, one. As to the minor planets, Mars has two moons; and, as far as is known, neither Mercury or Venus has a moon. Our earth has one moon, but, as we shall afterwards see, this is not to be regarded as a moon or satellite of the earth, but rather as a twin planet to the earth.

LaPlace's nebular hypothesis was proposed by LaPlace during the year 1796. While there are many objections that can be brought against it, since it fails to account for all of the phenomena of the solar system, yet it is a significant fact now, in the year 1907, nearly a century and a quarter after the hypothesis was first announced, that although modified in many respects, there has not been any hypothesis proposed to entirely replace it.

While the nebular hypothesis of LaPlace is necessarily a matter that belongs to astronomy, yet it will be advisable to consider it here, since it explains the source of the original heat of both the earth and the moon, which we believe is the true cause of volcanoes.

In his nebular hypothesis, LaPlace assumes that all the materials of which the solar system is formed, were originally scattered throughout space in the shape of an exceedingly rare form of matter known as nebulous matter. He points out that if it be granted that this medium began to accumulate around a common centre, so as to form a huge globe or sphere, and if a motion of rotation on its axis from west to east were given to this sphere that, on strictly mechanical principles, a system of heavenly bodies corresponding to the solar system might have been evolved. Let us, therefore, try to understand how this might have been brought about.

The nebulous matter that LaPlace assumed originally constituted all the matter in the solar system, was highly[Pg 161] heated gaseous matter. In other words, it consisted of ordinary matter raised to a very high temperature; LaPlace thought at a temperature very much hotter than that of the sun.

As this great mass of matter commenced to cool, it began to collect around a centre and slowly rotate. Its contraction or shrinkage, while cooling, must have caused an increase in the speed with which it spun around or rotated on its axis. At first it spun but sluggishly, but as it cooled and began to shrink this rate of rotation began slowly to increase.

Now you must bear in mind that the huge rotating mass, as imagined by LaPlace, was very many times larger than the size of our present sun. Indeed, instead of having a diameter of only 866,500 miles, its temperature was so high that the nebulous matter of which it was composed had expanded it so much that it extended far beyond the orbit of Neptune, or had a diameter twice as great as 2,766,000,000 miles.

As the huge mass continued to shrink or contract, its rotation began to gradually increase until at last its centrifugal force was sufficiently great to cause it to bulge out at the equator, so as at last to separate a ring of gaseous matter. This ring was left behind by the sun, as it continued cooling, and formed the first planet that was born into the solar system. The ring might have continued to revolve around the sun for a time, and would, of course, revolve in the same direction as that in which the sun was rotating, that is, from west to east. Eventually, however, it broke up into smaller fragments, that afterwards collected in a single body, and, assuming a globe-like shape of the planet, formed the planet Neptune. Necessarily, too, the planet so formed not only would revolve in its orbit from west to east in the same direction[Pg 162] in which the sun was revolving on its axis, but would also rotate or spin on its axis in the same direction.

After, in this way, throwing off the first planet, the central sun continued to cool and grow smaller, until the increase in the rate of its rotation was again such as to permit its centrifugal force to form a second ring around its equator, which being left as the sun continued to contract, gave rise to another planet, or to Uranus, and so on until the four major planets and the four minor planets were born.

According to this hypothesis, the planet that was first born was the planet that is farthest from the sun, that is, Neptune, and the planet last born must have been the nearest planet, Mercury.

But while all this planet forming was going on, the separate planets also continued to shrink, and, therefore, began to rotate more rapidly on their axes. Under the influence of the centrifugal force, ring-like masses began to form around their equators, and these masses left by the planet constituted their moons or satellites. As you can see, according to this hypothesis, just as the planets would all revolve in their orbits from west to east, and rotate on their axes in the same direction as the sun, so, too, the moons or satellites of the planets would also rotate on their axes, from east to west, and revolve in their orbits in the same direction.

In order to show the extent to which LaPlace's nebular hypothesis explains the peculiarities of the solar system, we must inquire what are the most important of these peculiarities. We will take these from Young's general book on Astronomy, from which most of the facts in this chapter have been condensed. They are as follows:

The orbits of nearly all the planets and their satellites are nearly circular; they are all in the same plane; and all[Pg 163] revolve in the same direction. They are, moreover, with the single exception of Neptune, arranged at distances from the sun in accordance with Bode's Law.

All the planets increase in both directions, towards and from the sun, in density from Saturn, the least dense.

All the planets, with the exception probably of Uranus, rotate in a plane that is nearly the same as the plane of the orbit in which they revolve. Moreover, with the exception of probably both Uranus and Neptune, all the planets rotate in the same direction as that in which they revolve.

The satellites revolve in orbits whose planes nearly coincide with the plane of the planets' rotation, while the direction of the revolution of the satellites is the same as that in which their planets revolve.

Finally, the largest planets rotate most swiftly.

Now, LaPlace's nebular hypothesis explains nearly all of the above facts. The following modifications of the hypothesis, however, are necessary. Let us briefly examine some of these modifications.

In the first place it can be shown that the original nebulous mass instead of being at a higher temperature than that of the sun was probably at a much lower temperature, since the condensation of the gaseous matter must have increased the temperature. Instead, therefore, of the original nebulous mass being purely gaseous it was, as Young expressed it: "Rather a cloud of ice cold meteoric dust than an incandescent gas or a fire mist." Or in other words, the original nebulous mass from which the solar system was evolved, consisted of finely divided particles of solid or liquid matter surrounded by an envelope of permanent gaseous matter.

A doubt, too, has been raised as regards the manner in which the planets were liberated from the central sun.[Pg 164] Instead of separating in the form of a regular ring, it has been thought that probably in most cases this separation assumed the shape of a lump. It might, however, have occurred at times in the ring-like form as may be seen in the case of the planet Saturn.

Again, instead of the outer rings being separated first, and the others in regular order, so that the outer planets are much the older, it would seem possible, or, as Young states, even probable, that several of the planets may be of the same or nearly the same age, as they would be if more than one ring had been separated at one time, or, indeed, several planets may have been formed from different zones of a single ring.

As you will see, LaPlace's nebular hypothesis assumes that both sun and moon were in a highly heated condition when they were separated from the nebulous sun, so that we can understand that the former molten condition of their interiors was due to the heat they originally possessed.

[Pg 165]

CHAPTER XIX

THE EARTH'S HEATED INTERIOR, THE CAUSE OF VOLCANOES

As we have already seen, the nebular hypothesis of LaPlace would seem to make it more than probable that the earth was originally in a highly heated condition, and only reached its present state after long cooling. While this cooling has gone on for probably millions upon millions of years both before and during the geological past, yet in the opinion of perhaps the best geologists the interior of the earth is still very hot, only the outer portions or crust having hardened by loss of heat.

That there is a very hot region somewhere inside the earth is evident, since from some place or places below the surface there come out the immense streams of lava that, continuing to flow at irregular intervals, have at last built up such great masses of land as the island of Hawaii, the still greater island of Iceland, the even greater lava fields of the western United States, and the great plateau of the Deccan in southern Hindustan.

It certainly must have required a great quantity of lava to build up an island like Hawaii with its area of fully 40,000 square miles, for the highest point on the summit of Mt. Kea reaches 13,805 feet above the level of the sea, and, moreover, stands on the bed of the Pacific Ocean in water fully 12,000 feet deep.

But Iceland is only one of many similar cases. Volcanoes are to be found in practically all parts of the earth, not only in the equatorial regions, where they are[Pg 166]especially numerous, but also in the frigid and temperate zones. We must also remember the immense lava streams that are known to have come from the interior during the great fissure eruptions of the geological past. When all these facts are taken into consideration, it would certainly seem that there is only one source sufficiently great to supply this wonderful demand, and that is the entire inside of the earth.

But entirely apart from volcanic phenomena there are other proofs that the entire interior of the earth is in a highly heated condition. The differences of temperature caused by the sun during day and night do not affect the earth much below a depth of three feet, while the differences of temperature between summer and winter do not extend much further below the surface than forty feet. Below these depths, in all parts of the earth, the temperature of the crust rises at a rate, which, although not uniform, yet is not far from an increase of one degree of the Fahrenheit thermometer scale for every fifty or sixty feet of descent.

If the above rate of increase continues uniform the temperature of the crust would be sufficiently hot to boil water at a distance of about 8,000 feet below the surface, while at a depth of about thirty miles the temperature would be sufficiently high to melt all known substances at ordinary conditions of atmospheric pressure; that is, to melt all known substances if they were subjected to such a temperature at the level of the sea.

In considering the above we must not lose sight of the fact that this increase in temperature with descent below the surface of the earth's crust occurs, not only in places where there are volcanoes, but over all parts of the earth, thus seeming to point out that there is something hot below the surface which fills the entire inside of the earth.

[Pg 167]

It is true the greatest distance to which man has actually gone down through the earth's crust is but a few miles. We do not, therefore, know by actual experience that the interior is anywhere in a fused condition, yet the escape of lava or molten rocks in all latitudes, and in the enormous quantities referred to above, seems to show that the entire inside of the earth is at a temperature sufficiently high to melt all known substances under ordinary conditions.

It may be interesting in this connection to examine some of the proofs of this increase in temperature with descent below the surface. The following figures are given by Dana:

Borings to great depths have been made in various parts of the earth, both for artesian wells as well as for the shafts of mines. After passing the line of invariable temperature, the rate of increase for a total distance of 4,000 feet below the surface is in the neighborhood of from one degree for fifty-five to sixty feet, or an average of fifty-seven and a half feet for each degree of heat. In the case of the deep artesian well bored at Grenelle, Paris, where a temperature of eighty-five degrees Fahrenheit was reached at a distance of 2,000 feet, the rate of increase was somewhat more rapid, being one degree Fahrenheit for every sixty feet.

In a deep well bored in a salt mine at Neusalzwerk, Prussia, a depth of 2,200 feet showed a temperature of ninety-one degrees Fahrenheit at the bottom. This was at the rate of one degree for every fifty feet of descent. At Schladenbach, in Prussia, a well has been dug to the depth of 5,735 feet with a temperature of 134° F. A boring at Wheeling, in West Virginia, reached a depth of 4,500 feet, 3,700 feet below the level of the sea. Here the rate of increase of temperature in the upper half was[Pg 168] one degree Fahrenheit for every eighty feet, and in the lower half of one degree for every sixty feet.

It must not be supposed because the rate of increase of temperature is not uniform that the argument of a highly heated interior is weakened. On the contrary, it would be very surprising if the rate continued uniform; for it is evident that the conducting power of different materials in the earth's crust for heat must necessarily make a great difference in the rate at which heat should increase, as we go farther down into the earth. This is so important a matter that I will explain it at somewhat greater length.

Let us suppose that instead of the highly heated interior of the earth, we consider the simple case of a hot stove, the doors or other openings into which are closed so that it is impossible to see the red hot coals inside. Now, suppose holes were bored in the sides of this stove not deep enough to reach the red hot mass within, and that tightly fitting rods or plugs all of the same length and thickness, but of different kinds of materials such as wood, earthenware, glass, iron, copper, silver, and gold, etc., were so placed in the holes as to tightly fit them. Now, under these circumstances the end of all the plugs would be at the same distance from the heated inside. They would not, however, by any means show the same temperatures, the metallic rods would be too hot to touch, while the end of the piece of wood would hardly be hot enough to burn the hand when held against it. The piece of glass and earthenware though less cool would be much less hot than the different rods of metals. Their temperatures would be necessarily affected by their conducting power for heat. The wood, the glass, and the earthenware being poorer conductors than the metals would show much lower temperatures.

[Pg 169]

Now, the same thing is true with the different materials that constitute the rocks of the earth's crust. Some of these are much better conductors of heat than others, so that the rate of increase of temperature with descent below the surface must necessarily vary with the kind of materials that form the crust of different parts of the earth.

You may, therefore, safely conclude that the entire interior of the earth is in a highly heated condition, and that the source of this heat is to be traced to the heat the earth originally possessed when, in accordance to the nebular hypothesis of LaPlace, it was separated from the sun which gave birth to it, that the present crust of the earth has been formed on the outside by the loss of a portion of this heat.

The rapidity with which a body cools, depends, among other things, on the difference between its temperature and that of the medium in which it is placed. The greater this difference of temperature the greater the rapidity of cooling. Careful measurements made by Tait, the English physicist, show that our earth loses every year from each square foot of surface, an amount of heat that would be able to raise the temperature of one pound of water from the melting point of ice to the boiling point of water, or from 32° F. to 212° F. The rate of loss of heat, must, therefore, have been much greater when the earth was more highly heated than it is now, and will be much smaller than now many years from the present.

Now, let us suppose, what nearly everyone acknowledges to be true, that the earth was originally so hot as to be a molten globe, and that while in this molten condition, it began to revolve or move around the sun. Since the empty space through which the earth moves is very cold, something in the neighborhood of 45° below the[Pg 170] zero of the Fahrenheit thermometer scale, the loss of heat would take place very rapidly and a thin crust of hardened materials would be formed on the outside. Now all the time the earth is cooling, it is shrinking or growing smaller.

A very little thought will convince you that this cooling or shrinkage could not go on uninterruptedly; for, while the earth was cooling it was contracting, or growing smaller, and in this way a great pressure, or as it is generally called in science, a great stress was being produced. Every now and then this stress became so great that the crust of the earth was fractured or broken.

At first these fractures would not require a very great amount of stress or force, since the crust of lava was then very thin. After great periods of time, however, the crust grew thicker and thicker, and the amount of force required to break it continually increased, so that the fractures of the crust produced a greater disturbance.

Whenever the earth's crust was fractured in this way the earth was shaken by what are called earthquakes, while a part of the molten interior would run out or escape, making volcanoes. In the very early times neither the earthquakes or the volcanoes were as energetic as they were at later periods when the thickness of the earth's crust increased.

Now, having as we believe correctly come to the conclusion that the entire interior of the earth is in a highly heated condition, the next question that arises is as to the present condition of this interior. A long time ago it was believed that the interior of the earth is still melted, and that a cooled portion or crust surrounds a great molten mass that fills all the inside; that it is this mass which supplies the immense quantities of molten rock or lava that escape through the craters of[Pg 171] volcanoes or through the fissures in the crust. Without going into this question thoroughly, since it is a very difficult question to understand, it will be sufficient to say that there are many reasons why it is impossible to believe that the interior is still melted.

You will understand that if the interior of the earth were melted like a huge central sea of fire that each volcano would necessarily affect all the others. Now, as we have seen, this is never the case, so that this is one reason we cannot believe in the existence of a melted interior.

Another reason we cannot believe in a molten interior is an astronomical consideration. It can be shown that under the attraction of the sun and moon the earth could not possibly behave as it does if it were still liquid in the interior. That, on the contrary, the behavior of the earth to the attraction of the sun and moon is such as to make it necessary for us to believe that it is as rigid throughout as would be a globe of steel of the same size.

I can easily understand that you find it very difficult to see how it can be believed that the interior of the earth is solid and yet at the same time be sufficiently hot to melt. I can imagine hearing you ask if it is hot enough on the inside to melt any known materials, why it is not melted. The reason, however, is very simple when you come to think it over. For a solid to fuse or become melted, it is not only necessary for it to be heated to a temperature which is different for different substances, but that at the same time it is heated it shall have plenty of room in which to expand or grow bigger. In other words, the temperature required to fuse any substance increases very rapidly with the pressure to which that substance is exposed.

Now, try to think of the pressure to which the[Pg 172] materials that fill the inside of the earth are subjected at great distances below the surface. This pressure is enormous, not only by reason of the weight of the many miles of rocks that are pressing down, but also by reason of the enormous stress or pressure caused by contraction or shrinkage. When we say that the interior of the earth is hot enough to melt all known substances we mean hot enough to melt them if they could be brought from great depths to the level of the sea, but not hot enough to melt them when subjected to the great pressure that exists in regions far below the surface of the earth.

Briefly, the condition of things is believed to be as follows: The entire interior is filled with rock hot enough to melt at the level of the sea, but under too great pressure to melt. If this be granted, as it is by perhaps the greatest number of men who are competent to judge, the phenomena of earthquakes can be readily explained, as can, indeed, the phenomena of those great movements whereby great changes of level take place in different parts of the earth.

Now let us see how volcanoes can be explained on the assumption that the interior of the earth is hot enough to melt, but remains solid only because there is no room for the heated mass to expand in. Such a heated interior as we have imagined, must be constantly losing its heat and, therefore, shrinking. Every now and then this shrinkage must produce great fissures or cracks in the solid crust of the earth. Now should such cracks or fissures extend downwards to the heated interior, there must result a decrease in the pressure. The rocks would, therefore, begin to expand and would be forced by the great pressure to rise slowly in such cracks or fissures. The further they rise the greater the relief of pressure,[Pg 173] until they at last assume a molten condition in which they are forced out through the craters of volcanoes as molten rocks or lava.

But it is not only volcanoes that seem to indicate a highly heated plastic condition as existing in the earth's interior. As geologists well know, there are to be found in the various strata of the earth places where great fissures have been made at various times during the geological past. These fissures vary in width from a few inches to many hundreds of feet, and are frequently scores of miles in length. Lava either flows out of them, and covers adjoining sections of the country, or simply rises in them and, afterwards cooling, forms dikes. In many instances, however, the lava is forced in between more or less horizontal layers and in some cases has caused these layers to assume the shape of what geologists know as *subtruderant mountains*. Some of the eastern ranges of the Rocky Mountains have been formed in this manner.

We can, therefore, picture to ourselves the following as the manner of formation of an ordinary volcano. A fissure is first formed in the solid crust of the earth, extending downwards to the regions of great heat. There is thus produced a relief of pressure, so that at this point the highly heated rocks begin to be slowly forced up through the fissure. As they rise higher and higher they become less solid and finally expand into fused masses that can flow out of the crater or opening in the earth's surface. In this way a volcano is started.

But for this volcano to continue in eruption, it is necessary that the conditions shall continue that force the molten rock upwards from great depths. It is not enough for the lava to fill the crevice that exists upwards to the surface, it must continue to be forced upwards[Pg 174] until it escapes. If it is permitted to remain in the fissure for any time, it hardens, and only great dikes are formed. It would seem, therefore, that some other force must be called into action to keep the fissure open or, in other words, to prevent the chilling of the lava. Now, this force is generally believed to be the expansive force of steam or the vapor of water.

As Dana points out, by far the greater part of the vapor which escapes from the craters of volcanoes consists of steam or the vapor of water. Indeed, it can be shown that for every hundred parts of different vapors, at least ninety-nine of such parts consist of water vapor. It is for the greater part, to the pressure of steam or water vapor that the escape of lava from the tube near the top of the crater is due.

Of course, the question arises as to where the water comes from that produces this steam. There are three possible sources. From the rains; from leakage at the bed of the ocean; and from vapors existing at great depths below the surface.

It is not probable that either rain water, or water from the ocean, penetrates through the earth's crust for distances much greater than a few thousand feet. It is, however, very well known that in all parts of the earth, except in desert regions, whether they are near or far from the ocean, the rocks are always found fully charged with water. When, therefore, the slowly rising lava passes through the moist rocks that everywhere form the crust of the earth, there must be formed in them great quantities of steam under very high pressure. Moreover, many substances, especially those forming lava, possess the power of absorbing large quantities of steam and other gases. Therefore, as the molten material reaches the moist rocks in the earth's crust,[Pg 175] it becomes highly charged with steam, and as the lava rises towards the surface this steam expands.

Where the lava is in a very fluid condition the steam quietly escapes, as does the steam from the surface of boiling water. But where the lava is viscous, like tar or pitch, great bubbles are formed, which, on their explosion, throw the lava upwards for great distances into the air.

We can, therefore, account in this manner for both the non-explosive as well as the explosive type of volcanoes.

It must not be supposed, however, that it is the explosive power of steam which is the principal cause of the lava rising upwards from great depths. This is caused by the great pressure or stress set up by the contraction of a cooling crust. The pressure of this steam is added to this pressure which keeps the lava flowing upwards from great depths below.

The objection has sometimes been urged that it is impossible to believe the lava comes from a highly heated interior, because, as is well known, lavas are of different types even when coming from the same volcano at different times of eruption. While such an objection would have weight were it believed that the interior of the earth is still in a molten condition, it loses its weight when one believes that the interior is solid. It must, however, be acknowledged that the largest part of the interior of the earth would probably have the same chemical composition if it had ever been in a completely melted condition throughout.

I do not doubt you have already concluded that the reason the earth's volcanoes are practically limited to the borders of continents, or to the shores of islands, is the leakage of the ocean waters into the crust at these parts.[Pg 176] This was at one time believed by most geologists. That sea water has much to do with such volcanoes as Vesuvius there is no doubt, but it is now generally recognized that it is not so much the present outlines of the earth, or the present arrangement of its land and water areas, that determines the distribution of the world's volcanoes. It is rather believed that the location of the lines of fractures along which the earth's volcanoes are found were determined by conditions that occurred long before the earth assumed its present outlines.

But there is another explanation that has been suggested as regards the condition of the interior of the earth. Judd refers to this explanation as follows:

"Some physicists have asserted that a globe of liquid matter radiating its heat into space, would tend to solidify both at the surface and the centre at the same time. The consequence of this action would be the production of a sphere with a solid external shell and a solid central nucleus, but with an interposed layer in a fluid or semi-fluid condition. It has been pointed out that if we suppose the solidification to have gone so far as to have caused the partial union of the interior nucleus and the external shell, we may conceive a condition of things in which the stability and rigidity is sufficient to satisfy both geologists and astronomers, but that in still unsolidified pockets or reservoirs, filled with liquefied rock, between the nucleus and the shell, we should have a competent cause for the production of the volcanic phenomena of the globe. In this hypothesis, however, it is assumed that the cooling at the centre and the surface of the globe would go on at such rate that the reservoirs of liquid material would be left at a moderate depth from the surface, so that easy communication could be opened between them and volcanic vents."

[Pg 177]

I must caution you, however, not to think that the above theory of volcanoes is accepted by all scientific men. On the contrary, there are many who believe that the earth is solid throughout because it has completely lost its original heat; that it is only comparatively small areas that are to be found filled with molten or at least highly heated material. But these opinions are held largely by those who have given their attention almost entirely to the phenomena of earthquakes, or who base their reasonings on mathematical grounds only and have not sufficiently considered the phenomena of volcanoes. Since, however, they can be better understood after we have explained the phenomena of earthquakes, we will defer their discussion to the last chapters of this book.

[Pg 178]

CHAPTER XX

SOME FORMS OF LAVA

In describing the wonders of volcanoes, we must not fail to say something of the many remarkable forms that lava is capable of assuming.

All volcanic lavas contain large quantities of an acid substance known as *silica*, or what is known better as *quartz sand*. This material exists in lava combined chemically with various substances called bases, the principal of which are alumina, magnesia, lime, iron, potash, and soda.

Although there are many kinds of lava, yet all lavas can be arranged under three great classes according to the quantity of silica they contain.

Acid lavas are those in which the quantity of silica is greatest. In these lavas the silica, which varies from 66 to 80%, is combined with small quantities of lime or magnesia, and comparatively large quantities of potash or soda. Some of the most important varieties of acid lavas are known as *trachytes, andesites, rhyolites,* and *obsidians.*

Basic lavas are those containing from 45 to 55% of silica. They are rich in lime and magnesia, but poor in soda or potash. Some of the most important of basic lavas are the *dolerites* and *basalts.* Generally speaking, basic lavas are of a darker color than acid lavas, and fuse at much lower temperatures.

Intermediate lavas are those containing silica in the proportion of from 55 to 66%.

[Pg 179]

While the temperature of liquid lava has not been very accurately determined, yet, since we know that molten lava is able to melt silver or copper, its temperature must be somewhere between 2,500° F. and 3,000° F., the melting point varying with the chemical composition.

According to Dana lavas can be divided into the following classes according to their fusibility; i. e., *lavas of easy fusibility,* such as *basalts;* these lavas fuse at about 2,250° F.; *lavas of medium fusibility,* including andesites; these lavas fuse at about 2,520° F.; *lavas of difficult fusibility,* such as trachytes; these lavas fuse at about 2,700° F.

But what is, perhaps, most curious about lavas is that when the surface of a freshly broken piece of cold lava is carefully examined, it is found to contain a number of small crystals of such mineral substances as quartz, feldspar, hornblende, mica, magnetite, etc.

The best way to study the different forms of lava crystals is to prepare a thin transparent slice of hardened lava and then examine it with a good magnifying glass. It will be found that the slice consists of a mass of a glass-like material through which the crystals are irregularly distributed, not unlike the raisins and currants in a slice of not over rich plumcake.

When examined by a more powerful glass, such as a microscope, cloudy patches can be seen distributed irregularly through the glass-like mass. When these patches are examined by a higher power of the microscope they are seen to consist of small solid particles of definite forms known as *microliths* and *crystallites.* It has been shown by a careful study of these minute objects that they form the exceedingly small particles of which crystals are built up.

If we fuse a small quantity of lava and then let it[Pg 180] slowly cool, the glassy mass will be found to contain numerous crystallites. On the other hand, when fused lava is permitted to cool quickly, it takes on the form of a black, glass-like mass known as*obsidian* or *volcanic* glass, a very common form of lava in some parts of the world.

In some lavas there are found larger crystals that appear to have been separated from the glassy mass, under the great pressure that exists in the subterranean reservoirs at great depths below the volcanic crater, and then floated to the surface surrounded by the glass-like material. Now when we examine these crystals with a higher power of the microscope, we frequently find in them minute cavities containing a small quantity of liquid and a bubble of gas, thus causing them to resemble small spirit levels. The liquid in such cavities has been examined chemically and in most cases has been found to consist of water containing several salts in solution. Sometimes, however, the liquid consists of liquefied carbonic acid gas. These wonderful things will be discussed at greater length in the Wonder Book of Light.

When the mass of molten rock or lava that comes out of the crater of a volcano is thrown upwards in the air the condition it assumes by the time it falls back again to the earth depends on the height it reaches. If this height is great the lava chills or hardens before reaching the earth, and assumes various forms according to the size of the fragments. The largest of these fragments are called *cinders;* the finer particles*volcanic dust;* while most of those of intermediate particles are known among other things as *volcanic ashes.*

We have already seen that when an explosive volcanic eruption occurs there is suddenly thrown out of the crater of the volcano a huge column of various substances[Pg 181]that rises sometimes as high as 30,000 feet or even more. The smaller fragments of lava are quickly cooled and form volcanic ashes, sand, cinders, or dust. These are rapidly spread out by the wind in the form of a black cloud, that not only covers the mountain but reaches out over the surrounding country, completely shutting off the light of the sun. From this cloud particles of red hot ashes, cinders, sand, etc., begin to fall, the largest particles near the crater of the volcano, and the smaller particles at much greater distances. In very powerful explosive volcanic eruptions such as Krakatoa, the finer dust may be carried to practically all parts of the world.

Volcanic ashes consist of a fine, light, gray powder. These particles take the name ashes from their resemblance to the ashes left after the burning of pieces of wood or coal in an open fire. The name, however, as Geicke points out, is unfortunate, since it is apt to lead one to suppose that volcanic ashes consist of some burned material. Such an idea is erroneous, however, since ashes do not consist of anything that is left after burning, but merely of fine particles of molten rock that have hardened by cooling. When in the shape of what is known as volcanic dust these particles are so exceedingly small that they can readily make their way through the smallest openings in a closed room just as does the finest dust in the rooms of our houses when they are shut up. There are cases on record where people have been suffocated by the entrance of volcanic dust in closed rooms to which they have fled for safety during volcanic eruptions.

Volcanic sand consists of the coarser particles of chilled lava that are partly round and partly angular. They are of various sizes up to that of an ordinary pea. Volcanic sand is formed by the breaking up of the lava[Pg 182] by the explosion of the vapors as they escape from the lava on relief from pressure. Volcanic dust when examined by the microscope is found to consist of very small particles that are more or less crystalline.

But besides the above there are larger fragments known as *lapilli*, consisting of rounded or angular bits of lava varying in size from that of a pea to an ordinary black walnut. These sometimes consist of solid fragments, but are usually porous, sometimes so much so that they readily float on water.

A curious form sometimes assumed by lava consists of what are called *volcanic bombs*. These are formed during explosive eruptions, when masses of liquid lava are hurled high up into the air. During their flight they take on a rotary motion, which tends to make them globular, so that cooling, while still revolving, they assume the form of a more or less spherical mass. At times, however, they are still sufficiently soft when they strike the earth to be flattened out in the form of flat cakes. When of a spherical form these are very properly called volcanic bombs.

That volcanic bombs have actually been subjected to a spinning motion while in the air can sometimes be shown by the fact that masses of scoriæ are frequently found in the interior with air cells largest at the centre of the bomb.

Volcanic bombs are sometimes thrown from the crater to great distances. During one of its recent eruptions, Cotopaxi threw out bombs that fell at a distance of nine miles from the crater.

According to Dana another form of lava bombs is sometimes found on the slopes of the active volcanoes of Hawaii, where masses of lava acquire a ball-like shape while rolling down an inclination.

[Pg 183]

What are sometimes called volcanic bombs, but which are more properly *volcanic vesicles*, are produced by small fragments of lava which are thrown up in the air for only a moderate height and, on cooling, assume pear-like forms. Fig. 25 represents the appearance of volcanic vesicles. The direction in which these vesicles moved through the air while in a molten state is indicated by their shape, the blunt end being the end towards which the particles were projected.

FIG. 25. VOLCANIC VESICLES
From Dana's Manual of Geology

But by far the greater portion of the hardened lava; i. e., the coarser, heavier particles, fall back on the mountain, and collecting around the crater build up volcanic cones, as already described in the case of mountains of the Vesuvian type.

There are two different ways in which the melted lava is broken up into fine particles when it is thrown upwards from the crater of the volcano. Nearly all lava contains large quantities of steam that are shut up, or occluded in the mass, being prevented from escaping by reason of the pressure to which the lava is subjected. The lava is released from this pressure as it is thrown out of the crater. The steam or gases escape explosively and thus break the lava into fine liquid spray, which rapidly hardens.

There is another way in which small particles of lava are formed. Sometimes large pieces of hardened lava are shot upwards into the air with a velocity as great as that with which a heavy projectile leaves the muzzle of a large gun. These heavy particles striking against one another, either while rising or falling, are broken into smaller fragments. Sometimes, indeed, these fragments[Pg 184] fall back again into the crater from which they are again violently thrown out, and are again broken into smaller fragments either while rising or falling.

You will, probably, remember several instances of volcanic eruptions where masses of rock were thrown violently up into the air out of the crater. These larger masses are known as *volcanic blocks*. They probably consist of masses of hardened lava that have collected in the tube of the volcano during some of its periods of inactivity. Sometimes, however, they consist of fragments of rocks that are not of volcanic origin. Cases are on record where volcanic blocks have been thrown out of the craters in so great quantities as to cover the surface of many square miles of land with fragments hundreds of feet deep.

There is sometimes formed on the surface of a pool of lava as it collects in the craters of such volcanoes as Mt. Loa or Kilauea, when the volcanoes are not in eruption, a material resembling froth or scum. The same thing sometimes occurs on the surface of some kinds of lava as it runs down the side of the mountain. In this way a very light variety of highly cellular lava known as *pumice stone* is produced. The action which thus takes place is not unlike that which occurs during the raising of a lot of the dough from which bread is made, where the carbonic acid gas which is formed during the raising of the dough expands, and produces the well-known open cellular structure of well-raised bread. In the case of pumice stone, however, this raising goes on to such an extent that the mass consists often of less than 2% of solid matter, the remainder being a tangled mass of air.

THE LAVA FLOW OF THE CRATER OF KILAUEA, HAWAIIAN ISLANDS
From a Stereograph, Copyright, by Underwood & Underwood

Fragments of lava that possess a cellular structure form what are known as *scoriæ*. The lightest of all kinds[Pg 185] of scoriæ is what is known as *thread-lace scoriæ*. Here the thin walls consist of mere threads. Figs. 26 and 27 represent the appearance of thread-lace scoriæ from Kilauea. The separate threads are very fine, being only from one-thirtieth to one-fortieth of an inch in thickness. As can be seen, this form of scoriæ have six-sided or hexagonal shapes. You can form some idea of the great lightness of such scoriæ when you learn that they contain only 1.7% of rocky material. Indeed, they contain so little solid material that a layer of volcanic glass only one inch thick, if blown out into scoriæ, would be able to produce a layer sixty inches thick.

FIG. 26. THREAD-LACE SCORIÆ FROM KILAUEA
From Dana's Manual of Geology

Another curious form sometimes assumed by lava, especially in the case of Kilauea, is where the lava is spun out in the form of long silk-like hairs. This is called by the natives *Pele's hair*, after the name of their goddess. Inasmuch as the origin of this form of lava was at one time generally attributed to the action of the wind in drawing out thread-like pieces from the jets of lava thrown upwards from the pool, it will be interesting if its true cause is explained.

FIG. 27. THREAD-LACE SCORIÆ FROM KILAUEA
From Dana's Manual of Geology

[Pg 186]

Dutton, in his report on the Hawaiian volcanoes, refers to the formation of Pele's hair as follows:

"The phenomenon of Pele's hair is often spoken of in the school books, and receives its name from this locality. It has generally been explained as the result of the action of the wind upon minute threads of lava drawn out by the spurting up of boiling lava. Nothing of the sort was seen here, and yet Pele's hair was seen forming in great abundance. Whenever the surface of the liquid lava was exposed during the break-up the air above the lake was filled with these cobwebs, but there was no spurting or apparent boiling on the exposed surface. The explanation of the phenomenon which I would offer is as follows: Liquid lava coming up from the depths always contains more or less water, which it gives off slowly and by degrees, in much the same way as champagne gives off carbonic acid when the bottle is uncorked. Water-vapor is held in the liquid lava by some affinity similar to chemical affinity, and though it escapes ultimately, yet it is surrendered by the lava with reluctance so long as the lava remains liquid. But when the lava solidifies the water is expelled much more energetically, and the water-vapor separates in the form of minute vesicles. Since the congelation of all siliceous compounds is a passage free from a liquid condition through an intermediate state of viscosity to final solidity, the walls of these vesicles are capable of being drawn out as in the case of glass. The commotion set up by the descending crust produces eddies and numberless currents in the surface of the lava. These vesicles are drawn out on the surface of the current with exceeding tenuity, producing myriads of minute filaments, and the air, agitated by the intense heat at the surface of the pool, readily lifts them and wafts[Pg 187] them away. It forms almost wholly at the time of the break-up. The air is then full of it. Yet I saw no spouting or sputtering, but only the eddying of the lava like water in the wake of a ship. The country to the leeward of Kilauea shows an abundance of Pele's hair, and it may be gathered by the barrelful. A bunch of it is much like finely shredded asbestos."

You have probably often seen the beautiful frost pictures that collect on the panes of glass in a room where the ventilation has been neglected. These pictures consist of groupings of ice crystals that collect on the surface of the windows, when the moist vapor-laden air in the room is chilled by contact with their cold surfaces. Now the crystals formed in cooling lavas are sometimes grouped in forms closely resembling frost pictures. A few of such forms are represented in Figs. 28 and 29 in lava from Mt. Loa and Mt. Kea.

FIG. 28. FROST-LIKE LAVA CRYSTALS
From Dana's Manual of Geology

FIG. 29. FROST-LIKE LAVA CRYSTALS
From Dana's Manual of Geology

Certain varieties of lava, especially that which is found in dikes, form cool, beautiful columns called basaltic columns. They are due to the contraction that occurs on the cooling of the material. Instances of basaltic[Pg 188] columns are seen in the Giant's Causeway, on the northern coast of Ireland, as well as in the Isle of Cyclops on the coast of Italy. The general appearance of the latter is represented in Fig. 30.

FIG. 30. BASALTIC COLUMNS, ISLE OF CYCLOPS, ITALY

It is a curious fact that the entire mass of basalt does not generally take the columnous form but only certain layers which terminate suddenly above and below at structureless masses of basalt, as shown in Fig. 31. These columns, however, are always found at right angles to the cooling surfaces as seen in the figures. They may, therefore, be inclined at all angles to the horizon.

[Pg 189]

FIG. 31. COLUMNAR AND NON-COLUMNAR BASALT

When molten lava is only thrown up a short distance into the air from a crater it is still partially molten when on falling it again reaches the earth, and therefore clings to any surface on which it falls. There are thus built up curious cones known as *driblet cones*, in which the separate drops covering the sides of the cone can be distinctly traced. Driblet cones are represented in Figs. 32 and 33. Here, as can be seen, the separate drops can be readily traced as they run down a short distance before cooling.

FIGS. 32, 33. DRIBLET CONES
From Dana's Manual of Geology

We have already referred briefly to the *lava caves* or *grottoes*, that are formed in some of the lava streams issuing from Vesuvius, Etna, or Hawaii. These caves[Pg 190] consist either of a number of communicating huge bubbles, or of the tunnels that are formed in the lava by the hardening of the outside of the lava streams as they flow down the sides of the mountain, and towards the close of the eruption are afterwards emptied by the molten lava within continuing to flow to a lower level before solidifying. Now, in the interior of these caves, there are often found on the walls, as well as on the portions of the floors of the caves, immediately below them, curious pendants, like icicles, or, more correctly, like the *stalactites of limestone* that are seen hanging to the walls of caves in limestone districts, where they are formed as follows: as the rain water sinks through limestone strata it dissolves some of the lime, when, slowly falling, drop after drop, from the roofs of the caverns, small particles of lime are deposited on the roof, and in this manner a pendant of limestone is formed. The water that falls to the floor of the causeway immediately below, also builds up a dome-like hillock called a stalagmite. In due time the pillar reaches downwards, and the opposite hillock upwards until the two meet, thus forming great natural pillars that appear to hold up the roof of[Pg 191] the vast cave in which they have been slowly formed. A number of *lava stalactites* are represented in Fig. 34.

FIG. 34. LAVA STALACTITES
From Dana's Manual of Geology

Now, in a similar manner these lava stalactites, formed in the lava caves or grottoes, are caused by the stream as it escapes from the walls of the caves depositing on them stalactites of various lava minerals it has dissolved as it slowly passed through them.

But the most important of all volcanic products is *volcanic dust*. This, as we have seen, is so light that it remains longest in the air, and is often carried by the winds to great distances from the volcano from which it escaped. It may interest you to know that some of the most fruitful of the great wheat fields of the western parts of the United States owe their extraordinary fertility to immense deposits of volcanic dust that have been thrown out from some of the great volcanoes of the geological past, now found in an extinct condition in these parts of the United States.

According to Russell, immense deposits of volcanic dust are spread over vast areas in Montana, Southern Dakota, Nebraska, and Kansas, as well as over parts of Oregon, and Washington,[Pg 192] and, indeed, over large areas of southwestern Canada and Alaska.

It is practically certain that many of the eruptions producing this dust occurred within historic times. There must, therefore, have been many times in these parts of our country when the dense ash clouds hiding the sun turned the day into night and destroyed the forests and other vegetation by showers of red hot ashes. There were produced, too, the same great dread, and possibly loss of life as common during historical eruptions. It is pleasing, however, to think that while these great catastrophes brought suffering and dread to the people who then lived on the earth, they were, nevertheless, but the forerunners of those fruitful fields that at a much later age were to bless the people who afterwards lived on them.

[Pg 193]

CHAPTER XXI

MUD VOLCANOES AND HOT SPRINGS

Mud volcanoes are the more or less conical hillocks from which, under certain conditions, mud is thrown out through the crust of the earth.

Geikie defines mud volcanoes as follows:

"Conical hills formed by the accumulation of fine and usually saline (salty) mud, which, with various gases, is continuously or intermittently given out from the orifice or crater in the centre. They occur in groups, each hillock being sometimes less than a yard in height, but ranging up to elevations of 100 feet or more. Like true volcanoes, they have their periods of repose, when either no discharge takes place at all, or mud oozes out tranquilly from the crater, and their periods of activity, when large volumes of gas, and sometimes columns of flame, rush out with considerable violence and explosion, and throw up mud and stones to a height of several hundred feet."

There are two kinds of mud volcanoes: those in which the mud is thrown out by the action of different kinds of gases, and those in which the mud is thrown out by the action of steam.

Mud volcanoes may or not be volcanic phenomena. Those which occur in the neighborhood of volcanoes whether active, dormant, or extinct, are probably of volcanic origin. There are others, however, which occur[Pg 194] in regions far removed from volcanoes. These are probably due not to volcanoes, but to chemical action and the eruptions are caused by the action of gases.

The gases producing these eruptions are either carbonic acid gas (the gas that is given off from soda water); carburetted hydrogen (the gas that is sometimes seen escaping from the bottom of marshy ground); sulphuretted hydrogen (a gas that is given off from rotten or decomposing eggs, and possessing the characteristic odor of decayed eggs) and nitrogen gas derived from the atmosphere. In mud volcanoes of the gaseous type the mud is generally cold, and the water salty. In this latter case the mud volcanoes are also called *salses*. Daubeny has pointed out that the mud volcanoes of this class that occur in the neighborhood of Sicily are due to the slow burning or oxidation of beds of sulphur.

Mud volcanoes which eject hot mud by the force of eruption of steam, which occur in volcanic districts, are of volcanic origin. They are caused by the passage of hot water and steam through beds of volcanic rock such as tufa, or hardened volcanic mud and other volcanic products. The hot water or steam raises the temperature of the mud through which it passes to the boiling point. As Dana remarks, the mud varies in consistency from very liquid muddy water to a thick mass like boiling soap, or in some cases like masses of mud or paint, and, in still other cases, to material like soft mortar, the consistency of the mud varying with the dryness of the season.

There are three regions where mud volcanoes are especially common. One of the best known is in the Yellowstone National Park, four miles north of Yellowstone Lake, and six miles from Crater Hill. Some of these mud volcanoes have circular craters about ten feet in depth[Pg 195] around which they have built mounds, the rims of which are several feet above the general level.

There are well-known regions of mud volcanoes in different parts of Iceland. Here, according to Lyell, they occur in many of the valleys where sulphur vapor and steam bursts from fissures in the ground with a loud hissing noise. In these regions there are pools of boiling water filled with a bluish black clay-like paste, that is kept violently boiling. Huge bubbles, fifteen feet or more in diameter, rise from the surface of the boiling mass. The volcanoes pile up the mud around the sides of their craters or basins.

Another part of the world where mud volcanoes are especially numerous is on the western shores of the Caspian Sea at a place called Baku. These are of the gaseous type and are attended by flames that blaze up to great heights often for several hours. These flames are due to the presence of natural gas and petroleum vapor that pass out through the water. Large quantities of mud are thrown out from the craters of these mud volcanoes.

There are also many mud volcanoes in a district in India about 120 miles northwest of Cutch near the mouth of the Indus. In this region the cone built up around the crater is sometimes as high as 400 feet.

The following description of mud volcanoes on Java is quoted from Daubeny's book on volcanoes.

"It would appear likewise from Dr. Horsfield's description, that Java exhibits phenomena of a similar kind to those noticed in Sicily and at the foot of the Apennines, and there known under the name of 'Salses.' In the calcareous district (which I suspect to belong to the same class of formations as the blue clay and tertiary limestone of Sicily) occur a number of hot springs, containing in solution a large quantity of calcareous earth, which[Pg 196] incrusts the surface of the ground near it. Of these, some are much mixed with petroleum, and others highly saline.

"The latter are dispersed through a district of country consisting of limestone, several miles in circumference. They are of considerable number, and force themselves upwards through apertures in the rocks with some violence and ebullition. The waters are strongly impregnated with muriate of soda, and yield upon evaporation very good salt for culinary purposes (not less than 200 tons in the year).

"About the centre of this limestone district is found an extraordinary volcanic phenomenon. On approaching the spot from a distance, it is first discovered by a large volume of smoke rising and disappearing at intervals of a few seconds, resembling the vapors arising from a violent surf, whilst a dull noise is heard like that of distant thunder. Having advanced so near that the vision was no longer impeded by the smoke, a large hemispherical mass was observed, consisting of black earth mixed with water, about sixteen feet in diameter, rising to the height of twenty or thirty feet in a perfectly regular manner, and, as it were, pushed up by a force beneath, which suddenly exploded with a dull noise, and scattered about a volume of black mud in every direction. After an interval of two or three, or sometimes four or five seconds, the hemispherical body of mud or earth rose and exploded again.

"In the same manner this volcanic ebullition goes on without interruption, throwing up a globular mass of mud, and dispersing it with violence through the neighboring places. The spot where the ebullition occurs is nearly circular and perfectly level; it is covered with only the earthy particles impregnated with salt water, which are thrown up from below; its circumference may be estimated at about half an English mile. In order to conduct[Pg 197] the salt water to the circumference, small passages or gutters are made in the loose muddy earth, which lead it to the borders, where it is collected in holes dug in the ground for the purpose of evaporation.

"A strong, pungent, sulphurous smell, somewhat resembling that of earth-oil (naphtha), is perceived on standing near the site of the explosion, and the mud recently thrown up possesses a degree of heat greater than that of the surrounding atmosphere. During the rainy season these explosions are more violent, the mud is thrown up much higher, and the noise is heard at a greater distance.

"This volcanic phenomenon is situated near the centre of the large plain, which interrupts the great series of volcanoes, and owes its origin to the same general cause as that of the numerous eruptions met with in this island."

There are, in many parts of the world, springs, whose waters issue from their reservoirs at temperatures either at or near the boiling point of water. These are called *hot* or *thermal springs*. Hot springs are found both in volcanic regions, as well as in regions where there are no volcanoes, but where there are lines of deep fissures or faults. According to Dana, in both of these classes, the cause is to be traced to heat of volcanic or deep subterranean origin. Hot springs are also found in regions where there are no volcanoes. In these cases the heat is due to the gradual oxidation of various sulphide ores, or to some other chemical action.

The waters of hot or thermal springs almost always contain various mineral substances in solution. All spring water contains some little dissolved mineral matter, but in hot springs the quantity of this matter is greater than in cold springs, because hot water can dissolve mineral substances much better than can cold water.

[Pg 198]

It might surprise you to hear that one of the commonest substances that is found in solution in the waters of many hot springs is silica; for silica is practically sand, and sand does not easily dissolve in water as does sugar. The very hot water, however, which comes from the hot spring, whose temperature below the earth's surface is very much higher than it is when it comes out of the spring, possesses the power of readily dissolving silica from the rocks over which it flows. When the waters of such springs reach the surface the silica is deposited in a solid condition around the outlets of the springs. In this way there are built up craters or mounds, or, more correctly, crater-shaped basins.

Sometimes the hot water contains calcareous substances dissolved in it, the solution being caused not only by reason of the hot water, but also by means of the carbonic gas it contains. When this water flows from the springs, it builds up the same crater-shaped mounds, only in this case the mounds are of lime instead of silica.

There are peculiar kinds of hot springs called *geysers*, that possess the power of throwing huge streams of water up into the air at more or less regular intervals. The word geyser is an Icelandic word meaning to rage, or snort, or gush, the name being given by reason of the manner in which the waters rush violently out during an eruption.

As Dana points out, when the water in a basin of a hot spring merely boils, whether this boiling is nearly continuous, or the water is alternately boiling and quiet, the spring is called a hot or thermal spring, but where the water is thrown violently out at more or less regular intervals, it is called a geyser.

The cause of the eruption of a geyser was discovered by Professor Bunsen, the celebrated German chemist, after[Pg 199] a careful study of the geyser regions in Iceland. The waters of geysers contain large quantities of either silica or lime in solution. Bunsen traced the cause of these curious eruptions to be the manner in which the hot springs pile up cones of silica or limestone around their mouths.

The water of a geyser generally issues from the top of a more or less conical hillock, reaching the surface through a funnel-shaped tube. Both the tube and the basin are covered with a smooth coating of silica or limestone. In the case of the Great Geyser in Iceland, the basin is over fifty feet high and seventy-five feet deep. Both the tube and the basin have been slowly deposited by the hot water of the geyser.

It is only when the tube of a geyser has reached a certain depth that the geyser is able to erupt. Moreover, as soon as this tube passes a certain depth the geyser can no longer erupt and forever afterwards becomes an ordinary hot spring. There are, therefore, to be found in most geyser regions, a number of what might be called young geysers or merely hot springs, that are not yet deep enough to erupt; others that have just commenced eruption, others that have reached their prime, while others that, old and decrepit, have again merely become hot springs.

Let us now try to understand the cause of the eruption of a geyser. Bunsen's explanation, which is now generally accepted, is as follows:

The heat of the volcanic strata through which the tube of the geyser extends, gradually raises the temperature of the water that fills the geyser tube. Since the boiling point of a liquid increases with the pressure to which it is subjected, far down in the tube of a geyser, the pressure arising from the weight of the water above it is sufficiently great to prevent the water from beginning to boil until[Pg 200] it reaches a temperature far higher than that at which it would boil in the upper parts of the tube. Suppose now, when the water in the funnel-shaped tube is nearly filled to the top, the water at last grows hot enough to begin boiling at some point near the middle of the tube. The pressure of the steam driven off from this portion of the water raises the column of water above it in the tube and begins to empty it out of the top of the geyser. All the water below this point being thus suddenly relieved of its pressure, and being now much hotter than is necessary to boil the water at that decreased pressure, suddenly flashes into steam, and violently shoots out all the water above it to a height that in some cases may be as great as 100 to 200 feet. The steam causes this eruption, then rushes out with a roar, and the geyser eruption is over.

Professor Tyndall in his charming book entitled "Heat as a Mode of Motion" speaks as follows concerning Professor Bunsen's discovery:

"Previous to an eruption, both the tube and basin are filled with hot water; detonations which shake the ground, are heard at intervals, and each is succeeded by a violent agitation of the water in the basin. The water in the pipe is lifted up so as to form an eminence in the middle of the basin, and an overflow is the consequence. These detonations are evidently due to the production of steam in the ducts which feed the geyser tube, which steam escaping into the cooler water of the tube is there suddenly condensed, and produces the explosions. Professor Bunsen succeeded in determining the temperature of the geyser tube, from top to bottom, a few minutes before a great eruption; and these observations revealed the extraordinary fact that at no part of the tube did the water reach its boiling point. In the sketch [not reproduced] I have given on one side the temperatures actually observed,[Pg 201] and on the other side the temperatures at which water would boil, taking into account both the pressure of the atmosphere and the pressure of the superincumbent column of water. The nearest approach to the boiling point is at A, a height of 30 feet from the bottom; but even here the water is 2° C., or more than 3-1/2° F., below the temperature at which it could boil. How then is it possible that an eruption could occur under such circumstances?

"Fix your attention upon the water at the point A, where the temperature is within 2° C. of the boiling point. Call to mind the lifting of the column when the detonations are heard. Let us suppose that by the entrance of steam from the ducts near the bottom of the tube, the geyser column is elevated six feet, a height quite within the limits of actual observation; the water at A is thereby transferred to B. Its boiling point at A is 123.8°, and its actual temperature 121.8°; but at B its boiling point is only 120.8°, hence, when transferred from A to B the heat which it possesses is in excess of that necessary to make it boil. This excess of heat is instantly applied to the generation of steam: the column is thus lifted higher, and the water below is further relieved. More steam is generated; from the middle downwards the mass suddenly bursts into ebullition, the water above, mixed with steam clouds, is projected into the atmosphere, and we have the geyser eruption in all its grandeur.

"By its contact with the air the water is cooled, falls back into the basin, partially refills the tube, in which it gradually rises, and finally fills the basin as before. Detonations are heard at intervals, and risings of the water in the basin. These are so many futile attempts at an eruption, for not until the water in the tube comes sufficiently near its boiling temperature, to make the[Pg 202] lifting of the column effective, can we have a true eruption."

The principal geyser regions of the world are in Iceland, in New Zealand, and in the Yellowstone National Park in the United States.

There are several geyser regions in Iceland. The best known lies in the neighborhood of Mt. Hecla. Here is a great geyser that shoots up a column of water to a height of about 100 feet every thirty hours. Fig. 35 represents the appearance of the crater of the great geyser in Iceland.

FIG. 35. CRATER OF THE GREAT GEYSER OF ICELAND

It is a well-known fact that in geyser regions generally, the throwing of stones or other materials into the tube will frequently hasten an eruption. This is probably due to the fact that the throwing in of these things results in the raising of the water in the tube, thus hastening the eruption.

[Pg 203]

The New Zealand region is in the neighborhood of Lake Rotomahama in the northern island.

The geyser region in the Yellowstone Park is by far the most interesting of all geyser regions. This region is situated principally around Fire-Hole Fork of the Madison, and near Shoshone Lake at the head of Lake Fork of the Snake River. There are many geysers in this region, as well as simple hot springs. The temperature of their waters varies from between 160° and 200° F. to the boiling point of water at this elevation. As you are probably aware, water boils at the temperature of 212° F. only under the condition of the ordinary atmospheric pressure that exists at the level of the sea. At higher elevations, such as on the slopes of mountains, or on high plateaus, water boils at a lower temperature. The height of the country in which the Yellowstone Park is situated is so great that the water boils at temperatures of from 198° to 199° F.

The conical hillock of geyser cones from which the waters flow assume various shapes, two of which are shown in Figs. 36 and 37.

FIG. 36. GIANT GEYSER
From Dana's Manual of Geology

FIG. 37. BEE HIVE
From Dana's Manual of Geology

That shown in Fig. 36 represents the shape of the cone of the giant geyser in the upper geyser basin of the Fire-Hole, Yellowstone National Park. This cone is about ten feet in height, and twenty-four feet in diameter. As shown in the figure it is broken on one of its sides. It[Pg 204] throws out, at long intervals, a column of water the height of which varies from ninety to 200 feet.

Fig. 38 represents the crater of a cone known as the Bee Hive in eruption.

Besides the above named geyser regions there is another region on the shores of Celebes, and a small region on San Miguel, in the Azores Islands, in the Atlantic Ocean.

Besides hot springs and mud volcanoes there are two other phenomena connected with volcanic action that we will now briefly describe.

When eruptions take place and the lava begins to flow down the side of a mountain, the different vapors and gases with which the lava is charged begin to escape or pass out from the boiling or fused mass. When these substances are of such a character that they produce fumes, or the vapors of various chemical substances, that become solid on cooling, they form what are called *fumaroles*, a word derived from a Latin word meaning "to smoke." For the greater part, fumaroles are found on the edge of craters, but sometimes are found in cavernous places either in the crater or in the lava streams.

There is, still, another class of openings through which only sulphurous vapors escape. These are called *solfataras*, a word derived from the Italian word *solfo*, or sulphur. Solfataras are generally found in regions distant from volcanic action. In the materials that escape from recently ejected lava, or molten lava, the temperature is high enough to volatilize many of the solid ingredients. But where the temperature is low, only sulphur vapors are driven off. It is for this reason that fumaroles are only found around the craters of active volcanoes, or on the lines of cracks or crevices of the lava stream where the temperature is very high.

[Pg 205]

FIG. 38. BEE HIVE GEYSER OF ICELAND
From Dana's Manual of Geology

Besides water vapor and sulphurous vapors there are[Pg 206] other substances that escape from the earth in volcanic districts. Sulphurous acid, together with hydrogen and nitrogen escape from nearly all lava. At Vesuvius chlorine gas is given off. This, however, as soon as it passes into the atmosphere becomes changed into hydrochloric acid. Sulphurous acid is frequently changed into sulphuric acid, which, combining with various substances, forms such materials as *gypsum*, or sulphate of lime, the chemical name for plaster of Paris; sulphate of soda or *Glauber's salt*; sodium chloride or *common table salt*; and *sal ammoniac*. You will remember in reading the description of Vulcano, in the Grecian Archipelago, that some of these products were collected at the chemical works that had been established on the volcano.

When a volcanic mountain is for the time being passing from an active to an extinct condition, it is sometimes said to be in the *fumarole stage*, since the presence of the fumaroles are the only indication of its activity. The volcanic heat is still great. When it reaches a still greater decline, the fumaroles disappear, and only solfataras are left. The amount of heat is now only sufficient to produce sulphur vapors and the vapor of water. This is called the *solfatara stage*.

Of course, as we have already pointed out, fumaroles and solfataras may occur in the neighborhood of a volcano at different distances from its crater.

[Pg 207]

CHAPTER XXII

THE VOLCANOES OF THE MOON

There can be no doubt that the moon was once the seat of very great volcanic activity. It was formerly believed that the very many volcanic craters which can be seen on its surface when it is examined by a comparatively small telescope, were all extinct. While this is nearly true, yet recent investigations have shown that in all probability a feeble volcanic activity still exists in a few of these craters.

The distinctness with which the surface of the moon is seen does not depend so much on the size of the telescope employed, as it does on the steadiness of the atmosphere when the telescope is being used. When one wishes to examine a very distant body like a star, it is necessary to use a powerful telescope, but in the case of a comparatively near body, like one of the planets or the moon, a big telescope is not necessary. It is, however, necessary to make the observations at some time of the year, or in some part of the world, when the air is apt to be free from winds.

A person on the earth's surface looking at the heavenly bodies through a telescope is practically in the position in which he would be were he at the bottom of the water in a large lake looking up through the water at some body in the heavens. He would have no difficulty in seeing such a body distinctly as long as the upper surface of the water remained quiet, and unruffled by waves. As soon, however,[Pg 208] as waves were set up, the images seen in the telescope are so distorted as to become practically worthless. It is for this reason that it is customary to build great astronomical observatories in parts of the world where there are apt to be many days in the year when the air is almost entirely free from wind.

Since the atmosphere is apt to be disturbed by winds in both the temperate and the polar latitudes, these parts of the world are not very satisfactory as sites for astronomical observatories. The conditions are more favorable near the equator, since, although at certain seasons of the year there are very severe storms in these regions, yet there are quite long periods when the air is almost entirely free from winds.

It is for this reason that Harvard University has erected an astronomical observatory at Arequipa, Peru, at an elevation of 8,000 feet above the level of the Pacific Ocean. Here, with a comparatively small object glass, of about twelve inches aperture, magnificent photographs have been obtained not only of the moon but also of the planet Mars.

According to Professor Pickering, from whose magnificent work, entitled, "The Moon," much of the information in this chapter has been obtained, the moon, which is generally spoken of as a satellite of the earth, ought rather to be called the earth's twin planet. Although the moon appears to revolve in a small elliptical orbit around the earth it should properly be said to revolve around the sun; for, together with the earth, it revolves around the sun once every year. As seen from any of the planets that lie near the earth the earth and moon would appear as a very beautiful double star.

In order the more readily to understand what will be said shortly concerning the origin of the moon, it may be[Pg 209] mentioned that the moon's diameter is 2,163 miles, or a little more than one-fourth the diameter of our earth.

You will, most probably, be surprised to learn that the origin of the moon is believed to be very different from the origin of the moons or satellites of Jupiter, Saturn, and the other planets. As we have already seen, according to the nebular hypothesis, all the planets except the earth probably had their moons formed from the rings that were left surrounding them when they shrunk on cooling to their present dimensions. Such a ring is still to be seen surrounding Saturn.

Now it is believed that our moon was formed in a different manner. It was not thrown off from the earth while the latter was in a highly fluid or gaseous condition, but after the earth had shrunken to nearly its present size and, most probably, after a solid crust had been formed on its surface. In order that our earth should be able to violently throw off a large portion of its mass, it is only necessary that at the time this separation occurred, its motion of rotation on its axis was sufficiently great to enable it to make one complete revolution in rather less than three hours instead of in the twenty-four hours it now requires. At this velocity of rotation, objects would fly off the earth in the neighborhood of the equator, under the influence of the high centrifugal force. Let us, then, endeavor to see if it was at all probable that the earth ever did turn so rapidly on its axis.

You all probably know that it is principally the attraction of the moon that produces the earth's tides. Of course, the sun also produces tides on the earth, but it is so far off from the earth that not withstanding its greater mass the tides it forms are much smaller than those produced by the moon. You also know that the moon produces at the same time two tides in every twenty-four[Pg 210] hours, on directly opposite sides of the earth; one on the side immediately under the moon, and the other on the side furthest from the moon. As the earth rotates between these two tides, they act as a break which serves to impede its motion. Every high tide, therefore, tends to make the earth rotate more slowly, and thus to slowly increase the length of the day. For this reason to-day is a trifle longer than yesterday, and still longer than a day a hundred years ago.

You must not suppose for a moment that this increase in the length of the day is large. On the contrary, it is so small that since the year A. D. 1, up to the present time, the day is only a very small fraction of a second longer.

But it was very different in the earth's geological past, when the inside of the earth was in a molten condition; for then great tides were set up in the melted interior of the earth that not only greatly changed the shape of the earth, but decreased the rate of rotation much more rapidly than it does when the earth's tides are limited as they are now to the waters on the earth's surfaces.

There was, however, at the same time, something going on that tended greatly to make the earth turn more rapidly on its axis. While the originally melted earth was cooling and shrinking, the rate of its rotation was necessarily increasing. As you know, the time of vibration of a pendulum, that is, the time it requires to make one complete to-and-fro motion, is shorter the shorter the length of the pendulum. A pendulum two feet long moves to and fro more slowly than a pendulum one foot in length. In the same way a rotating sphere will make one complete rotation in a shorter time when its radius, which corresponds to the length of a pendulum, is shorter. Therefore, as the earth shrunk, it rotated more and more rapidly, and at last reached a rapidity of motion at which[Pg 211] an immense quantity of matter flew off its surface nearest the equator and went out into space, never again to return. It was this mass that constituted the earth's moon.

Necessarily such a tremendous catastrophe was attended by an earthquake as well as by the most fearful volcanic phenomena that the earth has ever witnessed. The terrible catastrophe produced by the explosive eruption of Krakatoa was but as a small drop of rain falling on the earth, when compared with the catastrophe produced when the "five thousand million cubic miles of material left the earth's surface, never again to return to it."

It is not known whether this matter was torn off the earth at a single time or during successive times, but quoting the beautiful language of Professor Pickering:

"We may try in vain to imagine the awful uproar and fearful volcanic phenomena exhibited when a planet was cleft in twain, and a new planet was born into the solar system."

This terrible catastrophe took place at a time not when the earth was a gaseous mass, but when it had condensed into a comparatively small mass not much larger than it is at its present time, and possibly even after it had hardened sufficiently to form a solid crust on its outside.

If you look at a map of the earth on a Mercator's projection, such, for example, as that employed in illustrating the distribution of the world's volcanoes in Fig. 24, you can see, even without any very close examination, that the great water area of the Atlantic Ocean has its eastern and western shores almost parallel to each other, so that if you conceive the Eastern and Western Continents as being pushed together, they would, except at the south, almost completely fit together, and the same thing is true, if Greenland is pushed towards the northeastern coast of[Pg 212] North America. Of course, some portions of the coast would not fit exactly, but then these portions might either have been worn away, or, as is more probable, have been changed in shape by the deposit of immense beds of sedimentary rocks spread over the borders of the Atlantic by the great rivers that empty into it. This is so remarkable a fact that it will be well worth your while to turn to the map mentioned and convince yourself of the proof of what I have just said. As you will see, Europe and Africa would almost exactly fit against South America and North America, while Greenland would even more closely fit against the northeastern coast of North America.

Now, while we do not say that it was so, it has been suggested as just possible that the great depression of the Pacific Ocean represents the spot that was once filled by the moon. That the Eastern and Western Continents, then torn asunder by the great force of the convulsion, were left floating on the surface of a sea of molten matter, a greatly widened crack marking positions they assumed at the end of this cataclysm.

Of course, you must understand that all this is a mere supposition, and that we do not know whether the earth was actually cooled on the outside when this occurred, since it might have still been in a liquid condition throughout. It would seem, however, to have occurred rather recently, since it could not have occurred until the earth shrunk so much that it became so small in radius as to acquire a very rapid rate of motion on its axis.

It is an interesting fact that we are, perhaps, better acquainted with that side of the moon which is turned towards us than we are with the surface of the earth on which we live. Of course, I do not mean in the small details of the moon's surface, but with such portions as can be seen through a good telescope when the air is[Pg 213] quiet. While there are no parts of the moon's surface that have not been carefully examined in detail probably thousands of times by acute astronomers, there are still comparatively large areas of the earth that have never been once trodden by civilized man.

When I speak of all parts of the moon's surface, I only mean those parts that are turned towards us. You may possibly be ignorant of the fact that the moon always turns exactly the same face towards the earth. Not only has no man ever seen the opposite side of the moon, but he never can hope to see it while he remains on the earth. This is because the moon turns or rotates on its axis in exactly the same time that it revolves in its orbit.

When I say that the time of rotation is the same as the time of revolution of the moon, I do not mean that it is almost the same, but that it is exactly the same. If it differed even but a small fraction of a second, a time would come when we would be able to see the other side of the moon. Now, since astronomers have made careful pictures of the moon, many, many years ago, we can see by comparing them with photographs taken at the present time there has been no change whatever in that face of the moon which is turned towards us, and this, of course, proves beyond question, that the time of the moon's rotation during this great period has remained exactly the same as the time of its revolution.

It may possibly seem to you that it cannot be a matter of great importance in a book like this on the Wonders of Volcanoes and Earthquakes, whether or not the moon always turns its face towards the earth; on the contrary, it is a matter of the greatest importance since by it we can prove positively that the moon was at one time at least in a partly fluid condition. It was the presence of this partly fluid interior that resulted in the time of the moon's[Pg 214] rotation agreeing exactly with the time of its revolution. The tides of the earth set up in the moon's molten interior, tides, that instead of reaching twice every day the height of a few feet only, were set up in the molten mass in the moon's interior, probably reaching miles in height, rapidly decreased the time of the moon's rotation until the moon rotated once only during every complete revolution.

Even now that the moon is probably solid throughout, the time of its rotation and revolution exactly agree because, while in a molten condition, the action of the earth changed its shape from that of an exact sphere to a spheroid, with its longest axis in the direction of the earth. Even, therefore, if the moon at any time began to rotate faster than the earth, the earth acting on its projecting surface retarded it until the time of its rotation agreed exactly with the time of its revolution.

It was at one time believed that the moon had no atmosphere. It is now known, however, that it has an atmosphere. It is true this is a rare atmosphere, probably not greater in density than the one-ten thousandth of the earth's atmosphere. This important question was settled once for all on August 12th, 1892, at the Harvard Observatory at Arequipa, Peru, when a photograph was taken of an object on the moon. It could be readily seen on examining this photograph that the light coming from the moon experienced a bending, known as refraction, in passing from the space outside the moon to its atmosphere on to its surface.

Of course, when the moon was thrown off from the earth by reason of its great centrifugal force, it carried along with it a portion of the earth's atmosphere. But since the quantity of matter in the moon is only about one-eightieth of that of the earth, the force of gravity on the moon is much smaller than that on the earth, being[Pg 215] almost exactly one-sixth that of the earth's gravity. In other words, if you could succeed in reaching the moon's surface, you would only weigh one-sixth of what you weigh on the earth, but then you could carry a weight six times heavier with no greater effort, and, as for running, jumping, and other athletic exercises, the surface of the moon would, indeed, be a great place on which to break records, since one could readily jump six times higher, put the shot six times further, than on the earth, or go through most other athletic exercises with a corresponding increase.

Without going any further into this question it will be sufficient to say that the moon's present atmosphere is believed to consist of carbonic acid gas, and that while on the general surface of the moon this atmosphere must be very rare, yet, at the bottom of the great fissures that cross the moon's surface, it may possess a fairly great density, especially if the moon still possesses feeble volcanic activity; that carbonic acid gas is still being given off from the inside of the moon as we know it is being given off from inside the earth.

Under the best conditions of atmosphere and telescope, we can see the moon's surface as it would appear at a distance varying from 800 miles to 300 miles from the earth. With a fifteen-inch telescope, under perfect conditions of vision, objects can be seen as if they were at a distance of 800 miles from the earth, and with the most powerful glasses, and the best conditions of atmosphere this distance can be reduced to about 300 miles. This would enable us to clearly see large objects like rivers, lakes, seas, or forests, if they existed, but would not be sufficient to enable us to see houses, buildings, or roads.

When we come to examine the surface of the moon[Pg 216] under the most favorable conditions, we find that it is extremely irregular. There are plenty of high mountains. These mountains are not collected in ranges as they are on the earth's surface, but are completely separated from each other, and are scattered in great numbers over the moon's surface.

You may form some idea of the number of volcanoes that have been observed on the moon when I tell you that as many as 32,000 have been seen on that side of the moon that is turned towards the earth.

Now it is an interesting fact that almost all these mountains possess great craters that are not unlike some of the volcanic craters we see on the earth. The volcanic craters of the moon, however, are of very much greater size than those on the earth, many being from fifty to sixty miles in diameter, while some of them are more than 100 miles in diameter. Smaller craters, say from twenty to twenty-five miles in diameter, can be counted by the hundreds.

Like most of the moon's craters, the largest crater more closely resembles one of the pit-craters or calderas on the island of Hawaii. This volcanic crater consists of a huge circular ring with a small irregular peak that rises inside the ring. This peak, by the way, might at first appear to resemble the crater of Vesuvius, which after a long period of inactivity of the mountain during the eruption that destroyed Pompeii and Herculaneum was thrown up inside of what had been left standing of the old crater of Somma. But it has no crater at its summit, and, therefore, resembles rather the irregular pile or rock that rises from the surface of a lava lake in the craters of Mt. Loa or Mt. Kilauea in Hawaii.

Besides the numerous craters to be seen on the moon's surface there are many lines of deep, crooked valleys,[Pg 217] known as *rills*, that may at one time have been the beds of rivers. Besides the rills, there are many straight clefts about half a mile in width, that extend down into the surface of the moon for unknown depths. These clefts can be seen passing directly through mountains and valleys. They are believed to be cracks or fissures in the moon's surface.

On the moon is a great crater called Tycho. It is situated near the moon's south pole. The great crater of Tycho is by far the most prominent object on the moon's surface. It has a system of rays that extend for great distances around its craters.

You will also see if you examine the moon's surface by a powerful glass that there are immense plains called *oceans* or *seas*. By an appropriate custom the names of the different craters on the moon are the same as the names of the great astronomers and philosophers that have long since passed from their labors, such as Tycho, Copernicus, Kepler, Plato, etc.

Various explanations have been given as to the origin of the craters on the moon's surface, but without going into a discussion it may be said that they are now generally regarded as having been formed in the main just as were the craters of the earth's volcanoes.

The tremendous size of the moon's craters is of course due to the great decrease in the force of gravity. This would make the craters, approximately, six times as great as the craters on the earth. Professor Pickering points out that while the moon's craters resemble more closely those of Hawaii than those of any other of the earth's volcanoes, yet there is this difference in them: that while the earth's crater floors are generally considerably higher than the level of the sea, the moon's crater floors are generally below the level of the surrounding country.[Pg 218] Still, taking them all in all, the craters of the moon's volcanoes resemble those of the island of Hawaii, or again quoting from Pickering:—

"There seems, indeed, to be no feature found upon the moon which is not presented by these Hawaiian volcanoes, there is no feature of the volcanoes that does not also have its counterpart in the moon."

[Pg 219]

CHAPTER XXIII

EARTHQUAKES

An *earthquake* is a shaking of the earth. It may vary in intensity from a shaking so feeble that it requires the use of a delicate instrument to detect it, to a shaking violent enough to overthrow heavy buildings, and even to make great rents or fissures in the crust.

An earthquake then is an *earth-shake*. It may be caused by anything capable of shaking the earth; for example, as the falling of a heavy weight on its surface. Now, a shaking so caused is only felt in the immediate neighborhood of the place the weight strikes the earth. On the contrary, in an earthquake, the shaking spreads in all directions through the earth's crust, until, in the case of very violent earthquakes, it reaches portions that may be situated many thousands of miles away from where the shock started. This spreading of the earthquake waves through the solid earth is not unlike the spreading of the circular waves that are set up in a still water surface when a stone is tossed in.

Any shaking of the earth's crust produces what may be called an earth-shake or earthquake. The mere falling of a raindrop on the earth produces a slight shaking. The falling of a heavy stone produces a stronger shaking, and sets up a series of minute waves, generally called vibrations, that spread around the place in all directions from where the stone struck. These movements, however, while they spread in all directions, just as they do[Pg 220] in a surface of a lake, when a stone is thrown into it, are of course much more quickly stopped by the solid earth than similar movements are by the more readily movable water.

But, while any shaking of the earth's crust constitutes an earthquake, yet, strictly speaking, an earthquake is produced only by some force that acts suddenly on the earth, *at a point below its surface*, and, therefore, out of sight. This, of course, would rule out all such shakings as are caused by bodies striking the outer surface of the earth.

Earthquakes may occur in any part of the world, and at any time of the day or year. They do occur, however, most frequently in certain parts of the world, at certain seasons of the year and at certain hours of the day.

Earthquakes are far from being unusual occurrences. In some parts of the world, such as the island of Java, they are very common, and in Japan, under certain circumstances, scarcely a day passes without one or more shocks in some part of that little empire.

Professor Mallet, who has made a very extensive study of earthquakes, published in 1850 to 1858, in the Philosophical Transactions, brief abstracts or descriptions of all the more important earthquakes he could find records of during the past 3,456 years. The number of earthquakes thus recorded during this period reached 6,830. Of this great number nearly one-half occurred during the last fifty years.

It should not be inferred from the above figures that the number of earthquakes has really increased so greatly in the past half-century. The explanation of the apparent increase is that greater care has been taken recently in recording earthquakes, and that an apparatus called a[Pg 221] *seismometer*, or *earthquake-recorder*, has been invented which automatically produces a record of the smallest shocks; so that a great many have been recorded that would otherwise have passed undetected.

It is the opinion of Le Conte that if the records of all the earthquakes of 3,456 years had been thus made there would have been found during the entire time of Mallet's researches to have occurred no less than 200,000, while during the last four years of Mallet's records, the number would have probably reached two earthquakes per week.

Since Mallet's time, Prof. Alexis Perry published (1876) a much larger list of earthquakes. Perry finds that from 1843 to 1872 there have been 17,249 earthquakes, or 575 every year. Perry's list, however, is incomplete, since it fails to record earthquakes that occurred in mid-ocean, and in the unexplored and uncivilized parts of the world. So it seems likely that earthquakes are so common that our earth, at some part or other of its surface, is continually shaking or quaking.

Earthquakes are such tremendous phenomena that they were necessarily observed by the ancients. We find more or less complete accounts of them in various writings. Lucretius (Titus Carus Lucretius, a great Roman poet) speaks as follows, in his De Rerum Natura (On the Nature of Things). We use Munro's translation here:

"Now mark and learn what the law of earthquakes is. And first of all take for granted that the earth below us as well as above is filled in all parts with windy caverns, and bears within its bosom many lakes and many chasms, cliffs and craggy rocks; and you must suppose that many rivers hidden beneath the crust of the earth roll on with violent waves and submerged stones; for the very nature of the case requires it to be throughout like to itself. With such things then attached and placed below, the[Pg 222] earth quakes above from the shock of great falling masses, when underneath, time has undermined vast caverns. Whole mountains, indeed, fall in, and in an instant from the mighty shock tremblings spread themselves far and wide from that centre. And with good cause, since buildings beside a road tremble throughout, when shaken by a wagon of not such very great weight; and they rock no less, where any sharp pebble on the road jolts up the iron tires of the wheels on both sides. Sometimes, too, when an enormous mass of soil through age rolls down from the land into great and extensive pools of water, the earth rocks and sways with the undulation of the water just as a vessel at times cannot rest, until the liquid within has ceased to sway about in unsteady undulations....

"The same great quaking likewise arises from this cause, when on a sudden the wind and some enormous force of air gathering either from without or within the earth have flung themselves into the hollow of the earth and there chafe at first with much uproar among the great caverns and are carried on with a whirling motion, and when their force, afterwards stirred and lashed into fury, bursts abroad and at the same moment cleaves the deep earth and opens up a great yawning chasm. This fell out in Syrian Sidon and took place at Ægium in the Peloponnese, two towns which an outbreak of wind of this sort and the ensuing earthquake threw down. And many walled places besides fell down by great commotions on land and many towns sank down engulfed in the sea together with their burghers. And if they do not break out, still the impetuous fury of the air and the fierce violence of the wind spread over the numerous passages of the earth like a shivering-fit and thereby cause a trembling."

Of course, no one at the present time believes this ridiculous explanation as to the cause of earthquakes.

[Pg 223]

Aristotle, a Greek philosopher, speaks thus concerning earthquakes. We quote the translation employed by Mallet:

"Three theories on the subject have been handed down to us by three different persons; namely, Anaxagoras of Klazomene, before him Anaximenes the Milesian, and later than these Democritus of Abdera.

"Anaxagoras says that the ether of nature rises upward, but that when it falls into hollow places in the lower parts of the earth it moves it (the earth); because the parts above are cemented or closed up by rain, all parts being by nature equally spongy or full of cavities, both those which are above (where we live) and those which are below. Of this opinion it may perhaps be unnecessary to say anything, as being foolish, for it is absurd to suppose that things would thus exist above and beneath, and that the parts of bodies which have weight would not on every side be borne to the earth, and those which are light, and fiery, rise; especially since we see the surface of the earth to be convex and spherical, the horizon constantly changing as we change our place, at least as far as we know. And it is also foolish to assert on the one hand that it remains in the air on account of its great size, and on the other to say that it is shaken, when struck from beneath upwards. And besides these objections, it is to be remarked that he has not treated of the attendant circumstances of earthquakes, for neither every time nor place is subject to these convulsions.

"But Democritus says, that the earth being full of water, and receiving much also by means of rain, is moved by this. For when the water increases in bulk, because the cavities cannot contain it, in its struggles it causes an earthquake. And when the earth becomes partially dried up, the water being drawn from the full reservoirs[Pg 224] into those which are empty, in passing from one to the other, by its movements it causes an earthquake also.

"Anaximenes, however, says that the earth, when parched up and again moistened, cracks, and by the masses thus broken off falling on it, is shaken; wherefore earthquakes occur in drouths and again in times of rain; in drouths, because, as we have said, it cracks, when highly dried, and then, when moistened over again, it cracks and falls to pieces. Were this the case, however, the earth ought to appear in many places subsiding. Why then is it that hitherto many places have been very subject to these convulsions which do not present any such remarkable differences from others? Yet such ought to be the case. And, moreover, those who think thus must assert that earthquakes constantly become less and less, and at last cease altogether. For the continual condensation of the earth would cause this. Wherefore, if this be not the fact, it is plain that this is not the correct explanation."

Besides the above, there are numerous references to earthquakes in the works of other writers. Thales, Seneca, and Pliny all speak of these phenomena and appear to describe correctly the movement of the earth in waves both in the solid land, as well as on the sea.

Coming down to less ancient writers, Mallet refers to a book by Fromondi, published in Antwerp, in 1527, that contains much valuable and interesting information. Among other things Fromondi declares that in the year 369, in the reign of Valentinian, there was a great earthquake that shook nearly the entire world and that another earthquake of almost equal severity occurred in 1116. He also states that in 1601 an earthquake continued for nearly forty days; that a great earthquake in[Pg 225] Italy, in 1538, lasted fifteen days, and that another, in Spain, lasted for nearly three years.

This does not mean that these earthquakes actually continued to shake the earth violently for the times mentioned. These are only the times during which, at intervals of greater or less length, successive shocks were felt in these localities.

Another of the less ancient writers referred to by Mallet is Travagini, who published a book in Venice in 1683. This book contains a description of a terrible earthquake occurring in Italy on the 6th of April, 1667, which affected large portions of the country adjacent to Ragusa.

Without attempting at present to discuss the various theories of earthquakes, it will suffice to say that earthquakes can be divided, according to their origin, into two classes: *volcanic earthquakes*, or earthquakes that are caused by practically the same forces that cause volcanoes, and *tectonic*[1] *earthquakes*, or those produced by the slipping of a large mass of rock lying along the lines of old or new fractures.

Earthquakes of the first class are found especially in volcanic districts, while those of the second class are found in all parts of the world, whether in volcanic districts or elsewhere. According to Dana, earthquakes of the second class generally start in the neighborhood of mountains, where old lines of fractures are especially abundant.

As regards the direction of the shaking movements of the earth, earthquakes can be divided into three different classes: *explosive earthquakes*, or those in which the force acts vertically upwards; *horizontal earthquakes*, or those in which the force moves in a more or less horizontal[Pg 226] direction, or parallel to the general surface of the earth, and *rotary earthquakes*, or those in which the earth rotates or moves in great eddies or whirls.

When the earthquake wave is started below the earth's surface, it spreads through the crust in all directions. The direction these waves will have on emerging, or coming out of the surface, will depend on the distance of this point from the place the waves started. When a place is situated directly over where the wave started, the waves will emerge so as to move vertically upwards, so that the earth at this point will be shaken by an explosive earthquake. As the point where the waves pass out is situated further and further from the place where the waves start, the waves will emerge more nearly horizontally, the greater the distance from the source.

In explosive earthquakes, which, as just explained, occur at areas almost immediately above the point where the disturbance starts, the force is, generally speaking, the greatest. In earthquakes of this character the force is sometimes sufficiently great to throw large bodies high up into the air. In the case of the great Riobamba earthquake of 1797, the force was not only sufficiently great to fracture the earth in various places, but also to throw bodies lying on the surface great distances into the air. Bodies of men were thrown several hundred feet into the air and were afterwards found on the other side of a broad river or high up on the side of a hill.

It is possible that Humboldt did not inquire with as much care as he should have done into these reports. They were probably greatly exaggerated, since it is difficult to understand how a force great as this would have failed to detach the soil at these places, and hurl it after the people. This much, however, can be accepted, that the upward force was very great. [Pg 227]

In the great Calabria earthquake of March, 1783, Dolomieu states that the tops of the granite hills of Calabria were distinctly seen to rise and fall. In some cases houses were suddenly raised a great distance in the air, and were afterwards brought down again to a position of rest, at a higher level without any damage occurring to them. In a similar manner during the Caracas earthquake of March, 1812, the ground was seen to rise and fall in a nearly vertical direction. But, perhaps, one of the most terrible earthquakes of this character was the earthquake that destroyed the greater part of Jamaica in June, 1793. During this earthquake the entire surface of the ground at Port Royal assumed the appearance of a rolling sea. Houses were shifted from their old sites. Many of the inhabitants who had succeeded in escaping from the city to the neighboring country were thrown great distances into the air. Some of these, by good fortune, fell into the harbor, from which, in some cases, they escaped with their lives. Here again the projectile force was probably greatly exaggerated.

Vertical movements characterized the great earthquake of Lisbon, on November 1st, 1755, the city appearing to have been not far from the point of origin.

The commonest type of earthquakes is the horizontal, where the waves emerge at the surface in a direction either horizontal or parallel to the general surface, or at least inclined to it at a very small angle. Where the materials of the earth's crust, through which the waves spread, are of the same kind and of the same density in all directions, the area shaken is approximately circular, but where the materials of the crust are more or less dense in some directions than in others, the area of disturbance is of course oblong or elliptical.

In some cases earthquakes of the horizontal type are[Pg 228] limited almost entirely to a single direction. This is especially the case with earthquakes that occur in mountainous districts. These earthquakes are known as *linear earthquakes*, since they spread almost in a single line.

When earthquake waves pass from one medium to another, that is, from one kind of rock to another, the greater portion of the waves is refracted or bent out of their straight direction as they pass into the new medium; a part of the waves, however, are reflected. It is these reflected waves that probably cause rotary earthquakes.

The speed with which the surface waves move outwards in all directions, varies not only with the force of the wave, but also with the kind of material through which they pass. This velocity may be in the neighborhood of twenty miles per second, while in others the velocity is as great as 140 miles per second.

Naturally, one would suppose that the most severe earthquakes are those in which the waves move the most rapidly. On the contrary, however, the comparatively feeble shocks are sent through the earth with greater velocity.

In rotary earthquakes, as the name indicates, the ground is whirled or twisted in the manner of a violent eddy, and is often left in this twisted condition. In the great Calabria earthquake, huge blocks of stone forming obelisks were twisted on one another in a manner represented in Fig. 39. In this case the pedestals remained unaffected, but the separate blocks

80

of stone were partially turned around, as shown. During this earthquake the earth was so twisted that trees, which had been planted in straight lines before the earthquake, were left standing in zigzags. During the great Charleston earthquake, South Carolina, the chimney-tops of the houses were[Pg 229]separated at places where they joined the roof and were twisted around these places without being overthrown. In some of the houses wardrobes or bureaus were turned at right angles to their former positions, and in some cases were even found with their faces turned towards the wall.

FIG. 39. HEAVY STONE OBELISKS TWISTED BY CALABRIAN EARTHQUAKE OF 1783

Mallet suggests that in some cases the rotary motion is more apparent than real, being due only to a to-and-fro motion without any twisting, the apparent turning being due to the greater freedom of motion of the object in one direction than in another. A twisting motion, however, has actually taken place in some earthquakes.

While separate shocks, in a given locality, may follow one another at intervals for fairly long times, yet the principal shock or shake that produces the greatest damage is generally of exceedingly short duration. In the Caracas earthquake the greatest destruction was accomplished in about one minute. There were three[Pg 230] distinct shocks, each of which lasted but three or four seconds. The great Calabria earthquake, of 1783, lasted but two minutes. The earthquake of Lisbon, in 1755, lasted five minutes, but the first, and worst, shock, was only from five to six seconds.

[Pg 231]

CHAPTER XXIV

SOME OF THE PHENOMENA OF EARTHQUAKES

The nature of an earthquake and the movements of its waves from their starting place having now been briefly described, it remains to explain some of the strange phenomena that precede, accompany, or follow one.

Next to the violent shaking of the earth's crust, perhaps the most wonderful and impressive thing is the great variety of sounds and noises. These occur not only while the earth-waves are passing through the crust at any place, but also long before the principal shocks reach the place, as well as long after they have passed.

Earthquake sounds vary almost infinitely, both in intensity and character. Some are like the gentle sighings of the wind, or resemble faint mysterious whisperings; some are not unlike the confused murmurings of a crowded room; some resemble the sounds of a busy street. Some sounds are full and strong, like the deep bass notes of a large organ. Others resemble the din of a great battle with the reports of the large guns. Still others reach the intensity of continuous peals of thunder. But we can better understand the nature of earthquake sounds from an actual description of them in a number of great earthquakes, and by inquiring at the same time into any of the peculiar facts connected.

Humboldt in his great work, "Cosmos," thus describes the varied voice of the earthquake:

[Pg 232]

"It is either rolling or rustling, or clanking, like chains being moved, or like near thunder, or clear and ringing, as if obsidian or some other vitrified masses were struck in subterranean cavities."

That the sounds produced during earthquakes are carried through the ground faster than through the air appears clear from the fact that such sounds are sometimes heard in deep mines when they are not at all heard on the earth's surface.

In describing the earthquake that occurred in Kamtschatka, in 1759, Krashenikoff of St. Petersburg states that noises were heard like the rushing of a strong underground wind, accompanied by a hissing sound, which resembled the sizzlings heard when red hot coals are thrown in water.

In an earthquake that occurred in Lincolnshire, England, February 6th, 1817, a noise was heard closely resembling the sounds of wagons running away on a road. So complete

81

and convincing was the resemblance that several wagoners on one of the roads drew their teams to one side so as to permit the runaway to pass safely.

Another kind of noise heard during earthquakes is a loud hollow bellowing. Sometimes, however, the sounds are more musical in their nature, being not unlike those produced by a very large organ pipe. At other times they resemble the noises produced when steam is blown into cold water.

The following account of earthquake sounds is given by Daubeny, in his book on volcanoes. It appears that during March, 1822, the people living on the island of Melida, opposite Ragusa, in Dalmatia, were greatly alarmed by sounds that at first they believed due to cannonading either at sea or on the neighboring coast. They afterwards found that these sounds were due to something that was taking place under the ground. The[Pg 233] noises continued at intervals until August 23d, 1823, when a great earthquake occurred, during which one of the highest mountains on the island was cleft or split in one place. The underground noises continued from time to time and so frightened the people that they were about to leave the island permanently and emigrate to the mainland of Dalmatia. They were dissuaded from doing so by the government, and while the noises continued at intervals it so happened that no damage came to them. It is said, however, that twenty years after an active volcano broke out on the island.

There are various causes that produce earthquake sounds. A very slight rubbing or grinding together of rock surfaces may produce fairly loud noises, the volume of the sound being increased by transmission through the rock masses that lie in the path of the waves. An example of such an increase in the loudness of sounds is seen in the case of several of the large blocks of stone used for some of the piers of Kingston Harbor, in Ireland. When these rocks are moved together by blows of the waves they produce loud and appalling sounds, as if the whole island were being washed away. The same rocks, however, when left high and dry on the falling of the tide, can be caused to rub together, when moved by the hand. Under these circumstances, they produce but feeble sounds that can only be heard in their immediate neighborhood.

No doubt, some find it difficult to understand how it is possible for comparatively feeble sound-waves to be strengthened by their passage through large masses of solids. This is important and should be made clear. As everyone well knows, the ticking of a watch can only be heard at a short distance when the watch is held in the hand, because the sound-waves cannot readily pass[Pg 234] through the body of the person holding the watch to the earth, the materials of the body not being sufficiently elastic. If, however, the watch be placed on the bare surface of a large wooden table from which the tablecloth has been removed, so that the watch can come directly in contact with the wood, and nothing else is placed on the table but the watch, the sound-waves are transmitted to the mass of the table and its entire surface sends them out into the air. The ticking of the watch can then be heard distinctly in almost any part of a large room.

Mallet states that in nearly all great earthquakes sounds are heard before the principal shock, and in his description of the Calabrian earthquake Hamilton says:

"All agreed that every shock seemed to come with a rumbling noise from the westward, beginning with the horizontal and ending with the vorticose (rotary) motion."

According to Dolomieu, during the Lisbon earthquake, the shocks were preceded "by a loud subterranean noise like thunder, which was renewed for every shock.... This great shock," he says, referring to one of the great upward shocks, "occurred without the prelude of any slight shocks, without any notice whatever as suddenly as the blowing up of a mine.... Some, however, pretend that a muffled interior noise was heard almost at the same moment."

The noises do not generally continue long after the earthquake shocks. In some cases, however, a very loud noise is heard at intervals for a considerable length of time after the principal shock. This was the case at Quito and Ibarra, in which a great noise was heard for from eighteen to twenty minutes after the principal shock. In a similar manner during the earthquake of October, 1746, at Lima, and Callao, South America, peals of underground[Pg 235] thunder were heard at Truxillo for fifteen minutes after the principal shock. In such cases it seems probable that the noises were not caused by the same impulses that caused the original shock, but by the forces that caused the subsequent shock.

Humboldt relates that in 1784 there were noises heard at Guanajuato, from the 9th to the 12th of February. They were not, however, followed by an earthquake.

Humboldt also states that in an earthquake which occurred on the 30th of April, 1812, on the banks of the Orinoco River, in South America, a loud thundering noise was heard, without, however, any shock, but at this time a volcano on the island of St. Vincent, in the Lesser Antilles, although some 632 miles to the northeast, was pouring out streams of lava. Again in the great eruption of Cotopaxi, in 1734, underground noises were heard as if cannon were being fired. These sounds were distinctly heard at as great a distance as Honda on the banks of the Magdalena River. Now, bearing in mind that the crater of Cotopaxi is situated on the high plateau of Quito, in a region full of valleys and fissures, it would seem that for the sounds to have been sent through the 436 miles between the mountains and the valley of the Magdalena River, the waves must, for the greater part, have been transmitted through the solid earth at some considerable distance below the surface.

Mallet states that the underground noises which continued for more than a month from the midnight of January 9th, 1784, at Guanajuato, were not followed by any earthquake shocks, that it was if as thunder clouds occupied the space below the surface at that part of the earth and from these clouds there came the slow rolling sounds like short, quick, snaps of thunder.

Major Dutton in his book entitled "Earthquakes in[Pg 236] the Light of the New Seismology" gives the following as the principal signs that herald the coming earthquake in the open country.

"The first sensation is the sound. It is wholly unlike anything we have ever heard before, unless we have already had a similar experience. It is a strange murmur. Some liken it to the sighing of pine-trees in the wind, or to falling rain; others to the distant roar of the surf; others to the far-off rumble of the railway train; others to distant thunder. It grows louder. The earth begins to quiver, then to shake rudely. Soon the ground begins to heave. Then it is actually seen to be traversed by visible waves somewhat likes waves at sea, but of less height and moving much more swiftly. The sound becomes a roar. It is difficult to stand, and at length it becomes impossible to do so. The victim flings himself to the ground to avoid being dashed to it, or he clings to a convenient sapling, or fence-post, to avoid being overthrown. The trees are seen to sway sometimes through large arcs, and are said, doubtless with exaggeration, to touch the ground with their branches, first on one side, then on the other. As the waves rush past, the ground on the crests opens in cracks which close again in the troughs. As they close, the squeezed-out air blows forth sand and gravel, and sometimes sand and water are spurted high in air. The roar becomes appalling. Through its din are heard loud, deep, solemn booms that seem like the voice of the Eternal One, speaking out of the depths of the universe. Suddenly this storm subsides, the earth comes speedily to rest and all is over."

There are many other curious phenomena besides earthquake sounds or noises. Among some of the more interesting are the fire and smoke that are seen to come out of fissures that have been rent in the ground.

[Pg 237]

It is possible that in many cases these flashes of fire are in reality produced by electric discharges that momentarily light the clouds of dust thrown up out of the fissure. But sometimes true flames are seen escaping from the fissures. This was the case during the earthquake of Lisbon, in 1755, when fire burst through fissures at several places, burning with a lambent flame for some hours.

The clouds of dust that follow the rending of mountain masses by earthquakes are probably to be traced to the fracture of the rock masses, the dust so formed being violently thrown forth by the air squeezed out of the fissures, when they are suddenly closed. The violent compression of this air may raise this dust to incandescence.

Mallet asserts that in many cases the clouds of smoke observed do not consist of true smoke like that produced when wood or vegetable matters are incompletely burned, but is only ordinary air mixed with sulphurous acid gas, and various other gases.

But not only fire and smoke are seen at times coming out of fissures in the earth. A thing still more frequently thrown out is water, which often spouts forth along with great quantities of mud, sand, and the finely ground fragments of earthy materials generally. Among many other instances where the emission of water from the crevices was particularly noticeable, may be mentioned the earthquakes at Jamaica in 1687 and 1692. Here the water, in some places, was thrown out of the ground to considerable heights in the air.

Mallet calls attention to the fact that the waters of springs collect in reservoirs consisting either of fissures or crevices of the rocks, of small width but great depth, which are vertical or inclined to the horizon, or in reservoirs that are formed of extended beds of sand or gravel.

[Pg 238]

Now, when the earthquake waves moving horizontally over the surface produce movements that squeeze these fissures together, the water in the fissures is spurted out in high jets, and carries with it the finely divided rock or sand formed by the rubbing together of the rock surfaces. In the case of the reservoirs consisting of beds of sand or gravel, lying between impervious layers, if, during an earthquake motion, the land areas are suddenly lowered, the water rushing into the cavity thus left will afterwards be shot out with considerable force, when the land is suddenly raised again.

Where there are no direct openings in the ground the water will burst through the crust in the shape of great vertical jets, thus forming a circular hole, broken or fractured at its edges. Water jets of this character were especially numerous during the earthquake of Calabria in 1783. In a swampy plain, known as Rosarno, many of these circular wells or openings about the size of an ordinary carriage wheel, though in some cases much larger, were to be seen crowded together. The appearance of the openings are represented in Fig. 40.

Some of these were filled with water, but the greater number were dry and filled with loose sand. These latter, when examined by digging, were shown to be funnel-shaped, as seen in Fig. 41. As seen, the margins of the wells exhibit a series of cracks or crevices extending radially outward from the centre. Their origin is evident. As the water was violently expelled by the squeezing motion of the upper and lower impervious strata, it shot upwards, thus producing the funnel-shaped tube. At the same time the force of the eruption was sufficiently great to produce the radial fissures or fractures at the sides.

FIG. 40. CIRCULAR HOLLOW FORMED BY CALABRIAN EARTHQUAKE

FIG. 41. SECTION OF CIRCULAR HOLLOW FORMED BY CALABRIAN EARTHQUAKE

But greater fissures than these have been formed by[Pg 239] earthquakes, especially those of the class created by a slipping of the earth's strata. In the case of an earthquake on the South Island of New Zealand, in 1848, a fissure having an average width of eighteen inches could be clearly seen extending in a direction parallel to the[Pg 240] mountain chain for a distance of sixty miles, and during a later earthquake in the same region, in 1855, a fracture was formed that could be clearly traced for a distance of nearly ninety miles.

In some cases these fissures or fractured parts of the crust are left with one of their sides at a higher level than the opposite side. This was the case of the great Japanese earthquake of October 28th, 1891.

There are three kinds of waves produced by earthquakes; namely, the earthquake waves proper through the earth; the sound waves in the air, and great forced waves in the sea.

The sound waves of course reach the air from the point of origin below the earth's surface through the solid materials of the crust, and take on the curious varieties already described in connection with the sounds accompanying earthquakes.

We have already briefly described the manner in which the earthquake waves travel through the materials of the earth's crust. There remain to be discussed the great waves that are rolled up in the ocean during an earthquake shock. These waves are, perhaps, among the most destructive phenomena of great earthquakes. The following are only some of the more remarkable of such waves, and have been taken from Mallet's collection of earthquake data.

During some of the great earthquakes on the coasts of Chile and Peru, huge waves from the ocean did great damage when they reached the land. In the earthquake of 1590, ocean waves rushed for several leagues inland over the coast of Chile, carrying with them ships that were left high and dry as the wave receded. In the earthquake of 1687, Callao was inundated by a great wave from the Pacific Ocean, and ships were carried a[Pg 241] full league into the country. During the earthquake of 1746, Callao was again swept away by a huge ocean wave. At later times earthquake waves have caused great damage to several other parts of the coast of South America.

Ocean waves of this character are formed by successive upward and downward movements at the bottom of the ocean, following each other at very brief intervals. Le Conte points out that the sudden upheaval of the bed of the ocean forms a huge mound in the surface of the water which results in a large wave that spreads rapidly in all directions. Waves produced in this manner sometimes reach a height of fifty to sixty feet. They are not readily observed in the deep ocean, but as soon as they reach the shallow waters near the shore they rush forward, forming waves from fifty to sixty feet in height and, rushing over the land, sweep everything before them.

During the great Lisbon earthquake of 1755 a huge wave started at a point fifty miles off the coast of Portugal. Half an hour after the earthquake was over several waves, the largest of which was sixty feet in height, rushed over a part of the city and greatly increased the ruin already wrought by the earthquake. According to Le Conte the great waves so formed moved in all directions across the Atlantic Ocean. They were thirty feet high when they reached Cadiz, eighteen feet in height at Madeira, and five feet on the coast of Ireland. They even crossed the Atlantic, being observed on the coasts of the West Indies.

A great ocean wave accompanied the Japanese earthquake in 1854. As in the case of the Lisbon earthquake this wave started in the bed of the ocean off the coast of Japan and only reached the island half an hour afterwards. It was thirty feet in height, and completely swept away the town of Simoda.

Owing to water's greater freedom of motion earthquake[Pg 242] waves travel greater distances through the water than they do on land.

Of course, great earthquake shocks as a rule cause a very large loss of life. The following figures from Mallet give some idea of the extent of this loss, which is generally a matter of a few moments.

In the Lisbon earthquake, where the worst shock lasted a few seconds, 60,000 people were killed. During other earthquakes the losses have been as follows: 10,000 at Morocco; 40,000 in Calabria; 50,000 in Syria, and probably 120,000 in earthquakes that occurred in Syria in A. D. 19 and in A. D. 526.

But even these figures give only a meagre idea of the vast loss of life that has occurred during the past. It is said that during the reign of Justinian, earthquakes repeatedly shook the whole Roman world. The city of Constantinople was visited by earthquake shocks that continued at intervals for forty days. Deep chasms were opened in the earth and huge masses were thrown into the air. Enormous sea-waves were formed. At Antioch, during the earthquake of May 20th, A. D. 526, 250,000 people are believed to have been killed.

On the 31st of July, A. D. 365, in the second year of Valentinian, a dreadful earthquake shook the Roman world, and a great wave rolled in from the Mediterranean and swept two miles inland, carrying ships over the tops of houses. During this earthquake 50,000 people lost their lives at Alexandria.

In the earthquake of Messina in 1692, 74,000 people are said to have been killed; and, according to other accounts, 100,000. In the year A. D. 602, another earthquake at Antioch killed 60,000 people.

During the earthquake of Quito, in 1797, Humboldt estimates that 40,000 natives were either buried in crevices[Pg 243] in the earth, under the ruins of buildings, or were drowned in lakes and ponds that were temporarily formed.

In this connection Mallet writes as follows:

"Such are the numbers to be met with in narratives, and if we suppose that there occurs one great earthquake in three years over the whole earth and that this involves the entombment of only 10,000 human beings, and that such has been the economy of our system for the last 4,000 years, we shall have a number representing above 13,000,000 men thus suddenly swallowed up, with countless bodies of animals of every lower class. Sir Charles Lyell then with good reason suggests that even in our own time we may yet find the remains of men and of their habitations and implements thus buried deep and embalmed, as it were, by earthquakes that occurred in the days of Moses and the Ptolemies."

Necessarily the progress of a great earthquake wave will produce great changes in the earth's surface features; for example, landslides, where immense layers of clay or other material slip or slide to a lower level and are thrown across the course of a river, causing its waters to be dammed up and then by spreading to form great lakes.

Sometimes, after vast bodies of water have been collected in this manner, disastrous floods result later from a sudden giving way of the barrier, and the loss thus caused is occasionally far greater than that directly due to the earthquake.

Permanent changes of level are frequently caused by earthquakes, as, for example, the coast of Chile during the earthquake of November 19th, 1822, where the coast for many miles was raised from three to four feet above its former plane.

In other cases the level of the ground is permanently lowered. This occurred in the Bengal earthquake in[Pg 244] 1762, when an area of some sixty square miles suddenly sank, leaving only the tops of the higher points above water.

In some cases of changes in the level of the ground, large areas being raised in one place and lowered in another, rivers take new courses, and their old courses are completely obliterated.

[Pg 245]

CHAPTER XXV

THE EARTHQUAKE OF CALABRIA IN 1783

All students of elementary geography are quick to notice that the extreme southeastern part of Italy is shaped something like a boot, which appears to be kicking at the island of Sicily. This part of the Mediterranean Sea has for very many years been the arena or storm centre of more or less intense volcanic activity. To the northwest is the active volcano of Vesuvius, as well as the volcanic regions of the Phlegræan Fields. Immediately opposite the point of Italy, near the toe of the foot, is the active volcanic mountain, Etna, while not far from this point is the volcano of Stromboli.

In 1783 this part of the world was visited by a very severe earthquake. Since at that time the country was divided into two parts, known as Upper Calabria and Lower Calabria, this earthquake is sometimes spoken of as the earthquake of the Calabrias, or more simply as the Calabrian earthquake.

The great mountain range of the Apennines, mainly of granite formation, extends through the central part of Italy. The lands adjoining the mountains on each side are flat and marshy, and consequently unhealthy.

Numerous observers have compiled excellent accounts of the Calabrian earthquake. These, having been made by educated persons, are, to a large extent free from the inconsistencies and exaggerations apt to characterize descriptions by ignorant persons, especially when in a[Pg 246] condition of excitement or alarm. Among reliable writers was Sir William Hamilton, who made a personal examination of the region, soon after the first severe shock, and collected much valuable information for a paper which was afterwards published in the Philosophical Transactions of the Royal Society. Then, too, Dolomieu, another scientific man of high ability, made a careful study of the effects produced by the earthquake.

FIG. 42. MAP OF THE CALABRIAN EARTHQUAKE OF 1783

As can be seen by an examination of the map presented in Fig. 42, the part of Italy included in the Calabrias covers an area from north to south almost equal to two degrees of latitude. Although the shock extended beyond[Pg 247] the limits of Calabria, since it reached as far north as Naples, as well as over a great part of the Island of Sicily, the territory in which the greatest damage was done did not exceed in area about 500 square miles.

The southern part of Italy is subject to frequent earthquake shocks. Pignatari, an Italian physician, asserts that this region was visited during 1783 by no less than 949 earthquakes, of which 501 were of the first class, or degree of intensity, while in 1784, there were 151 earthquakes, of which ninety-eight were of the first class.

It seems that the city of Oppido, marked on the above map as midway between the two coasts, was the point from which the severe earthquake of 1783 started. If one draws a circle, with a radius of twenty-two miles, around Oppido as a centre, the portions of the Calabrias that were the most affected will all lie within this circle.

The great Calabrian earthquake was attended by numerous shocks. The first and the most severe shock, that of February 5th, 1783, was only two minutes in destroying most of the houses in all cities, towns, and villages on the western side of the Apennines in this part of Italy.

Another severe shock occurred on the 28th of March. This shock was almost as severe as that of February 5th.

In order to understand many of the effects produced by this earthquake, inquiry must be made into the geological character of the region. According to Dolomieu, the flat country at the slopes of the Apennines, known as the Plain of Calabria, is covered with sand and clay mixed with sea shells. These strata have been deposited by the sea from materials that have been obtained by the decomposition of the granite mountain ranges in the Apennines. The plain is quite level except where it is crossed by deep valleys or ravines, which have been[Pg 248] eroded or cut by the swift mountain torrents. In many cases, these ravines or valleys have depths as great as 600 feet. Their sides are generally almost perpendicular. Consequently, as Lyell remarks, throughout the length of the mountain chain, the soil, which adheres but loosely to the granite base of the mountain chain, could therefore be easily separated from the mountain, and sliding over the solid steeps of the mountain could readily move, especially through the ravines or gorges, to distances in some cases as great as from nine to ten miles.

This peculiarity of the country must be thoroughly understood, since, otherwise, it would seem impossible that lands could be carried several miles from their former position, and often bear along with them almost undisturbed houses, olive groves, vineyards, and cultivated fields.

The heaving of the surface of the earth like the waters of the sea, so common in severe earthquakes, occurred during the Calabrian earthquake. In some places this heaving so shook the trees that they bent until their tops touched the ground near their base.

Parts of the ground were violently thrown upwards into the air as in the explosive type of earthquakes. In many instances the large paving stones were thrown into the air and afterwards found with their lower portions upwards.

During the earthquake deep fissures were made in the earth at various localities and there were, moreover, marked changes of level. At Messina in Sicily the shore was fissured and rent and while before the convulsion the surface had been level, it was afterwards found to be inclined toward the sea.

According to Dolomieu the following curious incident occurred during the passage of the earthquake waves.[Pg 249] A well in the ground of one of the convents of the Augustines, lined on the inside with stones, was so affected by the upward thrust given to the land that its stone lining was left projecting above the level of the earth in the form of a small tower some eight or nine feet in height.

Frequent instances occurred of deep fissures in the surface of the earth. Many of these remained open after the earthquake, although in other cases they were firmly closed together before the earthquake shocks ceased.

FIG. 43. FISSURES CAUSED BY THE CALABRIAN EARTHQUAKE

Fig. 43 represents the appearance of certain fissures in a part of Calabria during this earthquake. These cracks, it will be noticed, radiate or pass outward in all directions from a central point, just like the cracks that are formed in a glass window pane when it is fractured by a stone thrown against it.

Of course, the most violent effects were near the origin of the earthquake at Oppido. Here the formation of deep fissures was common. In another part of the country a number of buildings were suddenly swallowed up in a[Pg 250] central chasm, which almost immediately closed, thus permanently burying all these objects.

Some idea of the force with which the fissures were afterwards closed can be formed by reflecting on a case where, in order to recover some of the buried articles, the ground was dug up at these points, and it was found that the materials, human bodies and other objects, were so jammed together as to make one compact mass.

To Sir William Hamilton a place was shown where the fissures, though, when he saw them, they were not more than a foot in width, had opened sufficiently wide during the shock to swallow up a hundred goats as well as an ox.

An earthquake that caused such marked changes in the appearance of the earth's surface, naturally made great changes in the direction of the rivers. In one case the end of a small valley was so completely filled with stones and dirt that the water was dammed up, producing a lake two miles in length and one mile in breadth. In a similar manner no less than 215 lakes were formed in different portions of Calabria.

Of course, in the flat country at the base of the Apennines, frequent landslides occurred, the land sliding into great chasms and continuing to move down them for considerable distances, so that in many places pieces of land containing olive trees, vineyards, and green fields, were bodily transported for distances of several miles. This, moreover, was done so quietly as to leave the houses entirely uninjured, and the trees and other vegetation continuing to grow up with apparently no marked decrease in vitality.

As is usual in such cases, the sudden and strong blows acting on the waters of the sea, killed great numbers of fish just as does the explosion of dynamite at a point[Pg 251] below the surface of the water; and in a similar way the fish that usually live at the bottom of the sea in the soft mud, being disturbed by the earthquake shocks, came near the surface where they were caught in vast numbers.

It is an interesting fact that during this earthquake the volcano of Stromboli showed a marked decrease in the volume of smoke it gave out. Etna, however, was observed to emit large quantities of vapor during the convulsion.

Lyell tells the following story of the Prince of Scilla, who with many of his vassals sought safety in their fishing boats. Suddenly, on the night of February 5th, while some of the people were sleeping in the boat, and others were resting on a low plain near the sea, in the neighborhood, another shock occurred, a great mass was torn from a neighboring mountain and hurled with a crash on the plain, and immediately afterwards a wave, twenty feet or more in height, rolled over the level plain, sweeping away the people. It then retreated, but soon rushed back again, bringing with it many of the bodies of the people who had perished. At the same time all the boats were either sunk or dashed against the beach, and the Prince with 1,430 of his people was destroyed.

The total number of deaths caused by this earthquake in the Calabrias and Sicily were estimated by Hamilton at 40,000. Besides these about 20,000 more perished in epidemics that followed the earthquake, or died for lack of proper food.

[Pg 252]

CHAPTER XXVI

THE GREAT LISBON EARTHQUAKE OF 1755

Lisbon, the capital of Portugal, on the Tagus River, is built along both banks for five miles, and on several small neighboring hills. It is supplied with water by means of an aqueduct, called the Alcantara, which brings the water from springs about nine miles to the northwest. For portions of its length the aqueduct is placed underground, but where it crosses the deep valley of the Alcantara it is supported, for a distance of 2,400 feet, by a number of marble arches, which in one place are 260 feet in height. This fact is put forward not merely for the sake of its artistic interest, but because, strange to relate, this part of the aqueduct remained uninjured during that great earthquake, the greatest of modern times.

On the 1st of November, 1755, this frightful catastrophe, according to Lyell, from whose excellent account much of the information contained in this chapter has been obtained, struck the beautiful city almost without any warning. Terrible sounds came suddenly from underground; almost instantly afterward a violent shock threw down the greater portion of the city; in less than six minutes 60,000 people were killed.

The place from which this earthquake started must have been situated on the bed of the ocean at some distance from the coast; for the great wave thus raised in the Atlantic Ocean did not reach the mouth of the Tagus River until about half an hour after the most severe[Pg 253] shocks were over. The arrival of this wave at the mouth of the Tagus was announced by the sea retiring to such an extent as to leave the bar dry. Then a huge wave, sixty feet in height, rolled in from the ocean and completed the work of destruction that had been commenced by the earthquake.

So great was the shock that the mountains in the neighborhood were violently shaken and some of them split or fractured in a most wonderful manner.

Particularly large was the loss of life in the churches whither hundreds hastened for refuge when the shakings of the earth began, for most of these buildings fell and buried the worshippers. Another immense loss of life was caused by the destruction of a large marble quay or wharf that was suddenly swallowed up by the sea. While the buildings in the city were being overthrown by the violent shakings of the earth, a multitude sought the quay as a flat place where they could not be injured by the falling buildings. Suddenly, however, this structure sank into the water and not only were all the people drowned, but none of the bodies was ever afterwards found.

Failure to find any remnants of the pier or any of the people who perished on it has been attributed to the formation of eddies or whirls that were sufficiently strong to carry down vessels by suction similar to that of the famous maelstrom off the coast of Norway. Of course, in a time of boundless excitement like that of the Lisbon earthquake, accounts are apt to be highly exaggerated. For example, assertions are made in many books that the water left in the harbor after the sinking of the quay was unfathomable. Now, in point of fact, the depth of this place has been measured and found to be less than 100 fathoms.

[Pg 254]

When it is remembered that not one of the bodies of the people on that quay was ever again seen, it is possible, as Lyell suggests, that a deep fissure or chasm opened immediately on the ground on which the quay stood, so that it, together with all on it, were dropped into the chasm, which, closing, buried them deep in the earth.

The Lisbon earthquake was especially noted for the extent of country affected by it. Humboldt estimated this area as being more than four times the size of Europe. In parts of this area immense mountain ranges, such as the Pyrenees, Alps, etc., were violently shaken. When the size of these mountains is considered one realizes that it must have required a mighty force to shake them. These shakings were so severe that they produced a deep fissure in the ground in France. Continuing towards the north the solid earth was shaken as far as the shores of the Baltic and Norway and Sweden, generally. This, of course, included the flat country of Northern Germany. The hot springs of Toplitz disappeared for a time, but, breaking out afterwards, discharged such quantities of muddy water that the surrounding country was inundated.

The waves crossed the Atlantic, causing high tides on the island of Antigua, Barbadoes, and Martinique, of the Lesser Antilles, where, instead of the usual tides of two feet, tides of twenty feet high were observed. Further to the north the waves reached the eastern shores of North America, and shook the continent as far west as the Great Lakes, and spread in the North Atlantic as far as Iceland.

Toward the south the waves affected parts of northwestern Africa, where much loss of life occurred in the villages some eight leagues distant from the city of Morocco. Here from 8,000 to 10,000 people were killed,[Pg 255] being swallowed up by deep fissures in the earth, which afterwards closed on their bodies.

Severe shocks were in many cases felt on vessels at sea. In one instance, although the vessels were at considerable distances from where the waves started, the captains reported that the shocks were so great that on several occasions it was believed the vessel had struck a rock, till, on heaving the lead, they found that they were in very deep water. In another instance, such was the shock to the vessel that the planks on the deck had their seams opened. In still another case several of the sailors were thrown into the air for a distance of about one and a half feet.

It has been frequently observed that when great earthquakes happen, curious changes take place in the level of the waters of lakes entirely disconnected with the ocean; for example, mountain lakes, far above the level of the sea, the water suddenly rising and then resuming its original level. Sometimes the waters of such lakes have suddenly disappeared, probably being drained off through a fissure formed in the bed of the lake. In such event the lake generally remains dry after the passage of the earthquake.

At the time of the Lisbon earthquake it was observed that the water of Loch Lomond in Scotland first rose above its ordinary, then sank again to its usual level. This difference of level is explained by Lyell as follows: when the earthquake waves reached the lake, the water being unable to take the sudden shove given to it by the earthquake waves, dashed over that side of the basin which first received the shock. Assuming this to be the case, since the rise of the level in the water of Loch Lomond was two feet and four inches, it is comparatively easy to calculate the speed of movement that the earthquake[Pg 256] waves had, when they reached this body of water. Calculated in this way it would seem that the waves had a speed of about twenty miles a minute.

But what especially characterized the Lisbon earthquake were the great waves that were produced in the ocean. Besides the huge wave that entered the Tagus, a wave of the same height swept eastward along the southern coast of Spain, and the northwestern coast of Africa. At Tangier in Africa it swept the coast as a very high wave no less than eighteen times, or, in other words, eighteen huge waves rolled in from the ocean. At Funchal, on the Madeira Islands, this wave rose fifteen feet above the high water mark.

Many attempts have been made to explain the manner in which the great sea waves are started in earthquake movements. Some believe that they are due to the sudden raising or heaving up of the water, far above ordinary level. But, as Lyell points out, this explanation would not be satisfactory for the waves produced in the case of the Lisbon earthquake, since it would fail to account for the fact that both on the coasts of Portugal as well as on the island of Madeira the high wave was preceded by a movement of the water toward the point of origin; that is, the waters moved away from Lisbon and the Madeira Islands, so as to leave the water very low at those points, when shortly afterwards a huge wave rushed in from the sea and swept over the land.

Earthquake waves move much more rapidly through the solid rocks of the earth's crust than through the waters of the ocean. The shock transmitted through the solid earth from Lisbon to the Madeira Islands took only twenty-five minutes to reach the islands, while the waves in the ocean took about two and a half hours to cover the same distance.

[Pg 257]

CHAPTER XXVII

THE EARTHQUAKE OF CUTCH, INDIA, IN 1819

Cutch is one of the Provinces of India lying on the western coast of Hindostan, east of the delta of the Indus River.

A great earthquake occurred in this region on June 16th, 1819. As indicated by the map presented in Fig. 44, by Lyell, the district of Cutch lies on the coast of the Arabian Sea. Cutch is at times a peninsula, being washed on the south and east by the Arabian Sea and the Gulf of Cutch, and on the north by a depression known as the Runn of Cutch which, during unusual tides, is overflowed by the waters of the sea, but for the rest of the year is dry.

The earthquake of Cutch was apparently central at the town of Bhooj, where the destruction was extreme, hardly a house being left standing. The shock extended over a radius of about 1,000 miles from Bhooj, reaching to Khatmandoo, Calcutta, and Pondicherry.

At Anjar the fort, together with its tower and guns, were completely ruined. The shocks continued at intervals after the principal shock until June 20th, when the volcano of Denodur is said by some to have emitted flames, although this is denied by others.

Great changes were produced in the eastern channel of the Indus, which forms the western boundary of the Province of Cutch. The water in this inlet had become so low that it was readily fordable at low tide at Luckput, and was only covered with six feet of water at high tide.[Pg 258] After the earthquake it deepened at the port of Luckput to over eighteen feet at low tide, while in other parts of the channel the water had deepened from four to ten feet at high tide, where before the earthquake shock it had never been deeper than from one to two feet. Indeed, after these changes the inland navigation of the country again became possible after having been closed for many centuries.

FIG. 44. MAP SHOWING DISTRICT VISITED BY THE EARTHQUAKE OF CUTCH OF 1819

The Cutch earthquake resulted in a marked depression of the country, especially north of Luckput, where the[Pg 259] fort and village of Sindree were so quietly sunk that the fort, with its tower and walls, was left projecting slightly above a body of water that not only completely covered the old site but also formed a large lake marked on the preceding map, at Sindree, by the dark shading. It was this change of level that deepened the eastern channel of the Indus, just mentioned.

FIG 45. SINDREE BEFORE THE EARTHQUAKE OF 1819

Fig. 45, from Lyell, gives an idea of the appearance of the fort at Sindree before the earthquake. The appearance of the fort after its submergence is represented in Fig. 46, where, as will be noticed, only the top of the tower and the walls remain above the surface of the water. That the masonry was not affected either by the earthquake, or by the inrush of waters, is evident from the fact that the ruins were still standing in March, 1838, as represented in the figure.

[Pg 260]

In heavy shading on the map in Fig. 44 is a large area lying in the northern part of the province known as the Runn of Cutch. This is a flat region of about 7,000 square miles. It owes its level surface to its being the deserted or dried-up bed of a sea. For the greater part of the year its bottom is dry and hard, and is covered with a crust of salt half an inch or so in thickness.

FIG. 46. SINDREE AFTER THE EARTHQUAKE OF 1819

According to Lyell, from whom most of the facts concerning this earthquake have been obtained, the Runn of Cutch is connected with a vast inland sea, not only by the water driven into it through the Gulf of Cutch, but also through the eastern channel of the Indus at Luckput. These changes occur especially during the monsoon, when the seas are high, and especially after the heavy rains that come with these winds, when the wet condition of the soil permits the sea water to spread rapidly.

Traditions of the natives tend to confirm belief that Cutch a long time ago was a true peninsula, and that the Runn of Cutch was then an arm of the sea.

That a change of this character did occur in the Runn of Cutch seems to be proved by the ruins of old towns now far inland that are said to have been ancient seaports,[Pg 261] and as apparent evidences of this many pieces of wrought iron and ships' nails have been found in parts of the Runn.

At the same time that the sinking of the land around the fort and village of Sindree took place a considerable elevation occurred in the neighborhood. Immediately after the earthquake, the people in Sindree saw that a low hill or mound had been thrown up in a place that before had been a low and perfectly level plain. They named this elevation the Ullah Bund, or *the Mound of God*, in order to distinguish it from several embankments that had been built directly across the eastern mouth of the Indus; for the Ullah Bund had been raised by the earthquake across the same branch of the Indus.

For several years after the earthquake of 1819 marked changes kept developing in the channels of the Indus. During 1826 a large body of water entered into the eastern branch of the Indus above the Ullah Bund and finally forced its way through the mound, thus establishing a direct course to the sea. The Ullah Bund, being thus cut in two, an opportunity was afforded of seeing the materials of which it was composed. These were found to consist principally of clay filled with shells.

The opening of the river resulted in throwing such large quantities of fresh water into Lake Sindree that its waters were rendered fresh for several months, but at last regained their saltiness.

Dana states that in 1845 another earthquake occurred in this district which converted Sindree Lake into a salt marsh.

[Pg 262]

CHAPTER XXVIII

THE SAN FRANCISCO EARTHQUAKE OF APRIL 18, 1906

About twelve minutes past five o'clock on the morning of the 18th of April, 1906, the inhabitants of San Francisco were rudely awakened by a few frightful earthquake shocks. Their houses were violently shaken to and fro, and on all sides were heard the awful crashings of falling walls, chimneys, and buildings, together with the death-shrieks of those caught in the ruins. Rushing madly into the streets they could see on every side evidences of destruction; for, in almost every direction, were heaps of fallen buildings, still being violently shaken by the earthquake waves that rapidly passed through the solid earth. Huge cracks or crevices had been formed in the streets, while the heavy rails of the trolley tracks had been bent and twisted by the mighty forces.

Before describing in detail the great San Francisco earthquake, the location of the city and its surroundings demand consideration.

As can be seen from the map, Fig. 47, San Francisco is situated on the western coast of California, at the northern end of a peninsula, some twenty miles in length and about six miles in width. This peninsula is formed by the magnificent Bay of San Francisco on the east, a navigable strait called the Golden Gate on the north, and the Pacific Ocean on the west.

FIG. 47. MAP OF WESTERN COAST OF CALIFORNIA SHOWING POSITION OF SAN FRANCISCO

San Francisco Bay, accessible by the Golden Gate, is the principal harbor on the Pacific Coast, and is, indeed,[Pg 263] one of the most magnificent harbors in the world. It is land-locked, that is, surrounded by a continuous land border except at its entrance through the Golden Gate. Including San Pablo Bay, it has a length of about fifty-five[Pg 264]miles, and varies in breadth from three to twelve miles. The entrance to the harbor, however, is impeded by a bar across the mouth of the Golden Gate, over which there is a depth of but thirty feet of water at low tide.

San Francisco has over 750 miles of streets, 200 miles of which are paved. The city is lighted by both electricity and gas, and has an extensive system of water-works, the water being brought from the Pilarcitos and Calaveras Creeks, situated from twenty to forty miles respectively from the city.

San Francisco is in a region where earthquakes are common. It might, therefore, be visited at any time by a great catastrophe. There have occurred between 1850 and 1888, no less than 254 earthquake shocks in the State of California, these shocks having been especially frequent in the country surrounding San Francisco Bay. The most severe were the earthquake of 1868, which injured San Francisco; the Owens Valley earthquake of 1872; the Vacaville earthquake of 1892; the Mare Island earthquake of 1898; and a smaller earthquake in 1900. Since 1900 there was a period of rest until the 18th of April, 1906.

As in the case of practically all severe earthquakes, that which destroyed San Francisco consisted of a few momentary shocks: then all was over. According to a preliminary report of the State Earthquake Commission, appointed by the Governor of California, April 21st, 1906, these shocks, as recorded in the observatory at Berkeley, began at twelve minutes and six seconds after five A. M., Pacific Standard Time. Their entire duration was only one minute and fifty seconds, but, as frequently happens, there were a number of minor shocks, following at regular intervals during the next few hours as well as the next few days.

[Pg 265]

While the most severe shocks were in the neighborhood of the Peninsula of San Francisco, yet minor disturbances were felt as far north as Coos Bay, Oregon, and as far south as Los Angeles, California. As shown by recording instruments at the seismograph station at Washington, D. C., Sitka, Alaska; Potsdam, Germany; and Tokio, Japan, a series of waves were propagated through the earth, as well as over its periphery.

The damage done within the city limits was wide-reaching. Among the buildings almost completely destroyed were the City Hall, on which about $7,000,000 had been expended, the United States Post Office, besides many business blocks, hotels, department stores, theatres, banks, churches, and dwelling houses.

Amid the terrors of such a calamity it is difficult to obtain observations possessing any scientific value. Fortunately, however, there was in the city a physicist trained to observe phenomena of this character, Professor George Davidson of the University of California. Like others, he had been awakened by the first severe shock. At once recognizing the nature of the phenomenon, and desirous of obtaining the exact time of its occurrence, he counted seconds while he ran towards the table on which he had placed his watch, and in this way estimated that the shock occurred at twelve minutes past five in the morning. The closeness of this observation is emphasized by the fact that it differed from the recorded time by only six seconds. He states that the motion, at the time of its greatest intensity, closely resembled that of a rat vigorously shaken by a terrier.

The destruction caused by the earthquake was, however, but a small part of the total loss to the city. Fires were almost immediately started in the ruined houses by the fires in the kitchens and other parts of the houses, by[Pg 266] the ignited jets of the illuminating gas, and, perhaps, especially, by the crossing of numerous electric light wires.

The manner in which the woodwork and other combustible materials of the buildings were loosely tossed together by the shocks helped the quick spread of the fires, and this, too, was probably greatly aided by the illuminating gas from the broken gas pipes and mains. Eight severe conflagrations were, therefore, soon raging in different parts of the doomed city. What made these fires especially dangerous was the fact that the earthquake shocks had destroyed the water pipes. Thus the firemen were handicapped in their heroic endeavors to extinguish the flames.

At the time of the fire a strong wind was blowing from the northeast. Since the firemen were unable to check the flames, the fire line rapidly advanced. Its path led towards the best residential parts of the city through portions of the mission section containing a dense population of poor people. The dwellings in this latter section consisted of frame houses, through which the flames rapidly spread.

There was but one way to save the city from total destruction—a free use of dynamite! This was intelligently employed until the supply gave out, when it seemed that the city was doomed to utter destruction. But at the last moment, as it were, came a lucky change in the direction of the wind. Instead of blowing from the northeast, the steady southwest winds set in, and beat back the fire on itself, so by Friday, the 18th being Wednesday, it was under complete control and the rest of the city was saved.

A SAN FRANCISCO PAVEMENT TORN BY THE EARTHQUAKE
From a Stereograph, Copyright, 1906, by Underwood & Underwood

The extent of the fire is thus described in an article in the "Outlook," for Saturday, April 28th, 1906, as follows:

[Pg 267]

"The turn in the direction of the fire endangered for a time the great Ferry House, at the foot of Market Street. While the section actually destroyed is not, geographically speaking, much more than one-third of the city limits, yet it is in the heart of San Francisco, and includes the chief business streets and the Mission District, inhabited by poor people, and a large part of the so-called Nob Hill Quarter, where were the finest and costliest residences of the city. Another fine residence section, Civic Heights, escaped, together with that known as the Western District.

"The unburned district, though large in extent, was in the nature of suburbs, and was not closely built up, so that estimates made, as late as Saturday, declared that three-fourths of San Francisco's improvements in real estate had been destroyed."

The burnt district was about two miles from east to west and from two to four miles from north to south, with, of course, very irregular outlines.

Naturally, the great destruction wrought by the earthquake of April 18th, 1906, attracted the almost universal attention of scientific men especially interested in earthquake phenomena. We are, therefore, able to speak authoritatively about the probable causes.

The great San Francisco earthquake of April 18th, 1906, appears to have been a *tectonic* quake. Ransome, in an article entitled, "The Probable Cause of the San Francisco Earthquake," says:

"The region thus amply fulfils the conditions under which tectonic earthquakes arise. It is in unstable equilibrium, and it is cut by long northwest faults into narrow blocks which are in turn traversed by many minor dislocations. Under the operation of the unknown forces of elevation and subsidence, stresses are set up which finally overcome the adhesion of the opposing walls of one or[Pg 268] more of the fault fissures; an abrupt slip of a few inches, or a few feet, takes place and an earthquake results. The region extending for some hundreds of miles north and south of the Bay of San Francisco may be considered as particularly susceptible to shocks on account of the number and magnitude of the faults and the evidences that these furnish of very recent slippings and the marked subsidence in the vicinity of the Golden Gate."

[Pg 269]

CHAPTER XXIX

SOME OTHER NOTABLE EARTHQUAKES

It would, of course, be impossible within the limits of this book to attempt a description of all the remarkable earthquakes in the annals of science; but before leaving this part of the theme a brief account of a few more among the many may be worth while.

Jamaica, one of the West Indian Islands, about ninety miles south of Cuba, suffered a very destructive earthquake in 1692. During this earthquake the ground was agitated like the waves of the sea. These movements were so violent that numerous fissures were made in the ground, as many as 300 being formed at the same time, rapidly opening and closing. Many of the inhabitants were swallowed up in these fissures. In some cases, however, their bodies were afterward thrown out of the fissures, along with quantities of water.

The Jamaican earthquake was characterized by marked sinkings of the ground. At the city of Port Royal, which was then the capital, many houses on the harbor side sank in from twenty-four to forty-eight feet of water. As in the case of the earthquake at Cutch, many of these houses were left standing, the chimney tops of some being seen above the water, with their foundations and other parts apparently uninjured, and some of them were standing at a date as late as 1780. At a little later date, 1793, they were mostly ruins.

During the Jamaican quake a tract of land containing[Pg 270] at least 1,000 acres near the town was sunk, and a wave of the sea rolled over it. This wave is said by Lyell to have carried a frigate over the roofs of the houses and left it stranded on one roof. When the wave rolled back to the sea, the weight of the frigate made it fall through the roof.

Perhaps one of the most remarkable things about the Jamaican earthquake was the swallowing up of several plantations, which disappeared, together with all their inhabitants, their former place becoming a lake. But the lake soon disappeared, leaving a mass of sand

and gravel which obliterated any least sign that dwellings and trees had once adorned the spot.

The forces developed during this earthquake were sufficiently powerful to make several rents in the Blue Mountains, and the shock of blows on the waters of the sea killed fish by the hundred thousands so that the silver shine of their dead bodies stretched for miles and was beheld for days "on the face of the deep."

Portions of the world that have been frequently visited by mighty earthquakes, are the coasts of Chile. On the 24th of May, 1751, a part of the Chilian coast near the ancient town of Concepcion, sometimes called Penco, was destroyed by an earthquake, and the powerful earthquake waves that afterwards rushed in from the sea. So complete was this destruction that the ancient harbor was rendered useless and the people had to build another town about ten miles from the coast, so as to be beyond the reach of earthquake waves from the sea.

Another great earthquake occurred on the coast of Chile on the 19th of November, 1822. This shock was felt simultaneously over a distance of 1,200 miles from north to south. It reached its greatest intensity about 100 miles north of Valparaiso. This earthquake caused a[Pg 271] rising of the coast to a height of from three to five feet. From careful examinations it appears that the area over which a permanent elevation of the country took place must have been equal to 100,000 square miles, an area equal to about half of the area of France, and five-sixths that of Great Britain and Ireland.

"If we suppose," says Dana, "the elevation to have been only three feet on an average, it will be seen that the mass of rock added to the continent of America by the movement, or, in other words, the mass previously below the level of the sea, and after the shock, permanently above it, must have contained fifty-seven cubic miles in bulk; which would be sufficient to form a conical mountain two miles high (or about as high as Etna) with a circumference at the base of nearly thirty-three miles.... Assuming the Great Pyramid of Egypt, if solid, to weigh in accordance with the estimate before given 6,000,000 tons, we may state that the rock added to the continent by the Chilian earthquake would have equalled more than 100,000 pyramids.

"But it must always be borne in mind that the weight of rock here alluded to constituted but an insignificant part of the whole amount which the volcanic forces had to overcome. The thickness of rock between the surface of Chile and the subterranean foci of volcanic action may be many miles or leagues deep. Say that the thickness was only two miles, even then the mass which changed place and rose three feet, being 200,000 cubic miles in volume, must have exceeded in weight 363,000,000 pyramids."

The shocks of this earthquake continued from the time of its occurrence, on November 19th, 1822, to the end of September, 1823, and even then there were scarcely two days that passed without a shock.

[Pg 272]

On the 20th of February, 1835, the same part of the world was in the throes of an earthquake that was felt nearly 1,000 miles from north to south, or from near the town of Concepcion to the Isle of Chiloe, and from east to west a distance of about 500 miles, from Mendoza to the island of Juan Fernandez, which you probably know better as Robinson Crusoe's Island. By this earthquake the new town of Concepcion and several other towns were partly destroyed.

There were the same phenomena connected with great sea waves that are common in earthquakes of this character. Both this and the preceding earthquakes probably began on the bed of the ocean at some distance from the coast; for, in the last earthquake, the sea retired from the Bay of Concepcion and vessels were grounded that had been anchored in seven fathoms of water. Shortly afterwards waves from sixteen to twenty feet in height rushed in from the ocean and swept over the land.

It is interesting in this connection to note that the volcanoes of the Chilian Andes were in an unusual state of activity before, during, and after the earthquake.

Another characteristic of this quake was the great number of severe shocks. Between the day of the first great shock; i. e., on February 20th, 1835, and March 4th, there were more than 300 severe shocks.

In this as in the preceding quake a notable elevation of the land near the coast occurred, amounting to from four to five feet, and a part of the bed of the ocean near the coast was raised permanently above the level of the sea.

In the description of the explosive eruption of Krakatoa in 1883, the fact was noted that the island of Java is very frequently visited by earthquakes. Here a terribly severe earthquake occurred on the 5th of[Pg 273] January, 1699. There were no less than 208 shocks of great intensity. Considerable property in the city of Batavia was destroyed, and a neighboring river, that has its head waters by a volcano near the city, ran high and muddy and brought down multitudes of fishes that had been killed, together with many buffaloes, tigers, rhinoceroses, deer, and other wild beasts. Seven hills bordering on the river sank down, damming up the streams of the region and thereby causing wide destruction from floods.

During portions of the years 1811 and 1812 an earthquake occurred in the United States, in the Mississippi Valley near the town of New Madrid, Missouri, at the mouth of the Ohio River. These shocks continued almost incessantly for several months, and were accompanied by a sinking of the ground over large areas. This depressed area, known in the neighborhood as *The Sunk Country*, extended along the course of the White Water River and its tributaries for a distance of about eighty miles from north to south, and several miles from east to west. Most of it was converted into a marshy lake characterized by thousands of submerged trees. The area was covered for the greater part with water to a depth of about three to four feet.

As the earthquake shocks continued at intervals for several months there was an ample opportunity for studying the peculiarities of the earth waves. The ground rose and fell like large waves in the sea, and after the crest of the waves had reached great heights, the ground burst, and threw large quantities of water, sand, and earth into the air.

[Pg 274]

FIG. 48. NEW ZEALAND

Throughout the disturbed district there were numerous depressions known as *sink-holes*, or irregularly shaped pits, varying from ten to thirty yards across, and having a depth of about twenty feet. These were formed by[Pg 275] the forcible ejection of large quantities of water mixed with sand.

New Zealand has been subject to earthquake shocks for a long time, the years 1826, 1841, 1843, 1848, and 1855 being especially marked by such visitations. It is a characteristic of the New Zealand earthquakes that they have produced a marked change in the coast line. This was particularly the case with those of 1848 and 1855.

The 23d of January, 1855, an earthquake occurred that was most violent in the narrowest part of Cook's Strait, a body of water separating the two principal islands that constitute New Zealand; or, as they are called, the North Island and the South Island. These shocks were felt at sea by ships 150 miles from the coast. The entire area shaken, including the water, has been estimated at three times the area of the British Isles. In the vicinity of the southern shores of the North Island a tract of land having an area of 4,600 square miles is believed to have been permanently raised from one to nine feet.

The earthquakes in New Zealand are evidently of the tectonic type. During that of 1848 a rent or fissure was formed, which, though but eighteen inches in average width, yet extended for a distance of sixty miles in a direction parallel to one of the mountain chains.

On the 31st of August, 1886, an earthquake of considerable intensity occurred in the United States in the neighborhood of the city of Charleston, South Carolina. The details of this earthquake were carefully studied by Major Dutton of the U. S. A., and published in the Ninth Annual Report of the United States Geological Survey of 1888.

Charleston is situated on a narrow tongue of land between the Ashley and the Cooper Rivers, about seven miles from the Atlantic Ocean. There are in this area[Pg 276] numerous creeks connected with the drainage of these rivers. As the city limits extended, the creeks were filled in, forming "made land," all buildings or structures erected on this land being supported by pilings.

It appears that the point at which the earthquakes started was situated sixteen or seventeen miles from Charleston.

The earthquake shock affected a large area of the United States. Fig. 49 shows curved lines called isoseismal connecting places, having the same degree of seismic intensity. This map shows that these isoseimals are marked by figures or numbers from two to ten. These numbers are the numbers of the Rossi-Forel earthquake scale. They indicate varying degrees of intensity, beginning from the least intense shock which is marked as two and ending with the severest shock marked as ten. There is one degree not marked on this map, the least, called the micro-seismic shock.

The shocks then increase in intensity as follows: II. Extremely feeble shocks; III. Very feeble shocks; IV. Feeble shocks; V. Shocks of moderate intensity; VI. Fairly strong shocks; VII. Strong shocks; VIII. Very strong shocks; IX. Extremely strong shocks; X. Shocks of extreme intensity.

The meaning of the map presented in the accompanying figure will now become more apparent in several ways. That portion numbered ten, denoting where shocks of greatest intensity have been experienced, clearly indicates the region just above the point where the earthquake originated.

Beyond this is a region marked nine where the earthquake shock has decreased in intensity to the next figure on the Rossi-Forel scale, and then to eight and a half, seven, six, five, four, three, and two.

[Pg 277]

FIG. 49. MAP SHOWING REGION AFFECTED BY THE CHARLESTON EARTHQUAKE OF 1886

The Charleston earthquake damaged property to a[Pg 278] considerable extent; for, although comparatively few buildings were completely destroyed, a considerable number were partially injured, and many, not thrown down by the shock, had to be torn down in order to insure public safety. The loss of life, fortunately, was comparatively small. During this earthquake a number of openings called *craterlets* were made in the ground by the forcible ejection of large quantities of water and sand.

The empire of Japan is another part of the world particularly subject to great as well as frequent earthquake shocks. Although Japan is also especially noted for its volcanic activity, its earthquakes are almost entirely of the tectonic type, or are due to the slipping of the land at faults in the earth's crust. Most of these quakes occur on the bed of the ocean on the sides of a steep slope that extends down to a very deep part of the Pacific known as the *Tuscarora Deep*.

On the 28th of October, 1891, Japan was visited by a great quake, generally known as the Mino-Owaro earthquake, from the name of the two provinces of Mino and Owaro in which it occurred.

This earthquake is correctly regarded as one of the most severe in Japanese records. Originating, as it did, in a densely populated section, it caused a great loss of life and property. The deaths reached about 7,000, while the number of houses entirely destroyed reached about 80,000 and those partly destroyed nearly 200,000. The total area markedly affected reached 250,000 square kilometres, while the area sensibly affected reached 900,000 square kilometres, or a little more than one-half the Empire.

The place at which this earthquake started was situated, not as usual on the bed of the ocean, but on the surface of the land. The first shock was the strongest and wrought[Pg 279]the greatest havoc. Besides the loss of life and property, the damage to the system of dikes or levees on the river where it passed through the delta plain near the river's mouth was heavy, and singular in some of its features. In one case, near the city of Nagoya, on the Bay near the southern coast of Niphon, one of these levees was lifted and shifted bodily more than sixty feet from its original position.

That this quake was of the tectonic type was evident from the great fault that was formed. According to Davison this fault was seventy miles in length and in places had a breadth of from two to five feet. It extended from east to west, crossing the entire width of the island.

Another great earthquake was that which hit northeastern Bengal and Assam in India on the 12th of June, 1897. According to the India Geological Survey, by whom a careful examination of the effects produced by this quake was made, it was, perhaps, the greatest quake that ever happened, not even excepting the Lisbon earthquake.

The place where the quake started appears to have been of unusual size and irregularity of outline. Its southern boundary was almost in the shape of a straight line extending from east to west about 200 miles, and covering a total area of nearly 6,000 square miles. Over all this vast area the intensity of the shock was exceedingly severe. The total area perceptibly shaken by the quake was about equal to 1,750,000 square miles.

That this quake was of the tectonic type became evident, when several faults were found in the ground afterwards. Some of these extended twelve miles, with a breadth at places as great as thirty feet.

Valparaiso, or, as the name means, Vale of Paradise, the second largest city of Chile and its chief seaport, lies[Pg 280] about ninety miles east of Santiago, the capital, with which it is connected by a railroad.

This beautiful sea city is built at the base of a cluster of hills about 1,600 feet above sea level. On August 16th, 1906, it was visited by an earthquake. There were two distinct shocks. Contrary to general rule it was not the first, but the second shock that did the most damage, coming about ten minutes after the first. As you will see from the above date the earthquake of Valparaiso occurred shortly after the catastrophe of San Francisco. In a general way, its coming was predicted by Dr. G. F. Becker of the United States Geological Survey, on April 19th, 1906, one day after the San Francisco disaster. Becker published an article in the "New York Tribune," in which he argued that the severe shock at San Francisco, having occurred on one part of the earthquake region extending around the Pacific, would probably soon affect other portions of this region along the Pacific coast line of this hemisphere.

As at San Francisco fierce fires immediately started in the ruins of the houses, but the Valparaisans were more fortunate in having a water supply available.

There were very many shocks following the first two of this earthquake. Indeed, during August 16th, 17th, 18th, and 19th, no less than 380 were noted.

Santiago, situated at the foot of the Andes, was also considerably damaged by the same earthquake. Estimates, probably conservative, put the total of dead in both cities at 1,000 and the number of people rendered homeless temporarily, at 100,000.

[Pg 281]

CHAPTER XXX

SODOM AND GOMORRAH AND THE CITIES OF THE PLAIN

The eastern border of the Mediterranean Sea or Syria, with that part of Arabia forming the Sinai Peninsula and which lies between the two northern arms of the Red Sea, is a region formerly characterized by extreme volcanic activity. This region includes the greater part of the land promised, according to the Old Testament, to the Children of Israel. Through a large part of this region flows that historic river, the Jordan, until it empties into the Dead Sea, also called the Salt Sea, the Sea of the Plain, and by some Lake Asphaltites because of asphalt or bitumen so abundant on its shores. This river has its source in the Mountains of Lebanon, some distance north of the Sea of Chinnerth, Tiberius, or the Sea of Galilee, which empties into the River Jordan.

As the map in Fig. 50 shows, this famous, though small river, flows between ranges of high hills, or low mountains, that lie on both its eastern and western boundaries; and these parallel ranges extend down to the Gulf of Akaba, which forms the eastern boundary of the Sinai Peninsula. The Sea of Galilee, the valley of the Jordan and the country between the Dead Sea and the Gulf of Akaba, are all, for the most part, considerably below the level of the Mediterranean or the Red Sea; the Sea of Galilee being about 626 feet and the Dead Sea 1312 feet below that line.

[Pg 282]

FIG. 50. SYRIA

That this country has been the scene of great volcanic[Pg 283] activities is evident from the volcanic rocks found over different portions of its surface. Moreover, the remains of several craters are still visible. On the western banks of the Jordan numerous dikes and streaks of basalt occur in the limestone that covers parts of the region. Besides there are thermal springs whose waters are at a temperature, according to Daubeny, of 114° F. Then, too, in the neighborhood of the Dead Sea, as well as in the neighborhood of the adjoining mountain ranges, there are quantities of sulphur and asphaltum or bitumen, while on the Dead Sea asphaltum is found floating in sufficient quantity to be a source of considerable revenue to the boatmen who collect it. It was in this region that Sodom, Gomorrah, and other cities of the plain were situated; cities so wicked that God utterly destroyed them by volcanoes and earthquakes.

Volcanic activity was evidently common in this land of the Bible during the times of the prophets of Israel; for in their poetic writings are frequent references to such phenomena—beautiful and majestic similes and metaphors derived from contemplation of live volcanoes.

Jeremiah says:

"Behold, I am against thee, O devouring mountain, saith the Lord, which destroyeth all the earth; and I will stretch out mine hand upon thee, and roll thee down from the rocks, and will make thee a burnt[1] mountain.

"And they shall not take of thee a stone for a corner, nor a stone for foundations; but thou shalt be desolate forever, saith the Lord." (Jer. li, 25-26.)

So, too, the prophet Isaiah says:

"Oh that thou wouldst rend the heavens, that thou wouldst come down, that the mountains might flow down at thy presence!

[Pg 284]

"As when the melting fire burneth, the fire causeth the water to boil, to make thy name known to thine adversaries, that the nations may tremble at thy presence!

"When thou didst terrible things which we look not for, thou cameth down, the mountains flowed down at thy presence." (Is. lxiv, 1-2.)

So, too, the prophet Nahum says:

"The mountains quake at him, and the hills melt, and the earth is burned at his presence, yea, the world, and all that dwell therein.

"Who can stand before his indignation? And who can abide in the fierceness of his anger? His fury is poured down like fire, and the rocks are thrown down by him." (Nahum, i, 5-6.)

Let us now examine briefly the description Moses gives of the destruction of Sodom, Gomorrah, and other cities of the plain. This destruction occurred during the life time of Abraham and his nephew Lot. The record says that God told Abraham He intended to destroy them because of their wickedness. Then follows in the 18th chapter of Genesis the eloquent pleading of Abraham for one of the doomed cities. At Abraham's earnest plea God promises to spare Sodom if fifty righteous men can be found therein. Obtaining this respite, Abraham repeatedly asks further mercy for the city, and at last receives the sacred promise that the city shall not be destroyed, if but ten righteous people can be found there. An evidence of the great wickedness of the city is seen in the fact that not even ten could be found. Whereupon the Lord gives notice to Lot that the cities were doomed and commands Lot to leave at once with his family.

"Escape for thy life; look not behind thee, neither stay thou in all the plain; escape to the mountain, lest thou be consumed!"

[Pg 285]

Moses describes what happened as follows:

"The sun was risen upon the earth, when Lot entered into Zoar.

"Then the Lord rained upon Sodom and upon Gomorrah brimstone and fire from the Lord out of heaven;

"And he overthrew those cities and all the plain, and all the inhabitants of the cities, and that which grew upon the ground.

"But his wife looked back from behind him, and she became a pillar of salt.

"And Abraham gat up early in the morning to the place where he stood before the Lord:

"And he looked toward Sodom and Gomorrah, and toward all the land of the plain, and beheld, and lo, the smoke of the country went up as the smoke of a furnace." (Gen. xix, 23-28).

This is clearly the description of a volcanic eruption, for throughout the Bible things are described as they appear to be. When Moses speaks of brimstone and fire being rained upon Sodom and Gomorrah out of heaven, he is describing the phenomenon as it would appear to one looking at it. Of course, we know that in volcanic eruptions such things come to the earth through the crater of the volcano. The lava is thrown high into the air, and the hardening, but still red hot, ashes, rain down on the earth from the ash cloud that forms over the mountain. But, looked at from a distance they appear to fall or be rained down from the skies. In exactly the same way, Livy, the Roman historian, tells about showers of stones that fell from heaven on Mt. Albano near Rome for two whole days during the second Punic War. So, too, even Pliny, who had some pretensions to be considered a naturalist, in describing the appearance of Mt. Vesuvius during the terrible eruption of A. D. 79, when Herculaneum[Pg 286] and Pompeii were destroyed, speaks of the red hot stones and ashes as falling from above. So, in reality, they did, although, as in the case of the cities of the plain, the materials forming the cloud came from the crater of the volcano below.

As to brimstone falling from the sky, this is by no means an unusual occurrence during many volcanic eruptions, since sulphur is a common material, often thrown out of the craters of some volcanoes.

Note also the statement that, when Abraham rose early in the morning and looked toward the place where Sodom and Gomorrah stood, he saw the smoke of the country go up like the smoke of a furnace. This was, probably, the smoke caused by the burning of the city, or even by the destruction of the crops in their fields, when ignited by the falling red hot ashes. It might also have been partly due to the burning of asphalt thrown out from the fissures in the ground, or to the showers of volcanic ashes that fell from the cloud formed during the eruption.

That the cities there were destroyed by a volcano far in the past appears from things outside of the Bible proper; for Strabo, the Greek geographer, refers to Jewish traditions that thirteen flourishing cities were swallowed up by a volcano, and this finds fair corroboration in the ruins along the western borders of the Dead Sea.

A writer referring to these eruptions says:

"The eruptions themselves have ceased long since, but the effects, which usually succeed them, still continue to be felt at intervals in this country. The coast in general is subject to earthquakes, and history notes several which have changed the face of Antioch, Laodicea, Tripoli, Berytus, Tyre, and Sidon. In 1793 there happened one which spread the greatest ravages. It is said[Pg 287] to have destroyed in the valley of Balbec upwards of 20,000 persons."

Attention has already been called to the fact that the valley of the Jordan occupies a depressed or sunken region far below the level of the Mediterranean and the Red Seas. It is the belief of some geologists that this depression was caused by an earthquake which accompanied the volcanic eruption that destroyed Sodom and Gomorrah and the cities of the plain. Indeed, some contend that the present site of the valley of the Jordan, including the Sea of Tiberius and the Dead Sea, is a great fissure that was made in the limestone of the valley during the time of that earthquake.

It would appear from the peculiar geography of this section of country that the Jordan River has not always emptied into the Dead Sea, but that before the time of the destruction of the Cities of the Plain the greater part of the country now occupied by the Dead Sea was a fertile valley, and the Jordan emptied directly into the Red Sea at the Gulf of Akaba; that during the disturbance through changes in the valley, or possibly by a lava stream flowing across a portion of the bed of the lower Jordan, or even by a huge accumulation of stones or ashes thrown out from a neighboring volcano, the discharge of the river into the Red Sea was cut off, and that in this way the waters of the rivers began to accumulate and to flow over the plain, thus forming the basin of the Dead Sea.

There is no difficulty in accounting for the saltness of the Dead Sea. There are large quantities of salt, and salty matters generally, in the volcanic rocks of the region, but, even if this were not so, when a river empties into a lake with no outlet to the sea, and which therefore loses its water by evaporation only, the water will gradually become very salt, since the remaining waters of such a[Pg 288] lake contain more or less salt, while the water they lose by evaporation contains none.

The waters of the Dead Sea are very salt, but not the saltest in the world. In every 100 pounds of Dead Sea water twenty-four pounds consist of salty matters. The waters of the Great Salt Lake, in Utah, contain eighteen per cent of salty matters. Lake Van, in eastern Turkey, is, perhaps, the saltest lake on earth, it containing no less than thirty-three pounds of salty substances in every 100 pounds of water.

Daubeny, an authority on volcanoes, and quite competent to give an opinion concerning what is possible in this line, describes what he believes took place, as follows:

"Briefly then to recapitulate the train of phenomena by which the destruction of the cities might have been brought about, I would suppose that the River Jordan, prior to that event, continued its course tranquilly through the great longitudinal valley, called El Arabah, into the Gulf of Akaba; that a shower of stones and sand from some neighboring volcano first overwhelmed these places; and that its eruption was followed by a depression of the whole of the region, from some point apparently intermediate between the lake of Tiberius and the mountains of Lebanon, to the watershed in the parallel of 30°, which occurs in the valley of El Arabah above-mentioned. I would thence infer that the waters of the Jordan, pent-up within the valley by a range of mountains to the east and west, and a barrier of elevated table-land to the south, could find no outlet, and consequently by degrees formed a lake in its most depressed portion, which, however, did not occur at once, and therefore is not recorded by Scripture as a part of the catastrophe, though reference is made in another passage of its existence *in what was before the valley of Siddim*."

[Pg 289]

As regards the turning of Lot's wife into a pillar of salt, Henderson, who has carefully studied this part of the country, remarks: "How natural is the incrustation of his wife on this hypothesis! Remaining in a lower part of the valley, and looking with a wistful eye towards Sodom, she was surrounded, ere she was aware, by the lava, which rising and swelling, at length reached her, and (whilst the volcanic effluvia deprived her of life) incrusted her where she stood, so that being, as it were, embalmed by the salso-bituminous mass, she became a conspicuous beacon and admonitory example of future generations."

[Pg 290]

CHAPTER XXXI

INSTRUMENTS FOR RECORDING AND MEASURING EARTHQUAKE SHOCKS

To attempt by the unaided senses a determination of the direction in which earthquake shocks reach any certain spot, the velocity with which they are travelling, their degree of intensity, their general character, whether horizontal or vertical, or any peculiarities which might show them to be exceptional would be futile for more reasons than one. Even a skilled scientific observer, familiar with what has already been discovered and eager to discover more, might in the excitement of an earthquake become so excited himself as to make him unable to take reliable observations.

But human ingenuity has succeeded in devising delicate instruments capable of recording not only the exact time of the arrival of an earthquake shock, but also of measuring the different parts of what may seem to be a single shock, the direction in which the shocks reach the place, as well as the variations of intensity in all the shocks.

Crude instruments to do some of these things have been in use from very early times. According to Mallet among the more important of these early instruments was the following: the instrument of Cacciatore of Palmero. This consisted of a circular wooden dish, about ten inches in diameter, placed horizontally, and filled with mercury to the brim of eight notches at equal distances apart. Beneath each notch was placed a small cup. On the passage[Pg 291] of the earthquake waves the vessel, being tilted in a direction dependent on the direction in which the waves were travelling, would cause some of the mercury to spill over into one or more of the cups, thus indicating by its amount the intensity of the wave, and by the particular cup or cups that were filled, the direction in which the waves reached the place.

Somewhat similar contrivances were of a vessel partly filled with molasses, or other sticky liquid; or a cylindrical tub, the sides of which were chalked or whitewashed and filled with some colored liquid. In either of these cases, on the passage of the earthquake waves, the vessels were tilted and showed by the height of the marks the intensity of the waves, and by the position of the marks the direction in which the waves first reached the instrument.

These instruments, though satisfactory for the study of earthquake shocks a long time ago, when an earthquake was regarded as practically consisting of but a single shock, or, at the most, of a very few shocks, would be worthless for the study of earthquakes now, for it is finally known that an earthquake consists of a series of many hundreds of vibrations, differing greatly in their rapidity and intensity, and following one another in a definite order.

The old forms of earthquake instruments were known as *seismoscopes*. The word seismoscope is a compound word from Greek consisting of the two words, seism and scope. It means literally any instrument capable of seeing, or calling attention to, a seism, or *earth-shake*. In other words, a seismoscope is any instrument capable of calling attention only to an earth-shake.

Of course, neither of the rude seismoscopes just mentioned would be able to give any valuable indications of the successive shakings to which the vessel containing the[Pg 292]viscid liquid had been subjected, since the liquid would simply be splashed a number of times over the same parts of the vessel. In order to get a record of the successive shocks another form of apparatus must be employed, a form known as a *seismograph*.

Concerning the complex character of the apparently single earthquake shock, Professor Milne makes this highly interesting and picturesque statement:

"An earthquake disturbance at a station far removed from its origin shows that the main movement has two attendants, one which precedes and the other which follows. The first of these by its characteristics indicates what is to follow, whilst the latter, in a very much more pronounced manner, will often repeat at definite intervals, but with decreasing intensity, the prominent features of what has passed. Inasmuch as these latter rhythmical, but decreasing, impulses of the dying earthquake are more likely to result from reflection than from interference, I have provisionally called them Echoes."

There are many different forms of instruments known as seismographs that are capable of recording all of these vibrations, but there is this objection to their use: that the records appear in so tangled a form that it is practically impossible to decipher or untangle them. This fact can be grasped by examining Fig. 51, which represents a record of this kind.

FIG. 51. COMPLEX RECORD OF SEISMOGRAPH

It is necessary, therefore, to employ a modified form of instrument called a*seismometer*, able not only to record all the different vibrations, but to record them in such a manner that they can be easily recognized. Fig. 52, for example, shows results obtained by the use of a seismometer, in which the different vibrations are separated, and so recorded on a sheet of paper, as to be readily understood. Such a record is called a *seismogram*, and[Pg 293] represents a *long distance seismogram*. Here the large arrow indicates the beginning of the record. And herein, as can be clearly seen, what would appear to an observer without an instrument only a single shock, lasting but the fraction of a minute, in reality consists of the *preliminary shake* as represented in ab and bc, the *principal shake*, as represented at c, d1, d2, and d3, and the *final portions of the shake* or the "echoes" of Professor Milne, as represented from d3 to e.

FIG. 52. LONG DISTANCE SEISMOGRAM

Except in a very general way there is for present purposes no need of explaining the construction and operation of the seismometer and seismograph. Suffice it to say, there are many forms of these instruments, any of[Pg 294] which are capable of recording the details of a passing shock. The most important thing in either a seismograph or a seismometer is to obtain what is known as a *steady point*, that is, a point consisting of some object or mass that will remain practically at rest, while everything around it, even the support which holds it, is affected by the earthquake.

It is, of course, not very easy to obtain a steady point, but it can be done; and it will be at once comprehended that if a plate or piece of paper were attached to such a steady point or mass, and a pencil or tracer had one of its ends resting on the plate, and its other end attached to the support that vibrates with the earth, a tracing or record would be drawn on the plate from which the character of the motion of the end of the tracer, and, therefore, of the earth, would be marked on the plate.

FIG. 53. VICENTINI VERTICAL PENDULUM

Various devices have been employed for the steady points. The most successful consists of a heavy mass of lead.

[Pg 295]

Fig. 53 represents a form of instrument invented by Professor Vicentini of Italy. Here the steady point consists of a heavy leaden bob, of 200, 400, or even 500 kilograms, suspended by three metallic rods united above by a brass cap, hung on a steel wire to a bracket fixed on the wall. This wire may have a length as great as fifty feet.

FIG. 54. VICENTINI PENDULUM AND RECORDER

Fig. 54 represents the recording instrument. Here a tracer is provided that is capable of multiplying the motion fifty times, or even eighty times. A record is traced on a sheet of paper passing over a roller which imparts a rapid motion to a sheet so as to make sure that the different parts of the shock or vibration will be recorded on separate portions of the paper.

[Pg 296]

CHAPTER XXXII

SEAQUAKES

As earthquakes are shakings of the earth's crust in places where it is uncovered by the waters of the ocean, so *seaquakes* are the shakings of those portions that lie on the bed of the ocean.

Mallet points out that the earthquake wave may start either in the interior of the continent, or on the bed of the ocean; that the latter place is the more common, since on the land vents—rude safety-valves, as it were,—are provided by the craters of the volcanoes; that, when earthquakes start on the ocean bed, the impulses are conveyed in different forms of waves, i. e., those through the solid earth, those through the water, and those through the air, with varying sounds like bellowings and explosions, or like the rolling of wagons over rough roads.

To learn when quakes occur on the sea is a much harder task, since on the land we can use seismoscopes, seismographs, or seismometers to indicate, record, or measure the shakings of the crust, while on the sea, where the water is always in more or less motion and the surface so far from the ocean's bed this is impossible, or, rather shall it be said, has hitherto been found so; for that the mind of man may surmount this obstacle is not impossible to conceive.

To detect the wave produced by the quaking of the bed of the ocean is exceedingly difficult, since those in very deep water are flat or possess but a small height. Indeed,[Pg 297] in the deepest parts of the ocean this height is probably to be measured only by inches instead of feet. When, however, the waves advance towards the shore they increase in height, and when they reach the shallows near the coast, they begin to curl over and break, thus creating the enormous waves mentioned so often as attending great earthquakes in the ocean.

During the great earthquake of Simoda in Japan, 1854, the waters of the bay were first greatly agitated, and then retreated, leaving the bottom bare in places where the water was formerly thirty feet deep. A wave, thirty feet high, then rushed in from the bay and, climbing the land, swept away everything in its path, covering the town with water to the tops of the houses. This monster wave then receded, but rushed back five times.

In 1751, an earthquake wave suddenly entered Callao, the port of Lima, Peru, sinking twenty-three vessels and driving a frigate inland, where it was left high and dry. This wave extended across the Pacific to the Hawaiian Islands, a distance of 6,000 miles.

On the 13th of August, 1866, an earthquake wave, that started a short distance from shore, produced a number of earthquake waves sixty feet high that reached the coast of Peru half an hour after the principal earthquake shock. These waves reached Coquimbo, 800 miles distant, in about three hours, and Honolulu, on the Sandwich Islands, 5,520 miles distant, in twelve hours, and the coast of Japan, more than 10,000 miles distant, on the next day. Le Conte remarks that these waves would have encircled the earth, had it not been for the barrier interposed by the Andes.

Another great seaquake, known as the Iquiqui seaquake, during 1868 in the same neighborhood damaged severely the towns of north Chile and southern Peru.

[Pg 298]

While, however, there is difficulty in readily observing the earthquake waves that form in the deep ocean, yet such is at times the violence of an earthquake that there is no difficulty in detecting its presence, even in deep water. Dr. Rudolph has made a careful study of the evidences of earthquakes produced in the deep sea, from a careful examination of a great number of the logs of ships. Logs, as everybody knows, are books in which the captain or commanding officer makes careful entries of all important happenings to the vessel, conditions of the weather and of the sea. From this source Dr. Rudolph obtained considerable information of much value concerning these phenomena.

I have already called your attention to portion of the Atlantic Ocean lying near the Equator, in the warmest part of the ocean, between Africa and South America, as being a region especially liable to submarine volcanic showers. While, generally speaking, there is nothing in this region to indicate the probability of submarine disturbance, yet suddenly, if a vessel happens to pass directly over the point of origin of the quake, there ensues a great quaking or quivering. Loose objects on the ship begin to shake and clatter. Noises arise from some invisible point deep down in the ocean. The disturbance grows, the noises begin to resemble distant thunder, the ship trembles and staggers as though it had struck rocks, and many believe she is about to go down; when, as suddenly as it began, the commotion ceases, the noises stop, and the ship shapes her course as calmly, and as gallantly, as before.

Rudolph gives two excellent examples of seaquakes in this region, both of which were, doubtless, due to submarine eruptions.

On the 25th of January, 1859, as the ship *Florence* was[Pg 299] in lat. 0° 48' N., long. 29° 16' W., about ten miles N. W. by N. from St. Paul's Rock, the people on board felt a sudden shock that began with a rumbling sound like distant thunder. This lasted only forty seconds. The glass and dishes of the vessel rattled so violently that it was feared they would be broken. The shakings were so strong that several objects on the vessel were thrown down. Everyone believed the ship had struck on rocks. The captain leaned over the taffrail in order to see the position of the reef, but soon saw that the vessel had struck nothing, and informed his crew "it was only an earthquake shock."

Another of the log books examined by Rudolph was that of a ship in the same part of the Atlantic Ocean. This record showed that suddenly on a morning, in 1883, strange noises were heard that soon increased and became not unlike the firing of great guns or the peals of distant thunder. The ship vibrated as if its anchor had been suddenly let go, and at the same time a feeling came over all the crew, as if they had been electrified.

In some cases the vibrations were sufficiently severe to throw heavy objects from the deck, as appears in an account given by a French geologist of a quake in the Mediterranean off the shores of Asia Minor.

"Our ship was over the epicentre,"[5] he says, "and was so severely shaken that at first the Admiral feared the complete destruction of the corvette." He then makes the statement that the shocks which were directly upwards were so strong as to throw heavy objects in the air; for example, a heavy gun and its carriage. While it is possible, as Dutton remarks, that this incident of the heavy gun and carriage was grossly exaggerated, yet it[Pg 300] should not be forgotten that in the case of submarine eruptions such as that which resulted in the production of the island of Sabrina, an immense column of water, weighing probably many times more than a gun and its carriage, was observed to be shot high into the air.

Where the seaquake is produced by a strong submarine volcanic eruption, there is a violent commotion of the water itself, so that a vessel passing over such a point may be greatly injured, and, indeed, even destroyed. Such disasters, however, are fortunately exceedingly rare.

Among other common effects of seaquakes is the destruction of fish already mentioned by the sudden blow to the water stunning and killing them, just as the explosion of dynamite or other high explosives does in a lake or pond.

The most marked effect, however, of seaquakes is the starting of the great wave on the coasts of continents and islands.

There are certain parts of the ocean that are especially liable to seaquakes. Some of the more important of these, as shown by Rudolph's researches, are:

The region already referred to in the narrowest parts of the Atlantic Ocean between Africa and South America almost immediately under the equator. Here there are two well marked regions. One is in lat. 1° N., long. 30° W., where there is a submarine ridge, the tops of which form what are known as St. Paul's Rock. The ocean here is very deep, the slopes of the ridge descending rapidly. It is on these slopes that earthquakes are very apt to occur just as they do on the steep slopes of mountain ranges. The other region, called by Rudolph the *Equatorial District*, lies a little further to the east on both sides of the equator in long. 20° W.

[Pg 301]

It appears from Rudolph's researches that between 1845 and 1893 no less than thirty-seven seaquakes were reported in the logs of ships in the neighborhood of St. Paul's Rock, and between 1747 and 1890, in the equatorial district, there were forty-nine seaquakes. It must not be supposed, however, that these were all the quakes in the regions during these times, since, of course, many shocks must have happened that were not felt even by vessels in the neighborhood and many more, when this portion of the ocean was free from any craft.

In the North Atlantic there is a portion of the ocean's bed known as the *West Indies Deep*. Here the bed is marked by great depths and by many irregularities and is, therefore, a region where seaquakes are common.

Still another district is found in the North Atlantic in the neighborhood of the Azores. This is the region in which the Lisbon earthquake is believed to have started.

Another region where seaquakes are common is in the Pacific along the coast of South America from the equator to 45° S. lat. "Here," says Dutton, "especially in the vicinity of the angle where the Peruvian and Chilian coasts meet have they been most numerous and formidable. The harbors of Pisco, Arica, Tacua, Iquiqui, and Pisago have been repeatedly subject to these destructive invasions."

There has been considerable discussion as to the exact manner in which the earthquake waves are set up. Whatever be the cause or causes, the action must be sudden, such as an upheaval of the bottom, or a collapse of a large section of the ocean's bed, with a dropping of a vast body of water. Or, possibly, a submarine volcanic eruption causes the water to lift suddenly under pressure of steam generated by escape of the lava and other hot volcanic products.

[Pg 302]

Dr. Rudolph attributes earthquake waves to submarine volcanic eruptions alone. It would seem, however, as if each one of the other things above referred to might at times be the direct cause.

CHAPTER XXXIII

THE DISTRIBUTION OF EARTHQUAKES

Earthquakes may occur at any part of the earth's surface, at any time of the day, or at any season of the year, yet they are more frequent at certain parts, certain hours, certain seasons.

Since some earthquakes are unquestionably connected with volcanic eruptions, a map or chart of the volcanoes of the earth would also, to a certain extent, show the parts of the earth that are likely to be visited by earthquakes. Since, however, by far the most severe earthquakes are not directly connected with volcanoes, but are due to sudden slips of faulted strata, a volcanic chart would necessarily fail to indicate accurately the principal earthquake regions.

In the preparation of a map showing the distribution of earthquakes over the earth's surface, Mallet adopted the plan of colorings or tintings in such a manner that the depth of the colors would represent not only the parts shaken, but also the relative number of times shaken, as well as the intensity of the shocks. In order to determine the depth of tint to be employed, Mallet divided earthquakes into the following classes according to their intensity:

Great earthquakes, or earthquakes of the first class; or those in which the area affected is of great size, in which many cities have been overthrown, and many people killed, and parts of the surface greatly altered.

[Pg 304]

Intermediate earthquakes, or those in which, although the area affected is great, yet the destruction of buildings, or loss of life, has been comparatively small.

Minor earthquakes, or those which, although capable of producing small fissures in the crust, generally leave but few or no traces of their occurrence.

The greatest distance to which earthquake waves of the first class extend is taken by Mallet as being over a diameter of 1,080 miles; those of the second class over a diameter of about 360 miles, and those of the third class over a diameter of about 120 miles.

According to the Rossi Forel scale already given, earthquake shocks are divided according to their relative intensity into ten separate classes, viz.: I. The micro-seismic; II. The extremely feeble; III. The very feeble; IV. The feeble; V. The moderately intense; VI. The fairly strong; VII. The strong; VIII. The very strong; IX. The extremely strong; X. Shocks of extreme intensity.

An earthquake map prepared according to Mallet's scale would show a greater depth of color or tint in the neighborhood of the volcanic districts of the earth and especially in the neighborhood of the mountain regions, where tectonic quakes are most frequent. Oceanic areas would be left almost untinted, not because earthquakes do not occur on the bed of the ocean, but because of the difficulty of observing such earthquakes at great distances from the land. So far from earthquakes being absent on the bed of the ocean it is most probable that they are more frequent there than elsewhere.

Prepared in this way, Mallet's map would show a preponderance of earthquakes along the borders of the continents, especially along the "Great Circle of Fire" on the borders of the Pacific Ocean.

[Pg 305]

Dutton as well as some others assert that the "Great Circle of Fire" on the shores of the Pacific has in reality no existence; that, instead of there being a continuous region of volcanoes, there is in reality nothing more than a considerable number of volcanoes arranged in groups along the borders of this ocean, but separated by spaces containing no marked volcanic activity. We do not think this a tenable position, since it is well known that volcanoes lie along great lines of fissures at different points or openings which are kept open by subsequent volcanic activity, while the remaining portions are closed soon afterwards; and, moreover, in parts of these so-called non-volcanic regions, there are probably extended regions of extinct volcanoes.

Since the time of Mallet many maps have been made to show the distribution of earthquakes. Among the best of such is that by M. de Montessus de Ballore.

Some idea of the great amount of work required for the preparation of Montessus' map may be formed when one learns that the catalogue of earthquakes collected by him for this purpose included for the years 1880 to 1900, 131,292 quakes.

De Montessus' earthquake map divides the grand divisions of the earth into numerous sub-divisions, too numerous, indeed, for even brief description in a work of this kind. From the map he thus laboriously prepared De Montessus drew the following general conclusions:

1. The parts of the earth that are most apt to be shaken by earthquakes are those which possess the greatest differences of relief between their highlands and lowlands, and that in such regions the most pronounced earthquakes are found on the steepest slopes.

2. Earthquakes are most common along those parts of the crust that are thrown up in huge wrinkles, or mountain[Pg 306] ranges, whether these masses be above the level of the sea or are covered by it.

FIG. 55. DAVISON'S EARTHQUAKE MAP OF JAPAN

3. Earthquakes are more common in mountainous districts than in plains. But not all mountains are characterized by earthquakes nor are all plains free from them. Sometimes the plain at the base of the mountain appears[Pg 307] to be especially liable to shocks, probably by reason of slips along faults at these points.

The great mountain ranges of the world are generally characterized by unequal slopes, the long gentle slope facing the interior of the continents, and the short, abrupt slopes being turned towards the coast. Now, Montessus points out that volcanoes are the most frequent on the short, abrupt slopes. In some cases, however, where the long slopes are the roughest, it is these slopes that are most frequently shaken.

The beds of the ocean that lie along rapidly descending lines, especially when they lie on the borders of large mountain ranges, are especially liable to earthquakes.

Dr. Charles Davison has made a map of the earthquakes of Japan in which he had adopted the plan of representing the origin or centres of earthquakes by a series of contour lines like those employed on topographical maps. The advantage of this type of map over that employed by Mallet is just this: Davison's earthquake map of Japan in which the active volcanoes are marked by dots, and the earthquakes by contour lines surrounding the points of origin, discloses the interesting fact that here the positions of the volcanoes and the earthquake centres coincide, since the mountainous districts where the active volcanoes are numerous are singularly free from earthquakes. This can be seen from an inspection of Fig. 55.

[Pg 308]

CHAPTER XXXIV

THE CAUSES OF EARTHQUAKES

Earthquakes occurred long before man appeared on earth. It is natural, therefore, that our early ancestors, experiencing these unwelcome phenomena, vaguely endeavored to explain their causes. These early attempts at explanation have in many cases been of an exceedingly fanciful character.

The ancient Mongolians and Hindoos declared that earthquakes are due to our earth resting on a huge frog and that they occur whenever the frog scratches its head.

In Japan, where earthquakes are very common, the ignorant people even at a much later day declared that there exists in the depth of the sea an immense fish which, when angry, dashes its head violently against the coast of the island, thus making the earth tremble. This is, doubtless, the biggest fish-story extant.

Another folk-lore explanation in Japan attributes the cause of the tremblings of the earth to a subterranean monster whose head lies in the north of the island of Hondo, while his tail lies between the two principal cities. The shaking of his tail causes earthquakes.

Fantastic and foolish as these explanations are, it is worthy of note that the first of the Japanese explanations shows no little observation on the part of the people, since it locates the starting-points of earthquakes as being not on the land, but on the bottom of the sea. In point[Pg 309] of fact, nearly all the great earthquakes in Japan seem to start somewhere between the coasts of the islands on the sea-bottom that leads down to a very deep part of the Pacific known as the Tuscarora Deep.

Many years ago nearly everyone believed that earthquakes were caused solely by the forces that produce volcanic eruptions; that all earthquakes, whether in the neighborhood of active volcanoes, or at great distances therefrom, were to be regarded solely as volcanic in their origin.

It is now recognized that the most severe and far-reaching earthquakes have no immediate connection with volcanic explosions, but are due to the sudden slippings of the earth's strata over lines of faults; or, in other words, earthquakes are most frequently of the tectonic type.

At the present time there is unfortunately much difference in opinion as to the exact cause of earthquakes. By this is not meant the immediate cause, but the ultimate cause. As to the immediate cause, practically all are agreed that quakes of volcanic origin are to be traced to the same forces that produce volcanic eruptions, while quakes of tectonic origin are due directly to the slipping of the strata along the faults. But when inquiry is instituted as to the nature of the forces that cause the volcanic eruptions, or that produce such an alteration of the strata as permits them afterwards to slip and thus jar the earth, there is much difference of opinion.

As can be seen from a few quotations of well-known authorities, only two kinds of earthquakes exist; namely, volcanic earthquakes and tectonic earthquakes.

Dana, for example, while acknowledging that small earthquakes may be caused by the sudden falling of large rock masses into cavities in the crust of the earth, says:

[Pg 310]

"But true earthquakes come, for the most part at least, from one or the other of the following sources of disturbance.

"1. Vapors suddenly produced, causing ruptures and friction.

"2. Sudden movements or slips along old or new fractures.

"Earthquakes due to the former of these methods are common about volcanoes, and at the Hawaiian islands shakings that are destructive over the island of Hawaii at the moment of some of the more violent eruptions, do not often affect the island of Oahu, a depth of 500 fathoms of water, the least depth between the two islands, being sufficient to stop off the vibrations....

"Earthquakes of the second mode of origin may occur in all regions, volcanic or not. They have their origin mostly in the vicinity of mountain regions, where old fractures most abound. The vibrations may begin in a slip of a few inches, in fact; but where there has been a succession of slips, up and up from 10,000 feet or more, as in the Appalachian, earthquakes of inconceivable volcanic activity must have resulted."

Dana points out that volcanoes stand on lines of fractures in the openings of which their existence began and that, during geological time, slips up or down these fractures have occurred, producing earthquakes and possibly starting eruptions.

Prestwich, a well-known English geologist, speaks very decidedly concerning the causes of earthquakes:

"For my own part, I am disposed to share the belief expressed by Dana that the tension or pressure, by which the great oscillations or plications of the earth's crust have been produced, have not entirely ceased; and that this is generally the most probable cause of earthquakes.[Pg 311] The uplifting of the great continental tracts and mountain ranges must have always left the interior of the crust in a state of unstable equilibrium, and any slight slide or settling along an old fracture, or in highly disturbed and distorted strata, would be attended by an earthquake shock.

"In volcanic areas the removal of the large volumes of molten rock from the interior to the surface must produce settlements and strains which might also result in some of these minor earthquakes to which volcanic districts are so subject. Where we have the two conditions combined, as they are in the Andes in South America, these earthquake phenomena are, as we should expect, developed on the grandest and widest scale."

Geikie, the Scotch geologist, says:

"Various conceivable causes may, at different times and under different conditions, communicate a shock to the subterranean regions. Such as the sudden flashing into steam of water in the spherodial state, the sudden condensation of steam, the explosion of a volcanic outpour, the falling in of the roof of a subterranean cavity, or the sudden snap of deep-seated rocks subjected to prolonged and intense stress."

Sir Charles Lyell, the great English geologist, holds the following views concerning the origin of earthquakes. He speaks as follows in his "Principles of Geology":

"1. The primary cause of the volcanoes and the earthquakes are to a great extent the same, and connected with the development of heat and chemical action at various depths in the interior of the globe.

"2. Volcanic heat has been supposed by many to be the result of the high temperature which belonged to the whole planet when it was in a state of igneous fusion, a temperature which they suppose to have been always diminishing[Pg 312] and still to continue to diminish by radiation into space....

"The powerful agency of steam or aqueous vapor in volcanic eruptions leads us to compare its power of propelling lava to the surface with that which it exerts in driving up water in the pipe of an Icelandic geyser. Various gases also, rendered liquid by pressure at great depths, may aid in causing volcanic outbursts and in fissuring and convulsing the rocks during earthquakes."

Major Clarence Edward Dutton, U. S. A., an acknowledged authority on seismology, speaks as follows:

"Thus far, then, we have two causes of earthquakes which are apparently well sustained: (1) the downthrows, which have often been observed to be accompanied by earthquakes, and (2) volcanic action. But neither of them have been shown to be connected with more than a comparatively small number. Much the greater part of the earthquakes still require explanation, and the indications are manifold that some of them are produced by some cause yet to be stated."

He acknowledges, however, this unknown cause may be traceable to volcanic agency. To quote him in full:

"It remains now to refer to the possibility that many quakes whose origin is unknown, or extremely doubtful, may, after all, be volcanic. This must be fully admitted, and, indeed, it is in many cases highly probable. Evidences that volcanic action has taken place in the depths of the earth without visible, permanent results on the surface abound in ancient rock exposures. Formations of great geological age, once deeply buried and brought to daylight by secular denudations, show that lavas have penetrated surrounding rock-masses in many astonishing ways. Sometimes they have intruded between strata, lifting or floating up the overlying beds without any[Pg 313] indication of escaping to the surface. Sometimes the lava breaks across a series of strata and finds its way into the partings between higher beds. Or it forces its way into a fissure to form a dike which may never reach the surface. In one place a long arm or sheet of lava has in a most surprising and inexplicable manner thrust itself into the enveloping rock-mass, and in the older or metamorphic rocks these offshoots or apophyses cross each other in great numbers and form a tangled network of intrusive dikes. In other places the intruded lava has formed immense lenticular (lense shaped) masses (laccolites), which have domed up the overlying strata into mountain masses. These intrusions, almost infinitely varied in form and condition, are often, in fact usually, inexplicable as mechanical problems, but their reality is vouched for by the evidence of our senses. What concerns us here is the great energy which they suggest and their adequacy to generate in the rocks those sudden, elastic displacements which are the real initiatory impulses of an earthquake. They assure us that a great deal of volcanic action has transpired in past ages far under ground, which makes no other sign at the surface than those vibrations which we call an earthquake."

Koto, the celebrated Japanese student of earthquakes, and a member of the Earthquake Investigation Committee appointed by the Japanese Government for studying the great Mino-Owaro earthquake, in Japan, 1891, is properly regarded as an authority on earthquakes. Living, as he does, in a country where earthquakes and volcanic eruptions are of almost daily occurrence, he has had abundant opportunity for studying these phenomena, especially in connection with the Seismological Institute of Japan. He speaks as follows:

[Pg 314]

"To make clear once for all my own standpoint, I may say plainly that the chain of volcanoes and the system of mountains of the non-volcanic earthquake, appear to me to have very intimate and fundamental relations with the so-called tectonic line."

Mallet regards earthquakes that can be directly traceable to volcanic origin as unsuccessful efforts on the part of nature to establish volcanoes. He speaks concerning this matter as follows:

"An earthquake in a non-volcanic region may, in fact, be viewed as an uncompleted effort to establish a volcano. The forces of explosion and impulse are the same in both; they differ only in degree of energy, or in the varying sorts and degrees of resistance opposed to them. There is more than a mere vaguely admitted connection between them, as heretofore commonly acknowledged—one so vague that the earthquake has been often stated to be the cause of the volcano (Johnson, 'Phy. Atlas,' Geology, page 21), and more commonly the volcano the cause of the earthquake, neither view being the expression of the truth of nature. They are not in the relation to each other of cause and effect, but are both unequal manifestations of a common force under different conditions."

Before closing this chapter on the causes of earthquakes it may be well to state briefly the explanations that have been suggested by those who hold that the earth is solid and cold throughout its entire mass, except that in the neighborhood of volcanic districts there are limited areas situated only a comparatively few miles below the surface where the rocks are highly heated.

Professor Mallet suggested that the source of heat for these local areas of melted rocks was to be found in the enormous mechanical force that is developed by the crushing of the strata in the earth's crust. The principal objection to Mallet's theory is to be found in the fact that, for[Pg 315] this heat to be available for the melting of rocks, it must be produced rapidly, and not spread out over long periods of time. Moreover, there would appear to be no other way to account for the production of the great force required to effect the crushing of the earth's strata save on the assumption of a highly heated interior still cooling and contracting.

In his "Aspects of the Earth" Shaler has suggested an hypothesis that may be regarded to a certain extent as explaining how heat, slowly generated, might be blanketed, or prevented from escaping and so possibly reaching a temperature sufficiently high to melt the materials in portions of the interior not far below the surface of the earth.

"We thus see that in the water imprisoned in the deposits of the early geological ages and brought to a high temperature by the blanketing action of the more recently deposited beds, we have a sufficient cause for the great generation of steam at high temperatures, and this is the sole essential phenomenon of volcanic eruptions. We see also by this hypothesis why volcanoes do not occur at points remote from the sea, and why they cease to be in action soon after the sea leaves their neighborhood....

"The foregoing considerations make it tolerably clear that volcanoes are fed from deposits of water contained in ancient rocks which have become greatly heated through the blanketing effects of the strata which have been laid down upon them. The gas which is the only invariable element of volcanic eruptions is steam; moreover, it is the steam of sea-water, as is proven by analysis of the ejections. It breaks its way to the surface only on those parts of the earth which are near to where the deposition of strata is lifting the temperature of water contained in rocks by preventing, in fact, the escape of the earth's heat."

[Pg 316]

Another very common theory is that of chemical action, or the heat produced by the oxidation of various substances inside the earth, such, for example, as iron pyrites, a compound of iron and sulphur.

When Sir Humphrey Davy discovered metallic sodium and it was found that this material, when thrown on water, possessed the power of liberating intense heat, the discovery was welcomed by geologists as affording a possible explanation of the cause of volcanoes and earthquakes.

110

It may be said generally concerning chemical action as the source of the earth's interior heat, that the chief objection against it is the fact that such heat is liberated too slowly to result in the production of a very high temperature. This objection does not exist in the case of such substances as metallic sodium, since here the heat is rapidly developed and is sufficient in amount to fuse the substances produced. But in the lava produced in such great quantities as it is in volcanic districts there must be liberated at the same time large quantities of gaseous hydrogen. Now, although hydrogen is, as we have already seen, sometimes given off with the gases that escape from volcanic craters, yet the quantity which escapes is so small that this theory of volcanic activity has been practically abandoned.

Quite recently, however, among the various chemical substances that are produced under the extremely high temperatures of the electric furnace have been found, or formed, a number of curious substances such as *calcium carbide, calcium silicide, barium silicide*, etc., that possess the property of becoming highly heated on coming in contact with water.

Now it is an interesting fact that the hydrogen and other gases which are given off by the action of water on these substances are absorbed in large quantities by the materials[Pg 317] themselves, so that the objection of the absence of hydrogen and similar gases in the craters of the volcanoes would not be quite as objectionable as in the case of such substances.

Of course, it is impossible to say whether such substances as calcium carbide, etc., actually exist inside the earth's crust, yet, as has been pointed out, the principal condition necessary for their formation, i. e., a high temperature, existed at times long after the earth, assuming the correctness of the nebular hypothesis, was separated from the nebulous sun.

There still remains to be discussed the most curious of all possible causes that have been suggested for the presence of the local heated areas at comparatively short distances below the earth's crust; namely, radio-activity.

In 1896, Henri Becquerel, a Frenchman, while investigating the power of the X-rays, when passing through certain substances, to produce phosphorescence, or causing the substances to shine in the dark, made the extraordinary discovery that some of the salts of uranium possess the power of emitting a peculiar radiation closely resembling the X-rays, that is able to pass through substances opaque to ordinary light as well as to affect photographic plates. But the most extraordinary part of this discovery was that the salts of uranium apparently possess the power of giving out this radiation continuously without being exposed to the sun's rays.

This peculiar property was called *radio-activity*, and was shortly afterwards found to be present in many other substances besides uranium, and notably so in two newly discovered elements known as polonium and radium.

Now it has been suggested that if there existed somewhere beneath the earth's crust in these locally heated[Pg 318] areas, large quantities of radio-active substances, these regions would at last become highly heated, and in this way likely to produce volcanoes and earthquakes. It would not, however, seem that this is probably their true cause.

From what has just been said it is clear how exceedingly difficult it has become to explain the source of the earth's interior heat when the fact of the earth's original highly heated condition is denied. We are, therefore, disposed with Russell to believe, as stated in the first part of this volume, that the ultimate cause of both volcanoes and earthquakes is to be found in the gradual cooling of an originally highly heated globe, and that the greater part of the interior is still in a highly heated condition, hot enough to be melted but yet in a solid condition by reason of the great pressure to which it is subjected.

[Pg 319]

CHAPTER XXXV

EARTHQUAKES OF THE GEOLOGICAL PAST—CATACLYSMS

There were numerous volcanoes in the geological past; therefore, since volcanic eruptions are generally attended by earthquake shocks, it follows that during that remote past the earth has been violently shaken by earthquakes. Indeed, if we assume, as we believe to be the case, that the cause of earthquakes is correctly to be traced to an originally heated globe which is gradually cooling, it follows that the earth was necessarily subject to great earthquakes almost from the time when it began to cool.

But to establish as a fact the occurrence of an earthquake at so remote a time in the earth's history is far more difficult than to detect the occurrence of a volcano at that time. While the earthquake shocks may produce fissures in the earth's crust, and may be accompanied by great changes of level, yet the great time that has elapsed between such occurrences and the present would permit the various geological agencies that are at work either to cover these fissures completely, or completely to remove by erosion, or in other similar ways, the rocks in which they occurred. It is different in the case of a volcano; for the volcanic craters are in many cases still left standing, and then there are the voluminous sheets of lava that have spread over great areas of the earth, as well as numerous volcanic cones. Besides, there are thousands of square miles of surface that have been[Pg 320] covered, often to great depths, by deposits of volcanic dust thrown out at one time or another from the craters of the then active volcanoes.

I am sure you will acknowledge that any force capable of causing great cracks or fissures in the earth's crust, must, while doing this, have produced violent shakings of the earth. Great cracks or fissures are to be found in the rocks of all the geological formations. These are a record of the earthquakes that must have attended these convulsions. And there is plenty of evidence to show that the earth's crust has been torn into these fissures in places deep down below the present surface; for, by the action of water, many of these portions have been uncovered so that these great cracks or fissures which have been afterwards filled with a molten rock that has hardened can be seen in the great dikes that still remain.

But there are still other evidences of the existence of earthquakes during the geological past. There are found in the different strata of the earth's crust fossil remains of the plants and animals that lived on the earth long before the creation of man. By a careful study of these fossils we know positively the kinds of animals and plants that lived on the earth, in its waters, or in its atmosphere, when these strata were being deposited. It is in this way possible for a geologist to trace the life of the earth and its development as it is written on the great book of which the earth's different strata form the separate pages. Now, a careful study of the earth's fauna and flora during the geological past, shows, beyond any question, that occasionally great changes have occurred in the earth; for, here and there, during different times, we find that certain species of animals and plants have completely disappeared, to be followed, after certain intervals, by[Pg 321] entirely different species. It is evident, therefore, that changes have occurred that have made it impossible for the animals and plants that formerly lived on the earth to exist under the changed conditions. These occurrences are known to geologists as *exterminations, catastrophes*, or *cataclysms*. They are also sometimes called *revolutions*, for they mark a more or less complete wiping-out of the animals living at the time they occurred.

If you will try to think you will readily understand how great a catastrophe must be, that would be able to wipe out or completely destroy an entire race of animals.

You have doubtless read with astonishment the terrible catastrophe that accompanied the eruption of Krakatoa, especially at the loss of life and property caused by the great waves that were set up in the ocean, but far reaching as these losses were they have nevertheless affected but a limited portion of the earth. The plain truth is even more stupendous, for catastrophes of the geological past appear to have been so far-reaching and powerful as to affect the whole surface of the earth, and to have annihilated entire races of animals and plants as if they had never existed.

Geologists are all practically agreed that there are only two ways in which such exterminations of the earth's life could have been caused, and these are changes in the earth's climate, or the starting of waves in the sea by great earthquakes. In the sea; for it must be borne in mind that in the geological past the greater part of the earth's surface was covered by water, and the land areas were comparatively small and low, so that waves created by earthquakes might easily have overwhelmed the entire land surface.

Of course, it is fair to suppose that in many cases these[Pg 322] exterminations may have been caused by sudden changes of climate, such as would naturally have resulted from any change in the direction of hot ocean currents which formerly flowed from the equator to the poles. The appearance of a fairly large mass of land in the central parts of the ocean might readily have turned aside the hot ocean currents that formerly swept over the polar regions, thus greatly lowering the earth's average temperature in these regions.

But it seems probable that the principal cause of the destruction of life in the geological past was produced by earthquake waves in the sea, sweeping over the continents. Let us, therefore, examine two of the earth's principal geological revolutions or cataclysms; namely, that which occurred at the close of an early geological time known as the Palaeozoic, and that which occurred at the end of a geological time intermediate between the Palaeozoic time or the time of ancient life, called the Mesozoic time, and the Cenozoic time, or the time immediately preceding the present time. These two revolutions are called by Dana, *the Post-Palaeozoic*, or *Appalachian Revolution*, and the *Post-Mesozoic Revolution*. Both were characterized by the making of great mountain systems, and were, therefore, especially liable to repetitions of tremendous earthquakes that must have produced enormous waves in the ocean.

"Palaeozoic time," says Dana, "closed with the making of one of the great mountain ranges of North America—the Appalachian, besides ranges in other lands, and in producing one of the most universal and abrupt disappearances of life in geological history. So great an event is properly styled a revolution."

Towards the close of the Palaeozoic time immense disturbances of the earth's crust occurred during the[Pg 323] uplifting of the Appalachian Mountain System. One may, perhaps, form some faint idea of the immensity of the forces at work, from the fact that there were great faults produced by the uplifting of the lands attended with displacement amounting to 10,000 or 20,000 feet or more; that in parts of southwestern Virginia there were flexure faults 100 miles in length.

As to the probability of the extensive exterminations that have occurred during these times being produced by earthquake waves, Dana speaks thus:

"The causes of the extermination are two.... (1) a colder climate.... (2) earthquake waves produced by orogenic movements (movements producing mountain ranges). If North America from the west of the Carolinas to the Mississippi Valley can be shaken in consequence of a little slip along a fracture in times of perfect quiet (the allusion here to the Charleston earthquake, in 1886), and ruin mark its movements, incalculable violence and great surgings of the ocean should have occurred and been often repeated during the progress of flexures, miles in height and space, and slips along newly opened fractures that kept up their interrupted progress through thousands of feet of displacements....

"Under such circumstances the devastation of the sea-border and the low-lying land of the period, the destruction of their animals and plants, would have been a sure result. The survivors within a long distance of the coastline would have been few. The same waves would have swept over European land and seas, and there found coadjutors for new strife in earthquake waves of European origin. These times of catastrophe may have continued in America through half of the following Triassic period; for fully two thirds of the Triassic period are unrepresented by rocks and fossils on the Atlantic border."

[Pg 324]

Coming now to the Post-Mesozoic revolution this period was marked by the making of the greatest of the North American mountain systems.

Dana points out that this revolution affected the summit region of the Rocky Mountains over a broad belt probably as long as the western side of the continent.

This great belt of mountain-making extended from the Arctic regions through North America, probably paralleled by like work, of equal extent, in South America, but on a more eastern line.

"The disappearance of species," says Dana, "at the close of Mesozoic time was one of the two most noted in all geological history. Probably not a tenth part of the animal species of the world disappeared at the time, and far less of the vegetable life and terrestrial Invertebrates; yet the change was so comprehensive that no Cretaceous species of Vertebrate is yet known to occur in the rocks of the American Tertiary, and not even a marine Invertebrate."

In tracing the causes of these disappearances, Dana points out that, perhaps, the principal cause was a decrease in the temperature of the ocean, since the destructions were limited in large measure to marine life. He regards, however, the other most probable cause as traceable to earthquake waves; for the making of a great mountain range along the entire length of the continent resulted in displacements of the rock formations along lines hundreds of miles in length. Such displacements must have been attended by a succession of earthquakes of unusual violence, causing the destruction by sudden shocks beneath, and resulting, directly and indirectly, in waves sweeping over the continent. Since at this time the land was still low for the greater part, the huge waves must have repeatedly swept over the greater part of the[Pg 325] land, leaving only the smaller species of animals and the vegetation.

It is evident, therefore, that during the geological past earthquakes occurred that were probably vastly greater than any that have occurred on the earth during more recent times.

[Pg 326]

CHAPTER XXXVI

THE KIMBERLY DIAMOND FIELDS AND THEIR VOLCANIC ORIGIN

The elementary substance carbon occurs in three forms, i. e., *charcoal*, *graphite*, and the *diamond*. The commonest form of carbon is to be found in charcoal, as well as in bituminous coal, anthracite coal, and *lignite*. Graphite, also known as *plumbago*, or *black lead*, is the substance you have seen so often in the lead of pencils. The diamond, as every one knows, is the highly prized precious stone that sparkles so brightly in the light, and is so hard that it is capable of scratching almost any other substance.

Diamonds are found in various parts of the world. We are now interested in them, however, only as they occur in certain parts of the world, as in the great Kimberly diamond fields in Southern Africa.

Dr. Max Bauer in his book on precious stones says that the discovery of diamonds in South Africa was made by a traveller named O'Reilly, who, in 1867, saw a child sitting in the house of a Boer named Jacobs, playing with a shining stone. Jacob's farm was a short distance south of the Orange River near Hopetown. This stone proved to be a diamond weighing some twenty-one and three-tenths carats and was afterwards sold for $2,500. The incident led to the discovery and consequent development of the Kimberly diamond fields.

Without going into a description of the different deposits in which diamonds are found, it will suffice to say[Pg 327] that in the Kimberly district the diamonds occur distributed through the materials that fill peculiar funnel-shaped depressions called *pipes* which extend vertically downward to unknown depths. The rock that fills a pipe consists of an entirely different material from that in which the pipe occurs. The upper extremity of the pipe is generally slightly elevated above the general surface for a few yards. The pipes vary in diameter from twenty to 750 yards, diameters of from 200 to 300 yards being quiet common.

In 1892, the diamond-bearing material found in the pipes of the Kimberly mines had been excavated vertically downwards a distance of 1,261 feet, without any signs of its being exhausted.

Now, the materials which fill the pipe of the great Kimberly mine are practically the same in all the mines in the neighborhood. At the upper part of the pipe the materials show the action of weathering by exposure to the air. Here the ground is of a yellowish color. Below, the materials have a blue color.

According to Bauer the diamond-bearing material that fills the upper part of the pipe consists of a soft, sandy material of a light yellow color, known to diamond miners as *yellow ground*, or *yellow stuff*.

In the case of the Kimberly mine, the yellow ground has a thickness of about sixty feet. Below it the material has a blue color and is known as the *blue ground*. This latter material possesses the character of a volcanic *tuff*, which is a hardened clay. It is of a green or bluish green color and has the appearance of dried mud that holds or binds together numerous irregular, tough, and sometimes rounded fragments of a green or bluish black serpentine.

The diamonds are found near the surface in the yellow[Pg 328] ground, as well as downwards through the blue ground. It was at one time thought that most of the diamonds existed in the yellow ground, and that they would soon disappear entirely at short distances below where the blue ground began. Under this belief some of the most valuable claims changed hands at prices far below their true value. It was soon found, however, that large and valuable stones existed in the blue ground, and, indeed, this ground has never been mined to a depth below where valuable diamonds appear.

The diamonds occur in very small quantities spread through the yellow and blue grounds. The following statement by Bauer will show this:

"A striking illustration of their sparing occurrence is furnished by the fact that in the richest part of the richest mine, namely, in the Kimberly mine, they constitute only one part in 2,000,000, or 0.00005% of the blue ground. In other mines the proportion is still lower, namely, one part in 40,000,000, a yield which corresponds to five carats per cubic yard of rock."

Of course, you will desire by this time to know the manner in which the pipes of the diamond mines of South Africa have become filled with the diamond-bearing rocks, and particularly what diamonds have to do with a book on volcanoes and earthquakes.

Dr. Emil Cohen, who has made a study of these regions, regards the pipes as volcanic vents or chimneys, and that the materials filling the pipes have been brought up from below by volcanic forces. He says:

"I consider that the diamantiferous ground is a product of volcanic action, and was probably erupted at a comparatively low temperature in the form of an ash saturated with water and comparable to the materials ejected by a mud volcano. Subsequently new minerals were formed[Pg 329] in the mass, consequent on alterations induced in the upper part by exposure to atmospheric agencies, and in the lower by the presence of water. Each of the crater-like basins, or, perhaps, more correctly, funnels, in which alone diamonds are now found, was at one time the outlet of an active volcano which became filled up, partly with the products of eruption and partly with ejected material which fell back from the sides of the crater intermingled with various foreign substances, such as small pebbles, or organic remains of local origin, all of which became imbedded in the volcanic tuff. The substance of the tuff was probably mainly derived from deep-seated crystalline rocks, of which isolated remains are now to be found, and which are similar to those which now crop out at the surface, only at a considerable distance from the diamond fields. These crystalline rocks from which the diamonds probably took their origin, were pulverized and forced up into the pipes by the action of volcanic forces, and imbedded in this eruptive material, these diamonds either in perfect crystals or in fragments are now found."

So far as the volcanic origin of the diamonds of the Kimberly diamond fields is concerned, Cohen's theory has been generally accepted with the following modifications: that the pipes were not filled by a single volcanic eruption, but by successive eruptions, and that in the case of the Kimberly mine, the pipes contain the results of as many as fifteen successive eruptions. There has, however, been another and more important modification proposed to Cohen's theory, which is far more probable. It will be noticed that Cohen's theory regards the action of the volcanic eruption as only serving to bring fragments of a deep-seated mother rock that contained the diamonds up from below with the material that fills the pipe. Now, Prof. Carvill Lewis proposes the following[Pg 330] very important change in Cohen's theory: that the blue ground does not consist of fragmentary material or tuff, but was forced up from below in the pipe in a molten mass and consolidated on cooling. In other words, the blue ground is filled with an ordinary igneous rock that was solidified in place in the vent or pipe.

In the great Kimberly mines the surface of the pipe is divided into numerous separate claims, each consisting of a small square lot. There are so many of these claims in the Kimberly mine that its surface is honey-combed by numerous square pits. The work is done largely by native Kaffirs employed there since the '70's. As the material was removed from the pit, the adjoining claims were separated from each other by high vertical walls.

At a later date, in order to remove the material and separate the lots, high staging provided with ropes and hauling machinery was erected. The number of these ropes is now so great that the mine has the appearance of a huge cobweb.

A very extensive series of investigations has been made at a comparatively recent date by Prof. Henri Moissan of France on various chemical products that are obtained under the influence of the high temperatures of the electric furnace. When a powerful electric current is caused to pass through a highly refractory material, that is to say, a material difficult to fuse, such as carbon, it raises it to an extremely high temperature. A still higher temperature can be obtained by causing a powerful current to flow between two carbon rods that are first brought into contact, and then gradually separated from each other, just as they are in the ordinary arc lights employed for lighting the streets of our cities. In the latter way a temperature that is estimated as high as 3,500° C. (6,332° F.),[Pg 331] can be readily obtained. Under these very high temperatures some very curious chemical products have been obtained in electric furnaces. These furnaces consist of small chambers made of highly refractory materials closely surrounding the incandescent carbon, or the carbon voltaic arc. Among some of the most curious of these products are artificially produced diamonds.

Moissan, however, was not the first to produce diamonds artificially. As soon as Lavoisier had experimentally shown that the chemical composition of the diamond and carbon are the same, efforts were made to convert charcoal into diamonds, and Despretz, as early as 1849, by means of the combined influence of a powerful burning glass, the oxyhydrogen blowpipe, and the carbon voltaic arc obtained a very high temperature. He claims by this temperature to have been able to change carbon into a few microscopic diamonds. It is quite possible, in the light of later investigations, that Despretz may have been mistaken in his belief that he had actually produced diamonds; but whether this be so or not, he was certainly one of the pioneers in this early transformation of charcoal.

Theoretically, all that would be required in order to change the non-crystalline form of carbon into the diamond, would be to subject the carbon to a temperature sufficiently high to fuse it and then permit it slowly to crystallize. Could this be done, there should be no trouble in transforming any amount of coal into any equal amount of diamonds. But the transformation is by no means as simple as might be supposed. It is not that the temperature of the carbon cannot be raised to its point of fusion, but that as soon as a certain temperature has been reached, the carbon, instead of fusing or melting, is suddenly volatilized or turned into vapor. There is no doubt that[Pg 332] this is done. Thousands of feet of carbon rods are volatilized every night in the arc lamps of our cities, but the trouble is that this carbon vapor so formed, when cooled, or condensed, is not converted into the exceedingly hard, clear, crystalline diamond, but into the soft, dull black graphite or plumbago.

Now the process adopted by Moissan in order to cause volatilized carbon, or carbon vapor, to condense in the form of crystalline diamonds was practically as follows: he placed pieces of pure carbon inside a very strong steel tube, such, for example, as would be formed by boring a short cylindrical hole in a piece of strong thick steel, and placing a small quantity of carbon inside the tube so formed. Closing the open end of the tube by means of a tightly fitting screw plug, he volatilized the carbon inside the tube. The steel, tube, and plug formed an electric furnace, for, as soon as he passed an electric current through it, the temperature at once became high enough to volatilize the carbon.

Under these circumstances the carbon vapor was subjected to great pressure owing to the limited space in which it was liberated. As soon as this mass of dense vapor had been formed, he seized the steel tube with a pair of furnace tongs, and plunged it below the surface of cold water in a bucket.

Of course, as the hot tube suddenly chilled, there was a great shrinking in the walls of the furnace, so that the already compressed carbon vapor was subjected to a still greater pressure which possibly liquified it. Of that, however, we cannot speak definitely. This, however, can safely be asserted, that when the tube was broken open a confused mass of small crystals was found inside, some of which, on examination with the microscope, were found to consist of small crystals of two forms of diamonds,[Pg 333] namely, the black diamond, or carbonado, and the regular crystallized diamond.

Moissan made a great number of experiments for producing diamonds in this way, and succeeded in forming some very beautiful, though microscopic, diamonds.

116

What may be said to characterize especially Moissan's experiments was the comparatively great number of diamonds, so small as to be scarcely distinguishable under the microscope. The high temperature to which the materials inside the tube were exposed resulted in the production of numerous minute crystals of different minerals. In order to get rid of as many of these as possible Moissan adopted the plan of subjecting the material to the action of powerful solvents, such as sulphuric acid, aqua regia, or a mixture of sulphuric and nitric acid, and hydrofluoric acid. These acids destroyed most of the minute crystals of other minerals, but left the minute crystals of diamonds unaffected.

Now it will be observed that the theory proposed by Prof. Carvill Lewis as to the probable origin of the diamonds of the Kimberly mines bears a wonderfully close resemblance to the method adopted by Moissan for the production of artificial diamonds, since it supposes the diamonds to have been formed by the sudden cooling or chilling within the pipe of various molten materials brought up from great depths by the volcanic forces. If this be true, then besides the comparatively large crystallized and perfect diamonds found in the blue ground of the Kimberly mines, there should also be found large quantities of microscopic diamonds, just as are found in Moissan's electric furnaces, in which he produced artificial diamonds.

Moissan, considering this, obtained a specimen of the blue ground from the Kimberly diamond pipe and on[Pg 334] subjecting it to the action of the different solvents before named, found in the mass that was left undissolved a great number of microscopic diamonds. It would seem, therefore, that there is no reasonable doubt but that the Kimberly diamond fields had their diamonds produced by the sudden chilling in the volcanic pipes of molten materials brought from great depths by the force of volcanic eruption.

[Pg 335]

CHAPTER XXXVII

THE FABLED CONTINENT OF ATLANTIS

Besides the sudden changes of level that frequently occur during earthquake shocks there are gradual changes of level that take place very slowly throughout long periods of time.

These are believed to be due to the warpings produced by the cooling of an originally highly heated globe.

It is not true, therefore, that the earth's surface is fixed, or that its land and water areas remain always the same. On the contrary, what is land at one time is water at another time, and so, too, water areas may become changed into land areas.

For the most part these changes go on so slowly as not to be noticeable in an ordinary lifetime. Indeed, in some cases, they are so extremely gradual that Methuselah himself might have gone to his grave in ignorance of their progress.

Let us briefly note a few well-known gradual changes of level.

One of the most extensive of these is the sinking of an immense area, over 6,000 miles in diameter, that covers a large part of the bed or floor of the Pacific Ocean.

It is an easy matter to observe the gradual changes of level on the coasts, since the old water line can be at once found, but it is very difficult to detect such changes in the bed of the ocean, hidden as it is by a covering of water. Yet many things that seem impossible to the uninitiated[Pg 336] are readily solved by those familiar with physical science. Little signs, meaningless to others, are easily read, and these prove beyond doubt the gradual sinking of the ocean's bed.

It was once believed that the coral polyps or animalculæ from the hard, bony skeletons of which coral reefs are formed, could live at the greatest depths of the ocean. These minute animals were, therefore, generally credited with filling up the deep ocean, in certain places, and converting it into dry land, and poetic philosophers were pleased to point to their indefatigable labors as an object lesson to the slothful.

But these charming, though fallacious, ideas were rudely overthrown by the sounding line and the drag-net. It had long been known that pieces of coral rock were brought up by dredging apparatus from the bottom of the ocean at all depths, but it was eventually shown that such pieces of coral rock never contained living animalculæ, when brought from water at greater depths than from 100 to 120 feet.

It puzzled scientific men no little at first to explain this apparent inconsistency. If the coral polyp could not live in water at greater depths than from 100 to 120 feet, how could the presence of coral rock at a depth of thousands of feet be explained? Happily, however, this problem was solved by the great naturalist, Charles Darwin, who showed that coral islands can only be formed in parts of the ocean whose beds are sinking at the same gradual rate at which the coral rock is being deposited. The presence, therefore, of coral islands on the bed of the Pacific, as well as along parts of its coasts, are, to scientific men, as good indications of its gradual sinking as if such facts had been written in the clearest language.

But there are other instances of gradual changes of[Pg 337] level besides the bed of the Pacific. About 600 miles along the coast of Greenland, from Disco Bay, near lat. 69° N., south to the Firth of Igaliko, lat. 60° 43' N., the bed of the ocean has been slowly sinking through 400 years. Old buildings and islands have been covered by the waters, so that fishermen have been compelled to provide new poles for their boats. As Sir Charles Lyell remarks:

"In one place the Moravian settlers have been obliged more than once to move inland the poles upon which their large boats are set, and the old poles still remain beneath the water as silent witnesses of the change."

Besides these gradual changes of level there are many others, but only one more need be cited: the gradual movements of the coasts of North America between Labrador and New Jersey that are rising in some places, and sinking in other places.

The evidences of these gradual changes of level are sometimes of such a character that he who runs may read them. One of the most interesting is, perhaps, that of the old Roman temple of Jupiter Serapis, at Pozzuli, on the borders of the Mediterranean. This temple, when completed, was 124 feet in length and 115 feet in width. Its roof was supported by forty-six columns, each forty-two feet in height, and five feet in diameter. Only three of these columns are now standing. They give, however, unquestionable evidence of having been submerged for about half their height. Nor, indeed, is the evidence wanting that this submergence continued a considerable time; for, while the lower twelve feet of the columns remain smooth and unaffected, yet, for a distance of nine feet above this portion, they have been perforated by various stone-boring mollusks of a species still living in the Mediterranean. This witnesses that the columns,[Pg 338] when submerged, were buried in mud for twelve feet, and surrounded by water nine feet deep. According to Dana, the pavement of the temple is still under water. The fact that another pavement exists below it shows that these changes of level had occurred before the temple was deserted by the Romans. It appears, that, prior to 1845, a gradual sinking of this part of the coast had been going on, but that since then there has ensued a gradual rising.

The evidences of these gradual changes of level in the land and water surfaces of the earth cannot be doubted by even the most skeptical. Again and again has the dry land disappeared below the surface of the waters of the ocean. Again and again, the ocean's bed has been raised to the surface and been converted into dry land. Suppose we attempt to follow one of the latter movements.

We will imagine an extensive area to have slowly appeared above the ocean. In due process of time this land surface, which we will assume to have continental dimensions, gradually becomes covered with plant and animal life. If it remains above the water for a sufficient length of time, its simple plants and animals acquire more and more complex forms, so as to make it difficult to detect any traces of the original species from which they have descended, or, more correctly, ascended. Moreover, where favorable conditions exist, the continent becomes peopled with men, who gradually advance from barbarism to semi-barbarism and eventually become a most highly civilized nation, sending to different parts of the world colonies, who carry with them the language and religious customs of the land of their birth.

But, a sudden or paroxysmal change of level occurs. The highly developed and densely populated region is suddenly swept out of existence and completely covered[Pg 339]by the waters of the ocean until, in a few thousand years, all traces of its existence have

118

so completely disappeared that but few, if any, can be found willing to acknowledge it ever had an existence.

Such, it is claimed, was the fate of the fabled Continent of Atlantis. It will, therefore, be interesting to endeavor briefly to review its past history and to read some of the things that have been written about this part of the world, which appears in the opinion of some of the ancients to have actually existed.

References to Atlantis have been made by various early writers. Solon, the great Athenian lawgiver, who flourished 600 years B. C., began a description of this place in verse. This description was never completed. At a later date one of Solon's descendants, Plato, who lived about 400 B. C., prepared a description of Atlantis, giving in detail its location, the general character of its surface, a description of its principal city, and the civilization of its inhabitants, as well as a brief reference to its sudden destruction. In another place this record of Plato will be given in full. It will suffice now to quote briefly what he says concerning its location.

"There was an island situated in front of the straits which you call the Columns of Heracles (Straits of Gibraltar). The island was larger than Libya and Asia put together, and was the way to other islands, and from the island you might pass through the whole in the opposite continent, for this sea which is within the Straits of Heracles is only a harbor, having a narrow entrance, but that other is the real sea, and the surrounding land may most truly be called a continent. Now, in the island of Atlantis, there was a great and wonderful empire, which had ruled over the whole island and several others, as well as over part of the continents; and, besides these, they subjected[Pg 340] the parts of Libya within the Columns of Heracles as far as Egypt, and of Europe as far as Tyrrhenia. The vast power, thus gathered into one, endeavored to subdue at one blow our country and yours, and the whole of the land which was within the straits, and then, Solon, your country shone forth, in the excellence of her virtues and strength, among all mankind, for she was the first in courage and military skill, and was the leader of the Hellenes. And when the rest fell off from her, being compelled to stand alone, after having undergone the very extremity of danger, she defeated and triumphed over the invaders, and preserved from slavery those who were not yet subjected, and freely liberated all the others who dwelt within the limits of Heracles.

"But afterwards, there occurred violent earthquakes and floods, and in a single day and night of rain, all your warlike men in a body sunk into the earth, and the island of Atlantis in a like manner disappeared, and was sunk beneath the sea. And that is the reason why the sea in those parts is impassable and impenetrable, because there is such a quantity of shallow mud in the way; and this was caused by the subsidence of the island." ("Plato's Dialogues," ii, 517, Timæus).

But besides Solon and Plato there are other ancient writers who refer to the lost island of Atlantis.

Ælian, in his "Varia Historia," lib. iii, chap. xvii, states that Theopompos, who flourished 400 B. C., refers to an interview between Midas, King of Phrygia, and Sielus, in which the latter speaks of a great continent larger than Asia, Europe, and Libya together that existed in the Atlantic.

Proclus quotes a statement from an ancient writer, who speaks about the islands of the sea beyond the Pillars of Hercules (Straits of Gibraltar).

[Pg 341]

Marcellus, in a book on the Ethiopians, refers to seven islands in the Atlantic whose inhabitants preserve legends of a greater island (possibly Atlantis), that had dominion over the small islands.

Diodorus Siculus asserts that the Phœnicians discovered a large island in the Atlantic beyond the Pillars of Hercules several days' sail from the coast of Africa.

Homer, Plutarch, and other ancient writers, refer to several islands in the Atlantic situated several thousand stadia from the Pillars of Hercules. (A stadium was a Greek measure of length equal to 600 feet. It was equal to one-eighth of a Roman mile, or 625 Roman feet.)

Ignatius Donnelly, in his book, called "Atlantis, the Ante-Diluvian World," claims that Plato's description of Atlantis which has generally been regarded as imaginary, was, on the contrary, historic; that the prehistoric continent of Atlantis was the cradle of the human race; that here man reached his highest civilization; that Atlantis was the site of the Garden of Eden, the Gardens of the Hesperides, the Elysian Fields, as well as Olympus; that, under the forms of the gods and goddesses of the ancient Greeks, the Phœnicians, the Hindoos, and the Scandinavians, are related the stories of the kings, queens, and heroes of Atlantis.

Much that has been claimed for the lost continent can hardly be regarded in any other light save that of imagination. For example, it has been asserted that it was from Atlantis that the colonies were sent out that peopled the coast countries of the Gulf of Mexico, of parts of the valley of the Mississippi, the basin of the Amazon, the western coasts of South America, parts of Europe, the shore lands of the Mediterranean Sea, the coasts of Europe, including the Caspian and the Black Seas, and even of parts of Africa.

[Pg 342]

It has also been asserted that this mighty nation of Atlantis carried the worship of the sun to Egypt, which was one of its first colonies, and, therefore, the civilization of Egypt was but an offshoot of prehistoric Atlantis.

But it will be reasonably objected that, if such a mass of land ever existed in the North Atlantic, some evidences should still be found on the bed of the ocean. Even though great periods of time have elapsed since the disappearance of Atlantis, some traces of its former existence should still remain on the floor of the ocean. Are there any evidences of an old land mass on this part of the floor of the Atlantic? The answer is unmistakable.

Deep-sea soundings show beyond question that there still exists in the North Atlantic in the region where Atlantis is said to have been located a submarine island, the summits of which appear above the waters in the Azores and the Canary Islands. This submarine island has been traced southwest over the bed of the ocean for a distance of several thousand miles with a breadth of fully 1,000 miles. Toward the south there is connected with it another submarine island, the summits of which reach above the surface in the islands of Ascension, St. Helena, and Tristan d'Acunha.

But the testimony of the submarine islands extends further than this. According to a number of careful soundings it appears that the bed of these parts of the ocean, instead of being characterized by a comparatively level surface due to the gradual accumulation of silt, possesses, to a great extent, the peculiarly sculptured surfaces which are only produced by exposure for a long time to the atmosphere.

Other facts might be adduced to show that some time during the first appearance of man on the earth there was a large land mass connecting the Eastern and Western[Pg 343]Continents. These facts include the wonderful resemblances existing between the plants and animals of the Eastern and Western Continents, the close resemblances of the myths and legends of the races of the Eastern and Western Continents, as well as the identity of their religious ideas, and the close similarity of their language so far as relates to certain fundamental ideas. These facts all point unquestionably to the existence of some large land mass between the two continents, and to this extent to throw light on the probable existence of prehistoric Atlantis.

[Pg 344]

CHAPTER XXXVIII

PLATO'S ACCOUNT OF ATLANTIS

The following is a translation of Plato's record in full:

Critias. Then listen, Socrates, to a strange tale, which is, however, certainly true, as Solon, who was the wisest of the seven sages, declared. He was a relative and great friend of my great-grandfather, Dropidas, as he himself says in several of his poems, and Dropidas told Critias, my grandfather, who remembered, and told us, that there were of old great and marvellous actions of the Athenians, which have passed into oblivion through time and the destruction of the human race—and one in particular, which was the greatest of them all, the recital of which will be a suitable testimony of our gratitude to you....

Socrates. Very good; and what is this ancient famous action of which Critias spoke, not as a mere legend, but as a veritable action of the Athenian State, which Solon recounted?

120

Critias. I will tell an old-world story which I heard from an aged man; for Critias was, as he said, at that time nearly ninety-years of age, and I was about ten years of age. Now the day was that day of the Apaturia which is called the registration of youth; at which, according to custom, our parents gave prizes for recitations, and the poems of several poets were recited by us boys, and many of us sung the poems of Solon, which were new at the time. One of our tribe, either because this was his real opinion, or because he thought that he would please Critias, said[Pg 345] that, in his judgment, Solon was not only the wisest of men but the noblest of poets. The old man, I well remember, brightened up at this, and said smiling: "Yes, Amynander, if Solon had only, like other poets, made poetry the business of his life, and had completed the tale which he brought with him from Egypt, and had not been compelled, by reason of the factions and troubles which he found stirring in this country when he came home, to attend to other matters, in my opinion, he would have been as famous as Homer, or Hesiod, or any poet."

"And what was that poem about, Critias?" said the person who addressed him.

"About the greatest action which the Athenians ever did, and which ought to have been most famous, but which, through the lapse of time and the destruction of the actors, has not come down to us."

"Tell us," said the other, "the whole story, and how and from whom Solon heard this veritable tradition."

He replied: "At the head of the Egyptian Delta, where the river Nile divides, there is a certain district which is called the district of Sais, and the great city of the district is also called Sais, and is the city from which Amasis the king was sprung. And the citizens have a deity who is their foundress: she is called in the Egyptian tongue Neith, which is asserted by them to be the same whom the Hellenes called Athene. Now, the citizens of this city are great lovers of the Athenians, and say that they are in some way related to them. Thither came Solon, who was received by them with great honor; and he asked the priests, who were most skilful in such matters, about antiquity, and made the discovery that neither he nor any other Hellene knew anything worth mentioning about the times of old.

"On one occasion, when he was drawing them on to[Pg 346] speak of antiquity, he began to tell about the most ancient things in our part of the world—about Phoroneus, who is called 'the first,' and about Niobe; and, after the Deluge, to tell of the lives of Deucalian and Pyrrha; and he traced the genealogy of their descendants, and attempted to reckon how many years old were the events of which he was speaking, and to give the dates. Thereupon, one of the priests, who was of very great age, said: 'O Solon, Solon, you Hellenes are but children, and there is never an old man who is an Hellene.' Solon, hearing this, said, 'What do you mean?' 'I mean to say,' he replied, 'that in mind you are all young; there is no old opinion handed down among you by ancient traditions, nor any science which is hoary with age. And I will tell you the reason of this: there have been, and there will be again, many destructions of mankind arising out of many causes.

"'There is a story which even you have preserved, that once upon a time Phaëthon, the son of Helios, having yoked the steeds in his father's chariot, because he was not able to drive them in the path of his father, burnt up all that was upon the earth, and was himself destroyed by a thunder-bolt. Now, this has the form of a myth, but really signifies a declination of the bodies moving around the earth, and in the heavens, and a great conflagration of things upon the earth recurring at long intervals of time: when this happens, those who live upon the mountains and in dry and lofty places are more liable to destruction than those who dwell by rivers or on the sea-shore; and from this calamity the Nile, who is our never-failing savior, saves and delivers us.

"'When, on the other hand, the gods purge the earth with a deluge of water, among you herdsmen and shepherds on the mountains are the survivors, whereas those of you who live in cities are carried by the rivers into the[Pg 347] sea; but in this country neither at that time nor at any other does the water come up from below, for which reason the things preserved here are said to be the oldest. The fact is, that wherever the extremity of winter frost or of summer sun does not prevent, the human race is always increasing at times, and at other times diminishing in numbers. And whatever happened either in your country or in ours, or in any other regions of which we are informed—if any action which is noble or great, or in any other way remarkable has taken place, all that has been written down of old, and is preserved in our temples; whereas you and other nations are just being provided with letters and the other things which States require; and then, at the usual period, the stream from heaven descends like a pestilence, and leaves only those of you who are destitute of letters and education; and thus you have to begin all over again as children, and know nothing of what happened in ancient times, either among us or among yourselves.

"'As for those genealogies of yours which you have recounted to us, Solon, they are no better than the tales of children; for, in the first place, you remember one deluge only, whereas there were many of them, and, in the next place, you do not know that there dwelt in your land the fairest and noblest race of men which ever lived, of whom you and your whole city are but a seed or remnant. And this was unknown to you, because for many generations the survivors of that destruction died and made no sign. For there was a time, Solon, before that great deluge of all, when the city which now is Athens, was first in war, and was preëminent for the excellence of her laws, and is said to have performed the noblest deeds, and to have had the fairest constitution of any of which tradition tells, under the face of heaven.'

[Pg 348]

"Solon marvelled at this and earnestly requested the priest to inform him exactly and in order about these former citizens. 'You are welcome to hear about them, Solon,' said the priest, 'both for your own sake and for that of the city; and, above all, for the sake of the goddess who is the common patron and protector and educator of both our cities. She founded your city a thousand years before ours, receiving from the Earth and Hephæstus the seed of your race, and then she founded ours, the constitution of which is set down in our sacred registers as 8,000 years old. As touching the citizens of 9,000 years ago, I will briefly inform you of their laws and of the noblest of their actions; and the exact particulars of the whole we will hereafter go through at our leisure in the sacred registers themselves. If you compare these very laws with your own, you will find that many of ours are the counterpart of yours, as they were in the olden time.

"'In the first place, there is the caste of priests, which is separated from all the others; next there are the artificers, who exercise their several crafts by themselves, and without admixture of any other, and also there is the class of shepherds and that of hunters, as well as that of husbandmen; and you will observe, too, that the warriors in Egypt are separated from all the other classes, and are commanded by the law only to engage in war. Moreover, the weapons with which they are equipped are shields and spears, and this the goddess taught first among you, and then in Asiatic countries, and we among the Asiatics first adopted.

"'Then, as to wisdom, do you observe, what care the law took from the very first, searching out and comprehending the whole order of things down to prophecy and medicine (the latter with a view to health); and out of these divine elements drawing what was needful for[Pg 349] human life, and adding every sort of knowledge which was connected with them. All this order and arrangement the goddess first imparted to you when establishing your city; and she chose the spot of earth in which you were born, because she saw that the happy temperament of the seasons in that land would produce the wisest of men.

"'Wherefore the goddess, who was a lover both of war and of wisdom, selected, and first of all settled that spot which was the most likely to produce men likest herself. And there you dwelt, having such laws as these and still better ones, and excelled all mankind in all virtue, as became the children and disciples of the gods. Many great and wonderful deeds are recorded of your State in our histories; but one of them exceeds all the rest in greatness and valor; for these histories tell of a mighty power which was agressing wantonly against the whole of Europe and Asia, and to which your city put an end.

"'This power came forth out of the Atlantic Ocean, for in those days the Atlantic was navigable; and there was an island situated in front of the straits which you call the Columns of Heracles: the island was larger than Libya and Asia put together, and was the way to other islands, and from the island you might pass through the whole of the opposite continent which surrounded the true ocean; for this sea which is within the Straits of Heracles is only a harbor, having a narrow entrance, but that other is a real sea, and the surrounding land may be most truly called a continent. Now, in the island of Atlantis there was a great and wonderful empire, which had rule over the whole island and several others, as well as over parts of the continent; and, besides these, they subjected the parts of Libya within the Columns of Heracles as far as Egypt, and of Europe as far as Tyrrhenia.

[Pg 350]

"'That vast power, thus gathered into one, endeavored to subdue at one blow our country and yours, and the whole of the land which was within the straits; and then, Solon, your country shone forth, in the excellence of her virtue and strength, among all mankind, for she was the first in courage and military skill, and was the leader of the Hellenes. And when the rest fell off from her, being compelled to stand alone, after having undergone the very extremity of danger, she defeated and triumphed over the invaders, and preserved from slavery those who were not yet subjected, and freely liberated all the others who dwelt within the limits of Heracles. But afterward there occurred violent earthquakes and floods, and in a single day and night of rain all your warlike men in a body sunk into the earth, and the island of Atlantis in like manner disappeared, and was sunk beneath the sea. And that is the reason why the sea in those parts is impassable and impenetrable, because there is such a quantity of shallow mud in the way; and this was caused by the subsidence of the island.' ('Plato's Dialogues,' ii, 517, Timæus.)...

"But in addition to the gods whom you have mentioned, I would specially invoke Mnemosyne; for all the important part of what I have to tell is dependent on her favor, and if I can recollect and recite enough of what was said by the priests, and brought hither by Solon, I doubt not that I shall satisfy the requirements of this theatre. To that task, then, I will at once address myself.

"Let me begin by observing first of all that nine thousand was the sum of years which had elapsed since the war which was said to have taken place between all those who dwelt outside the Pillars of Heracles and those who dwelt within them. This war I am now to describe. Of the combatants on the one side the city of Athens was[Pg 351] reported to have been the ruler, and to have directed the contest; the combatants on the other side were led by the kings of the islands of Atlantis, which, as I was saying, once had an extent greater than that of Libya and Asia; and, when afterwards sunk by an earthquake, became an impassable barrier of mud to voyagers sailing from hence to the ocean. The progress of the history will unfold the various tribes of barbarians and Hellenes which then existed, as they successively appear on the scene; but I must begin by describing, first of all, the Athenians as they were in that day, and their enemies who fought with them; and I shall have to tell of the power and form of government of both of them. Let us give the precedence to Athens....

"Many great deluges have taken place during the nine thousand years, for that is the number of years which have elapsed since the time of which I am speaking; and in all the ages and changes of things there has never been any settlement of the earth flowing down from the mountains, as in other places, which is worth speaking of; it has always been carried round in a circle, and disappeared in the depths below. The consequence is that, in comparison with what then was, there are remaining in small islets only the bones of the wasted body, as they may be called, all the richer and softer parts of the soil having fallen away, and the mere skeleton of the country being left....

"And next, if I have not forgotten what I heard when I was a child, I will impart to you the character and origin of their adversaries; for friends should not keep their stories to themselves, but have them in common. Yet, before proceeding further in the narrative, I ought to warn you that you must not be surprised, if you should hear Hellenic names given to foreigners. I will tell you[Pg 352] the reason of this: Solon, who was intending to use the tale for his poem, made an investigation into the meaning of the names, and found that the early Egyptians, in writing them down, had translated them into their own language, and he recovered the meaning of the several names and retranslated them, and copied them out again in our language. My great-grandfather, Dropidas, had the original writing, which is still in my possession, and was carefully studied by me when I was a child. Therefore, if you hear names such as are used in this country, you must not be surprised, for I have told you the reason of them.

"The tale, which was of great length, began as follows: I have before remarked, in speaking of the allotments of the gods, that they distributed the whole earth into portions differing in extent, and made themselves temples and sacrifices. And Poseidon, receiving for his lot the island of Atlantis, begat children by a mortal woman, and settled them in a part of the island which I will proceed to describe. On the side toward the sea, and in the centre of the whole island, there was a plain which is said to have been the fairest of all plains, and very fertile. Near the plain, and also in the centre of the island, at a distance of about fifty stadia, there was a mountain, not very high on any side. In this mountain there dwelt one of the earth-born primeval men of that country, whose name was Evenor, and he had a wife named Leucippe, and they had an only daughter, who was named Cleito.

"The maiden was growing up to womanhood when her father and mother died; Poseidon fell in love with her, and had intercourse with her; and, breaking the ground, enclosed the hill in which she lived all around, making alternate zones of sea and land, larger and smaller, encircling one another; there were two of land and three of[Pg 353] water, which he turned as with a lathe out of the centre of the island, equidistant every way, so that no man could get to the island, for ships and voyagers were not yet heard of. He himself, as he was a god, found no difficulty in making special arrangements for the centre island, bringing two streams of water under the earth, which he caused to ascend as springs, one of warm water and the other of cold, and making every variety of food to spring up abundantly in the earth. He also begat and brought up five pairs of male children, dividing the island of Atlantis into ten portions; he gave to the first-born of the eldest pair his mother's dwelling and the surrounding allotment, which was the largest and best, and made him king over the rest; the others he made princes, and gave them rule over many men and a large territory.

"He named them all: the eldest, who was king, he named Atlas, and from him the whole island and the ocean received the name of Atlantic. To his twin brother, who was born after him, and obtained as his lot the extremity of the island toward the Pillars of Heracles, as far as the country which is still called the region of Gades in that part of the world, he gave the name which in the Hellenic language is Eumelus, in the language of the country which is named after him, Gadeirus. Of the second pair of twins, he called one Ampheres and the other Evæmon. To the third pair of twins he gave the name Mneseus to the elder, and Autochthon to the one who followed him. Of the fourth pair of twins he called the elder Elasippus and the younger Mestor. And of the fifth pair he gave to the elder the name of Azaes, and to the younger Diaprepes.

"All these and their descendants were the inhabitants and rulers of divers islands in the open sea; and also, as has been already said, they held sway in the other direction[Pg 354] over the country within the Pillars as far as Egypt and Tyrrhenia. Now Atlas had a numerous and honorable family, and his eldest branch always retained the kingdom, which the eldest son handed on to his eldest for many generations; and they had such an amount of wealth as was never before possessed by kings and potentates, and is not likely ever to be again, and they were furnished with everything which they could desire both in city and country. For, because of the greatness of their empire, many things were brought to them from foreign countries, and the island itself provided much of what was required by them for the uses of life.

"In the first place, they dug out of the earth whatever was to be found there, mineral as well as metal, and that which is now only a name, and was then something more than a name—orichalcum—was dug out of the earth in many parts of the island, and, with the exception of gold, was esteemed the most precious of metals among the men of those days. There was an abundance of wood for carpenters' work, and sufficient maintenance for tame and wild animals. Moreover, there were a great number of elephants in the island, and there was provision for animals of every kind, both for those who live in lakes and marshes and rivers, and also for those which live in mountains, and on plains, and therefore for the animal which is the largest and most voracious of them.

"Also whatever fragrant things there are in the earth, whether roots, or herbage, or woods, or distilling drops of flowers, or fruits, grew and thrived in that land; and again, the cultivated fruit of the earth, both the dry edible fruit and other species of food, which we call by the general name of legumes, and the fruits having a hard rind, affording drinks, and meats, and ointments, and good store of chestnuts and the like, which may be used[Pg 355] to play with, and are fruits which spoil with keeping—and the pleasant kinds of dessert which console us after dinner, when we are full and tired of eating—all these that sacred island lying beneath the sun brought forth fair and wondrous in infinite abundance.

"All these things they received from the earth, and they employed themselves in constructing their temples, and palaces, and harbors and docks; and they arranged the whole country in the following manner: first of all they bridged over the zones of sea which surrounded the ancient metropolis, and made a passage into and out of the royal palace; and then they began to build the palace in the habitation of the god and of their ancestors. This they continued to ornament in successive generations, every king surpassing the one who came before him to the utmost of his power, until they made the building a marvel to behold for size and for beauty.

"And, beginning from the sea, they dug a canal three hundred feet in width and one hundred feet in depth, and fifty stadia in length, which they carried through to the outermost zone, making a passage from the sea up to this, which became a harbor, and leaving an opening sufficient to enable the largest vessels to find ingress. Moreover, they divided the zones of land which parted the zones of sea, constructing bridges of such a width as would leave a passage for a single trireme to pass out of one into another, and roofed them over; and there was a way underneath for the ships, for the banks of the zones were raised considerably above the water.

"Now the largest of the zones into which a passage was cut from the sea was three stadia in breadth, and the zone of land which came next of equal breadth; but the next two, as well a zone of water as of land, were two stadia, and the one which surrounded the central island was a[Pg 356]stadium only in width. The island in which the palace was situated had a diameter of five stadia. This, and the zones and the bridge, which was the sixth part of a stadium in width, they surrounded by a stone wall, on either side placing towers, and gates on the bridges where the sea passed in. The stone which was used in the work they quarried from underneath the centre island and from underneath the zones, on the outer as well as the inner side. One kind of stone was white, another black, and a third red; as they quarried, they at the same time hollowed out decks, double within, having roofs formed out of the native rock.

"Some of their buildings were simple, but in others they put together different stones, which they intermingled for the sake of ornament, to be a natural source of delight. The entire circuit of the wall which went around the outermost one they covered with a coating of brass, and the circuit of the next wall they coated with tin, and the third, which encompassed the citadel, flashed with the red light of orichalcum. The palace in the interior of the citadel was constructed in this wise: in the centre was a holy temple, dedicated to Cleito and Poseidon, which remained inaccessible, and was surrounded by an enclosure of gold; this was the spot in which was originally begotten the race of ten princes, and thither they annually brought the fruits of the earth in their season from all the ten portions, and performed sacrifices to each of them.

"Here, too, was Poseidon's own temple, of a stadium in length and half a stadium in width, and of a proportionate height, having a sort of barbaric splendor. All the outside of the temple, with the exception of the pinnacles, they covered with silver, and the pinnacles with gold. In the interior of the temple the roof was[Pg 357] of ivory, adorned everywhere with gold and silver and orichalcum; all the other parts of the walls and pillars and floor they lined with orichalcum. In the temple they placed statues of gold: there was the god himself standing in a chariot—the charioteer of six winged horses—and of such a size that he touched the roof of the building with his head; around him were a hundred Nereids riding on dolphins, for such was thought to be the number of them in that day.

"There were also in the interior of the temple other images which had been dedicated by private individuals. And around the temple, on the outside, were placed statues of gold of all the ten kings and of their wives; and there were many other great offerings, both of kings and of private individuals, coming both from the city itself and the foreign cities over which they held sway. There was an altar, too, which in size and workmanship corresponded to the rest of the work, and there were palaces in like manner which answered to the greatness of the kingdom and the glory of the temple.

"In the next place, they used fountains both of gold and hot springs. These were very abundant, and both kinds wonderfully adapted to use by reason of the sweetness and excellence of their waters. They constructed buildings about them, and planted suitable trees; also cisterns, some open to the heaven, others which they roofed over, to be used in winter as warm baths: there were the king's baths, and the baths of private persons, which were kept apart; also separate baths for women, and others again for horses and cattle, and to them they gave as much adornment as was suitable for them. The water which ran off they carried, some to the grove of Poseidon, where were growing all manner of trees of wonderful height and beauty, owing to the excellence[Pg 358] of the soil; the remainder was conveyed by aqueducts which passed over the bridges to the outer circles: and there were many temples built and dedicated to many gods; also gardens and places of exercise, some for men, and some set apart for horses, in both of the two islands formed by the zones; and in the centre of the larger of the two, there was a racecourse of a stadium in width, and in length allowed to extend all round the island, for horses to race in.

"Also there were guard-houses at intervals for the body-guard, the more trusted of whom had their duties appointed to them in the lesser zone, which was nearer the Acropolis; while the most trusted of all had houses given them within the citadel, and about the persons of the kings. The docks were full of triremes and naval stores, and all things were quite ready for use. Enough of the plan of the royal palace. Crossing the outer harbors, which were three in number, you would come to a wall which began at the sea and went all round; this was everywhere distant fifty stadia from the largest zone and harbor, and enclosed the whole, meeting at the mouth of the channel toward the sea.

"The entire area was densely crowded with habitations; and the canal and the largest of the harbors were full of vessels, and merchants coming from all parts, who, from their numbers, kept up a multitudinous sound of human voices and din of all sorts, night and day. I have repeated his descriptions of the city and the parts about the ancient palace nearly as he gave them, and now I must endeavor to describe the nature and arrangement of the rest of the country. The whole country was described as being very lofty and precipitous on the side of the sea, but the country immediately about and surrounding the city was a level plain, itself surrounded by mountains which[Pg 359] descended toward the sea; it was smooth and even, but of an oblong shape, extending in one direction three thousand stadia, and going up the country from the sea through the centre of the island two thousand stadia; the whole region of the island lies toward the south, and is sheltered from the north.

"The surrounding mountains were celebrated for their number and size and beauty, in which they exceeded all that are now to be seen anywhere; having in them also many wealthy inhabited villages, and rivers and lakes, and meadows supplying food enough for every animal, wild or tame, and wood of various sorts, abundant for every kind of work. I will now describe the plain, which had been cultivated during many ages by many generations of kings. It was rectangular, and for the most part straight and oblong; and what it wanted of the straight line followed the line of the circular ditch. The depth and width and length of this ditch were incredible, and gave the impression that such a work, in addition to so many other works, could hardly have been wrought by the hand of man. But I must say what I have heard.

"It was excavated to the depth of a hundred feet, and its breadth was a stadium everywhere; it was carried round the whole of the plain, and was ten thousand stadia in length. It received the streams which came down the mountains, and winding round the plain, and touching the city at various points, was there let off into the sea. From above, likewise, straight canals of a hundred feet in width were cut in the plain, and again let off into the ditch, toward the sea. These canals were at intervals of a hundred stadia, and by them they brought down the wood from the mountains to the city, and conveyed the fruits of the earth in ships, cutting transverse passages from one canal into another, and to the city. Twice[Pg 360] in the year they gathered the fruits of the earth—in winter having the benefit of the rains, and in summer introducing the water of the canals. As to the population, each of the lots in the plain had an appointed chief of men who were fit for military service, and the size of the lot was to be a square of ten stadia each way, and the total number of all the lots was sixty thousand.

"And of the inhabitants, of the mountains and of the rest of the country there was also a vast multitude having leaders, to whom they were assigned according to their dwellings and villages. The leader was required to furnish for the wars the sixth portion of a war-chariot, so as to make up a total of ten thousand chariots; also two horses and riders upon them, and a light chariot without a seat, accompanied by a fighting man on foot carrying a small shield, and having a charioteer mounted to guide the horses; also, he was bound to furnish two heavy-armed men, two archers, two slingers, three stone-shooters, and three javelin men, who were skirmishers, and four sailors, to make up a complement of twelve hundred ships. Such was the order of war in the royal city.

"That of the other nine governments was different in each of them, and would be wearisome to narrate. As to offices and honors the following was the arrangement from the first: each of the ten kings, in his own division and in his own city, had the absolute control of the citizens, and in many cases, of the laws, punishing and slaying whomsoever he would.

"Now the relations of their governments to one another were regulated by the injunctions of Poseidon as the law had handed them down. These were inscribed by the first men on a column of orichalcum, which was situated in the middle of the island, at the temple of Poseidon, whither the people were gathered together every fifth[Pg 361] and sixth years alternately, thus giving equal honor to the odd and to the even number. And when they were gathered together they consulted about public affairs, and inquired if any one had transgressed in anything, and passed judgment on him accordingly—and before they passed judgment they gave their pledges to one another in this wise:

"There were bulls who had the range of the temple of Poseidon; and the ten who were left alone in the temple, after they had offered prayers to the gods that they might take the sacrifices which were acceptable to them, hunted the bulls without weapons, but with staves and nooses; and the bull which they caught they led up to the column. The victim was then struck on the head by them, and slain over the sacred inscription. Now on the column, besides the law, there was inscribed an oath invoking mighty curses on the disobedient. When, therefore, after offering sacrifices according to their customs, they had burnt the limbs of the bull, they mingled a cup and cast in a clot of blood for each of them. The rest of the victim they took to the fire, after having made a purification of the column all round.

"They then drew from the cup in golden vessels, and, pouring a libation on the fire, they swore that they would judge according to the laws on the column, and would punish any one who had previously transgressed, and that for the future they would not, if they could help, transgress any of the inscriptions, and would not command, or obey any ruler who commanded them, to act otherwise than according to the laws of their father Poseidon.

"This was the prayer which each of them offered up for himself and for his family, at the same time drinking, and dedicating the vessel in the temple of the god; and,[Pg 362] after spending some necessary time at supper, when darkness came on and the fire about the sacrifice was cool, all of them put on most beautiful azure robes, and, sitting on the ground at night near the embers of the sacrifices on which they had sworn, and extinguishing all the fires about the temple, they received and gave judgment, if any of them had any accusation to bring against any one; and, when they had given judgment, at daybreak they wrote down their sentences on a golden tablet, and deposited them as memorials with their robes.

"There were many special laws which the several kings had inscribed about the temple, but the most important was the following: that they were not to take up arms against one another, and they were all to come to the rescue, if any one in any city attempted to overthrow the royal house. Like their ancestors, they were to deliberate in common about war and other matters, giving the supremacy to the family of Atlas; and the king was not to have the power of life or death over any of his kinsmen, unless he had the assent of the majority of the ten kings.

"Such was the vast power which the god settled in the lost island of Atlantis; and this he afterward directed against our land on the following pretext, as traditions tell. For many generations, as long as the divine nature lasted in them, they were obedient to the laws, and well-affectioned toward the gods, who were their kinsmen, for they possessed true and in every way great spirits, practicing gentleness and wisdom in the various chances of life, and in their intercourse with one another.

"They despised everything but virtue, not caring for their present state of life, and thinking lightly on the possession of gold, and other property, which seemed only a burden to them; neither were they intoxicated[Pg 363] by luxury, nor did wealth deprive them of their self-control; but they were sober, and saw clearly that all these goods are increased by virtuous friendship with one another, and that by excessive zeal for them and honor of them, the good of them is lost, and friendship perishes with them.

"By such reflections, and by the continuance in them of a divine nature, all that which we have described waxed and increased in them; but when this divine portion began to fade away in them, and became diluted too often, and with too much of the mortal admixture, and the human nature got the upper hand, then, they being unable to bear their fortune, became unseemly, and to him who had an eye to see, they began to appear base, and had lost the fairest of their precious gifts; but to those who had no eye to see the true happiness they still appeared glorious and blessed at the very time when they were filled with unrighteous avarice and power. Zeus, the god of gods, who rules with law, and is able to see into such things, perceiving that an honorable race was in a most wretched state, and wanting to inflict punishment on them, that they might be chastened and improved, collected all the gods into his most holy habitation, which, being placed in the centre of the world, sees all things that partake of generations. And when he had called them together, he spake as follows:"

The story abruptly ends here, for Plato left no further record.

[Pg 364]

CHAPTER XXXIX

NATURE'S WARNING OF COMING EARTHQUAKES

That there are signs of coming earthquakes which might be read by man, had he sufficient knowledge, there would seem to be but little doubt. These phenomena follow natural laws so that the approach of an earthquake must necessarily be in a definite order both as regards the phenomena which precede as well as those which follow it. There should, therefore, be signs that would enable one to predict its coming, although it must be acknowledged that these signs, so far as we actually know, are indistinct.

It may seem to the unthinking and unobservant that the awful catastrophe of an earthquake comes entirely unheralded; that, apparently, it is not until the earth's surface begins to rock to and fro under the mighty forces that are causing destruction that its presence can be known. There are, however, many reasons for believing that in, perhaps, the greatest number of cases, it might have been foreseen, if greater attention had been given to the slight indications of its probable approach a short time before its occurrence.

It is evident that the conditions of great pressure or stress in the earth's crust which finally result in a disastrous earthquake have been slowly accumulating for a long time, and that when the pressure at last reaches a point where the crust has to yield or slip, the ground is suddenly crushed and tossed to and fro while vast fissures[Pg 365] and chasms are produced in the subterranean regions. At those points of the earth immediately above or in the neighborhood of such regions it is possible that there are many signs of the coming quake; and, although indistinguishable by our duller senses, are readily appreciated by the more highly developed senses of the lower animals. Indeed, had we accustomed ourselves to reading the various indications of nature as the lower animals have, we, too, might be able to read these warnings of the coming earthquake.

At great distances from the place where the earthquake starts there would necessarily be a better opportunity for predicting its approach. As already stated, what is called an earthquake does not consist of a single shaking of the ground, but of a highly complex series of shakings. According to Mallet, the following waves start at the same time from the place of origin of an earthquake, when located on the bed of an ocean; i. e., an earth sound wave and a earth wave constituting the earth's shake; a sound wave through the ocean, another through the air; a sea wave called by him a forced sea wave, and finally the great sea wave.

These waves reach a distant point in the following order: the sound wave through the earth and the great earthquake or shake which produces the damage. Then a smaller sea wave called the forced sea wave. This is followed almost immediately by the sound wave through the sea. Next come the air sound wave and finally the great sea wave; which, rushing in on the shore, sweeps nearly everything before it.

In other words, the disturbances produced by the great earthquake follow in this order of sequence. If, therefore, the great earthquake wave proper transmitted through the earth should for any reason be delayed in[Pg 366] reaching a distant place, the great sound waves should be able to give warning of the coming disturbances.

Again, as we have already seen, the earthquake wave is preceded by a number of preliminary tremors, and is followed by a number of after tremors or *earthquake echoes*. Since, therefore, the preliminary waves reach a place first, it would seem that the approach of an earthquake must be heralded by the preliminary tremors. These, perhaps, at least in part, enable the lower animals to detect its coming.

Again, in almost all instances there are a number of preliminary shocks that precede the great earthquake shock. Some of these preliminary shocks continue at intervals for several days or even longer. Sometimes, indeed, these subterranean sounds fail to be followed by earthquakes. Milne thinks that these sounds are caused by the preliminary tremors which precede the principal shock of the earthquake and that they reach the place first. Here again then it is evident that, were we able to interpret properly these sounds, we would probably be able to foretell the coming quake with a fair degree of certainty.

There would appear to be no reasonable doubt that in some manner which we have not yet been able to discover, but probably along some of the lines indicated above, animals are capable of recognizing a coming earthquake. Long before the coming of the catastrophe they are said to exhibit extreme terror, and in many cases appear to seek the companionship of man, as if for protection.

That the senses of smell and hearing are far more acute in the lower animals than in man no one can reasonably doubt. The manner in which a trained dog can follow a scent, for a long time after the animal or thing[Pg 367] producing it has passed, far exceeds the power of scent possessed by man, and it is more than likely that this same power is possessed by all animals who live upon or prey upon other animals. It is probable that faintly odorous vapors or gases escape from the crust shortly before the great shock occurs, and that these faint odors are warnings to the animals of the approaching calamity. The sense of hearing also is much more acute in the lower animals.

Daubeny is evidently of this belief, as will be seen from the following:

"These gases and vapors (alluding to emanations given off from the ground during earthquakes) exert an influence on the barometer, which does appear to be indirectly affected by the earthquake. Then, similar properties also may occasion that uneasiness which animals are said to evince before any such event. Thus, according to the accounts of some writers, rats and mice leave their holes, alligators seek the dry land, quadrupeds snuff the ground, and manifest such signs of the impending calamity that in countries where earthquakes are common, the inhabitants take the alarm in consequence, and escape from their houses. It is right, however, to add, that more recent authorities dispute altogether the correctness of these statements."

Dutton doubts the ability of animals to foretell coming earthquake shocks.

But that the lower animals do exhibit signs of fear at the approach of an earthquake has been repeatedly asserted by good observers.

Hamilton, who made a careful examination of the neighboring country during the great earthquake at Calabria, asserts that horses and oxen during the shocks extended their legs widely in order to avoid being thrown[Pg 368] down, "and that hogs, oxen, horses, and mules, and also geese, appeared to be painfully aware of the approach of the earthquake of Calabria; and the neighing of a horse, the braying of an ass, or the cackling of a goose, even when he (Hamilton) was making his survey (after the occurrence of the great earthquake shock), drove the people out of their temporary sheds in expectation of a shock."

It is asserted that birds appear to be especially sensible to a coming earthquake shock. That geese will quit the water in which they were swimming before the earthquake and will not return to it. It is quite possible that these birds with their heads immersed in the water can hear the distant murmurings long before they become audible in the air.

Von Hoff makes the following statement:

"It has been remarked that at such times (immediately before the coming of an earthquake shock), domestic animals showed a decided uneasiness, dogs howled mournfully, horses neighed in an unusual manner, and poultry flew restlessly about. These latter phenomena might easily be produced by mephitic vapours, which often ascend to the surface of the earth before the breaking out of an earthquake."

Mallet states that there is abundant evidence that earthquake shocks, even when not of very great intensity, produce nausea in both men and women. This would seem natural, since, as everyone knows, until one is accustomed to sea-voyages, merely to be tossed to and fro by the motion of the waves results in the production of sea-sickness.

It has been also noticed that during earthquakes fish which under ordinary circumstances live in the mud at the bottom of bodies of water come near to the surface and at such times can be caught in great numbers.

[Pg 369]

Mallet cites the following effects produced by earthquakes:

"Amongst the effects supposed to be produced by the earthquake on the atmosphere were reckoned tempestuous winds, thunder-storms, meteors, coldness of the air, severe winters, heavy rains, miasmata, producing diseases and affecting vegetation. A very remarkable instance of the latter is quoted, namely, that in Peru, after the earthquake of 1687, wheat and barley would not thrive at all, though formerly the country was remarkably favourable for them."

Sir Charles Lyell notes the following phenomena attending earthquakes:

"Irregularities in the seasons preceding or following the shocks; sudden gusts of wind, interrupted by dead calms; violent rains at unusual seasons, or in countries where, as a rule, they are almost unknown; a reddening of the sun's disk, and haziness in the air, often continued for months; an evolution of electric matter, or of inflammable gas from the soil, with sulphurous and mephitic vapours; noises underground, like the running of carriages, or the discharge of artillery, or distant thunder; animals uttering cries of distress, and evincing extraordinary alarm, being more sensitive than men to the slightest movement; a sensation like sea-sickness, and a dizziness in the head, experienced by men. These, and other phenomena, less connected with our present subject as geologists, have recurred again and again at distant ages, and in all parts of the globe."

THE END

FOOTNOTES:

[1]A point on the other side of the earth directly opposite a given point.

[2]A fracture of a stratum, or a general rock mass, with a relative displacement of the opposite sides of the break.

The plane or fracture of a fault, known as the fault-plane, is seldom vertical. The higher side is called the heaved or upthrow side; the opposite side the thrown or downthrow side.

[3]*Tectonic Earthquake.* An earthquake due to the sudden slip of faulted strata.

[4]*I. e.*, burnt out mountain, extinct volcano.

[5]*Epicentre.* A point on the surface of the earth vertically above the point of origin of an earthquake, or the place where it starts.